CHILDHOODS OF THE GLOBAL SOUTH
Children's Rights and Resistance

Manfred Liebel

In collaboration with Rebecca Budde,
Urszula Markowska-Manista and Philip Meade

P

First published in Great Britain in 2023 by

Policy Press, an imprint of
Bristol University Press
University of Bristol
1–9 Old Park Hill
Bristol
BS2 8BB
UK
t: +44 (0)117 374 6645
e: bup-info@bristol.ac.uk

Details of international sales and distribution partners are available at
policy.bristoluniversitypress.co.uk

British Library Cataloguing in Publication Data
A catalogue record for this book is available from the British Library

ISBN 978-1-4473-7040-6 hardcover
ISBN 978-1-4473-7041-3 paperback
ISBN 978-1-4473-7042-0 ePub
ISBN 978-1-4473-7043-7 ePdf

Cover design: Robin Hawes
Front cover image: iStock/ShutterWorx; iStock/FrankRamspott; iStock/amtitus

Contents

Notes on the authors

Manfred Liebel was Founder and Director of the MA Childhood Studies and Children's Rights at the Free University of Berlin and University of Applied Sciences Potsdam, 2007–2021, and is now an independent social researcher and activist.

Rebecca Budde is a cultural scientist and was the Academic Coordinator of the MA Childhood Studies and Children's Rights, 2007–2021.

Urszula Markowska-Manista is Researcher and Assistant Professor at the University of Warsaw and was the Co-Director of the MA Childhood Studies and Children's Rights, 2016–2021.

Philip Meade is a social pedagogue and Lecturer in the MA Childhood Studies and Children's Rights. With Manfred Liebel, he is co-founder of the ProNATs Association to strengthen the rights of children and youth.

Presentation and acknowledgements

With this book, I follow up on reflections I set out in the book *Decolonizing Childhoods*, published by Policy Press in 2020. In particular, I am interested in exploring the meaning of children's rights for young people who suffer from postcolonial inequality and related forms of marginalization and oppression. I understand these rights as a possible tool for children's action that can facilitate the visibility and affirmation of their own individual and collective needs and interests. My own interest is focused on how children's rights can help strengthen the social position of these children. In this sense, I understand them as *rights from below* or *counter-rights in the hands of children*.

I group the children who are at the centre of the book under the term *childhoods of the Global South* and ask about the specific views, forms of action and life perspectives of these children. To make the meaning of rights comprehensible to them, I use historical examples to illuminate some legal traditions that attach particular importance to children's participation in social and political life. With a view to the present, I explore the question of how children cope with their precarious living conditions and under what conditions forms of *political subjectivity* emerge that can be understood as *resistance*.

With this book, I want to contribute to do these children justice and make visible their real lives in their objective and subjective diversity. As a 'White' adult who enjoys academic privilege and has not experienced racism first-hand, this is certainly only approximately possible for me. Moreover, I can only refer to some aspects of these children's lives. The focus is on Latin America, but occasionally I also draw on examples from other continents.

In the course of my involvement with the topic of children's rights, new questions have repeatedly come to mind that I believe have been inadequately addressed to date. These questions have been stimulated in various ways. Fundamental to my understanding of children's rights and their relevance to children's lives have been my experiences and studies with children in southern or postcolonial regions of the world, particularly in Latin America. In this context, I have been most inspired by meetings with working and Indigenous children and youth and their adult collaborators.

Many new points of view also arose from my teaching activities and the exchange with students in the international master's programme 'Childhood Studies and Children's Rights', which I co-founded at Free University Berlin in 2007 and which has been continued at the University of Applied Sciences Potsdam since 2017. Further important impulses came from the exchange with colleagues in different countries, from which new contours of a critical conception of children's rights studies emerged. I co-authored one chapter each with Rebecca Budde, Urszula Markowska-Manista and Philip Meade, with whom I have been working closely for years.

Spanish- and German-language citations I have translated, unless English-language publications of the cited writings were available.

In this book, we write the personal designations Black, White and Indigenous with capital letters in each case, insofar as they are group-related self-designations or socio-political categories of analysis.

Finally, I would like to thank the anonymous reviewers and the staff of Policy Press for providing advice during the writing of the book and for making its publication possible.

Manfred Liebel
Berlin, January 2023

Introduction: Colonization of childhoods and identities of resistance

In the following sentences, I set out the basic line of argument of this book. First, I clarify why I think it is necessary to consider issues of children and children's rights in relation to colonization and coloniality. I then explain how I understand children's rights and why I consider them indispensable for the lives of children in particular at the grassroots. I also show what must happen and be considered for these rights to be experienced by children as meaningful and that they can be used by them in their own interest. In order to get a concrete idea of children's living conditions and collective interests, I explain my understanding of the concepts of 'the popular' and of 'popular childhoods' as well as 'childhoods of the Global South'. Since I am primarily concerned with how identities of resistance emerge in these childhoods, I also consider it necessary to get an idea of colonization processes. In this book, due to my personal and professional biography, I focus on the subcontinent of Latin America and look for the traces colonization has left on social relations, on thoughts and feelings of young people, and how these can be counteracted. At the end of the Introduction, I give an overview of the individual chapters of the book.

Why and how do I speak of the colonization of childhoods?

Following the publication of the book *Decolonizing Childhoods: From Exclusion to Dignity* (Liebel, 2020), some people raised the question whether, analogous to the colonization of peoples and territories, it is possible to speak of a colonization of childhood(s). For this reason, I will explain how I understand colonization as a concept and why I find it meaningful to apply it to children and childhoods.

I understand colonization as a form of submission of people and living spaces against their will and to the detriment of the people in those living spaces. Certainly it must be borne in mind that the colonization is situated in a specific historical context, the era of European colonialism (and imperialism), and that it cannot be simply transposed to other historical or social contexts. It is equally important to bear in mind that the term has come to be understood in a broader sense as the 'internal colonization' of the lifeworld (Habermas, 1981). When I speak of the colonization of childhoods, I have in mind both meanings of colonization. However, I always see it in relation to what happened in the era of colonialism and continues today in a modified form in the postcolonial world order. The topicality is expressed in the concept of coloniality coined by the Peruvian sociologist Anibal Quijano, understood in the multiple and interrelated sense of 'coloniality of power' (Quijano, 2000; 2008; 2019), 'coloniality of knowledge' (Lander, 2000), and even more fundamentally as 'coloniality of being' (Maldonado-Torres, 2007).

To characterize coloniality or the postcolonial state of the world with its enormous inequalities of power and wealth, it has become a custom to distinguish between the *Global North* and the *Global South*. This distinction is not geographical but *geopolitical*. It does have references to specific regions of the world, but the Global South is also found in the geographic North, particularly with the massive migration processes. On the other hand, islands of wealth representing the Global North can be found in the geographic South. This is especially true of the megacities, where pompous luxury buildings and 'gated cities' dominate the cityscape within sight of growing slums. The difference between the Global North and the Global South is also expressed in the fact that the 'imperial way of life' (Brand and Wissen, 2017) that dominates in the geographic North, and the economic growth that underlies it, which is based on the exploitation of people and nature, lead to a global destruction of the foundations of human life. People in the geographic South are particularly affected by this destruction, which can be experienced above all in climate disasters, but the consequences are also becoming increasingly noticeable in the geographic North. In this respect, too, the North is being caught up with what it has done to the South through colonization and its continuation as coloniality.

When speaking of the colonization of childhoods, I am thinking in particular of children who are affected by coloniality and whose lives are particularly devalued, endangered, restricted or disadvantaged. In this sense, I describe these children's childhoods as *childhoods of the Global South*. In Latin America it is also common to speak of '*infancias populares*' or '*niñez popular*' (Liebel, 2021). Since this expression, which I translate as *popular childhood(s)*, is not yet very common in English, I will explain it in more detail later. In the sense of the Indian-born postcolonial social researcher Gayatri Spivak (1988), we could also speak of *subaltern* (or more precisely subalternized) *childhoods*. These childhoods are predominantly – but not exclusively – found in former colonized territories.

The colonization of these childhoods is manifest in both material and ideological ways. In material terms, the lives of these children tend to be shortened, destroyed and deprived of their past and future. Ideologically, their subjective dimensions are discriminated against and made invisible or distorted. This is expressed, for example, in the fact that these children are denied the possibility of having a childhood (often called 'children without childhood'), a way of speaking that is colonialist as it makes the Western-European model of childhood the (absolute) norm. It is also expressed in the fact that these children are pitied and denied any subjectivity. I see a challenge both in making visible the colonization of these childhoods in its material and ideological dimensions and in disclosing their subjectivities. This means tracing the other childhoods that emerge after colonization, that is, that are simultaneously produced and hidden by it, and making them intelligible.

These considerations can be related to the debate on *adultism* or *adult supremacy* (see Flasher, 1978; LeFrançois, 2014; Fletcher, 2015; Bergman, 2022; in German: Liebel and Meade, 2023). Having said this, adultism would not only have to be understood as a form of children's subjugation to adult power and the discrimination that accompanies it, but would also have to be situated in its colonial and postcolonial contexts. This would then have to be tantamount to recognizing the counter-forces and counter-movements among children and exploring the possibilities of children's self-liberation or agency. The recently introduced concept of *childism* (Wall, 2019) has this in mind, but has so far not been understood as a form of decolonization of childhoods, but rather as a critique of the structurally unequal relationship between adults and children or adulthood and childhood. I will come back to this concept later in the book.

Another possible point of departure could be the debate on *patriarchy*, especially from the perspective of so-called Black and decolonial feminisms (Collins, 2000; Lorde, 2007; Nash, 2019; Vergès, 2021). In these feminisms, the critique of male domination and the associated violence is combined with criticizing racism, which emerged as an ideology during colonialism. Again, I see a similarity with the 'infantilization' of colonized peoples, that is, their labelling as 'children' in the sense of the Western-European pattern of childhood, in other words, as immature, uncivilized and backward beings in need of development and civilization.

Rights from below

This book looks at children's rights from the point of view of what they mean for children at the grassroots, and how they can be used by children in their own interest (see Liebel, 2012a). To do this, these rights cannot be understood as if they speak for themselves, but must be contextualized to children's living conditions and experiences. This is the only way to avoid the mystification of children's rights, and the only way for children to perceive them as relevant for themselves. The discourse on rights is based on the assumption that they apply equally to all people, in the case of children's rights to all children, but what they mean to them, whether they benefit them and whether they can use them depends on the particular circumstances of each child's life.

Children's rights do not arise and do not exist in an ahistorical and socio-distant space. Their claim to universal validity encounters a world characterized by power inequalities and cultural diversities. Therefore, it is not enough to apply the rights, they must also be 'translated' so that they are compatible with the specific circumstances and experiences of children on the ground. Before appealing to children's rights, the question arises whether they can be an effective and feasible instrument for securing children's dignity and strengthening their position in society in any given situation. If we consider children as actors, that is as acting subjects with their own ways of seeing and expressing, a minimum set of preconditions must be met. This includes that children not only trust in themselves, but also have the necessary space to be able to act at all. This also includes that, at the legal level, they find contact persons who take the discourse on rights seriously and that there are political frameworks in place in which human rights are not completely ignored. Finally, this also includes that children find allies among adults who are ready to take up and support their legal demands. The origin of these assumptions, like the emergence of human rights, should not be understood as a kind of naturalistic fact, but as a result of social struggles, and can therefore be induced and changed.

It is essential to look at children's views and to understand children's rights in such a way that they can be used individually and collectively by children themselves as they grow older. And it must be borne in mind that the rights themselves are only of practical significance if they are accompanied by structural changes in the respective societies that lead to greater equality and social justice and, in particular, to strengthening the social position of children. This does not exclude the representation of children by adults and state institutions, but requires that every representation of others is also associated with risks that can only be countered by a broad participation and self-organization of children.

In any case, if we want children to take ownership of their rights and want them to learn how to exercise and benefit from them, it is necessary to contextualize them and make them relevant to their life experience. It is not enough to simply implement the rights that formally exist. It is essential to analyse them in their political, cultural and structural contexts and to weigh them in terms of the effects they can have on children's lives. In all of this, it is important to take into account that, for example, the life situations of girls and boys are very different, so that the same right may have different meanings for them. In some cases, rights will need to be further specified and expanded, always with the appropriate participation of children. Children deserve respect as people who, as they grow older, are very capable of participating in the construction of their rights and providing input on their management.

In my view, children's rights need to be understood not only in the sense of a state commitment, but in a much broader, subject-oriented sense, that is as rights that are in the hands of subjects and the societies and communities constituted and reproduced by them. This idea requires a concept of politics and law that does not cling to the state and the legal form of fixed codified rights, but sees rights, like legal systems, as the outcome of struggles and social movements that can change and continue to change permanently. The 'social relations of different forces' condensed in legal systems and 'legal concepts' are 'sediments of strategic and selective products of past conflicts' (Buckel, 2008: 127). This does not mean that the state is unimportant, nor does it mean that the state should not seek to protect rights. What it does mean is simply that we should not see the state as the final instance of rights-preserving obligations, but as part of a much broader social dynamic.

This shift in thinking is also important because by focusing on state commitments and obligations, we run the risk of reducing human rights in general and children's rights in particular to their bureaucratic and instrumental management. In the process:

> [L]aw and politics are brought together in institutional structures that operate procedurally, technocratically and in other ways that rend to hollow out the emancipatory and expressive dimensions of human rights. Without dismissing the positive benefits of the international human rights system, there is clearly a major problem with a reduction of human rights praxis that is organised through and orientated towards institutionalised structures of power. (Stammers, 2009: 225)

Indeed, the institutionalization of human rights tends 'to remove them from social contestation – sedimenting them within positive law and its supposed timeless majesty' (Stammers, 2009: 229) and generates an 'unquestionable, rigid, totalizing and self-enclosed magnetism' (Magistris, 2016: 33) that erases the everyday dimension of rights. Similar considerations are expressed by Vanessa Pupavac as follows:

> The prescription of higher law beyond the reach of political contestation undermines the right of the people to determine both the good and the political process by which the good is determined, hence is anti-democratic. As a consequence, instead of law deriving from and being contingent upon the will of subjects, law takes on the form of decree. (Pupavac, 2001a: 100)

Based on these arguments, I suggest going beyond the merely legalistic interpretation of rights, which turns them into *paper rights*, and to understand children's rights as a work in progress, as the result of a process in constant transformation. In this process actors (children) from below transform their realities, translate their needs and rights to a better life into demands for action and obligations on governments and power elites.

This concept of law as a process brings attention to the contingency and dynamic development of rights: rights are not fixed or predetermined; rather, they are the changing outcome of conflicting needs, ideas or interests, and the social and political action that emerges from these antagonisms. This dynamic has at least two dimensions. In the case of existing and codified children's rights whose legal wording may be very vague, we are faced with a problem of interpretation, specification of their meanings and their implementation. For example, what is the content of the concept of 'best interests'? What should be the balance between protection and participation rights? How should children's participation rights be implemented in different policy areas? Equally important, although much less researched in literature on the subject, are the efforts of different actors to express their perspectives and interests in rights that have not yet been codified. Therefore, it may be necessary to expand or modify the existing regime of children's rights, which is based on the UN Convention on the Rights of the Child (CRC).

This understanding of rights as work in progress makes us realize the need to think about the actors involved in this process. This includes the proclamation and interpretation of existing rights or the creation of new rights, the social conflicts that the creation and/or preservation of rights can cause, and the power and resources that different actors bring to these conflicts. With this, the widespread tendency to see human rights as 'a process of "top-down" elite construction' (Stammers, 2009: 231) can be contested. Instead, 'the processes of "bottom-up" agency in the historical and social construction of human rights' (Stammers, 2009: 231) come to the fore. In terms of children's rights, therefore, it is necessary to acquire *situated* or *liberatory knowledge* of the *lived realities* of children in popular, grassroots sectors. This would be a knowledge that enables and facilitates children themselves to claim certain rights in a concrete situation, and to formulate new rights individually and collectively that are appropriate for the situation at hand and to insist on their social and legal recognition.

Addressing the paradoxes of children's rights

Situated and liberating knowledge is characterized by the fact that it allows us to recognize the paradoxes of rights in claiming and using them. The human rights inscribed in international law have the problem that, although they are supposed to apply equally to all people, they can only be claimed by them to different degrees or not at all. This has to do with the fact that people's living conditions and political status (citizenship) are extremely unequal. The assumed equality of rights 'before the law' can thus have the consequence of further entrenching inequality. This is sometimes referred to as the paradox of human rights.

To counter this paradox, human rights have been specified over the past decades for groups of people who are considered particularly disadvantaged or marginalized. For example, special rights have been created for women, people with disabilities, Indigenous peoples and children. In contrast to the general human rights as codified internationally in the Universal Declaration of Human Rights of 1948 and the UN Covenants on Political and Civil Rights as well as Social, Economic and Cultural Rights of 1966, these rights are tailored to the special needs of these groups. This is because equal rights are not equal for all people, as they encounter unequal starting conditions and thus risk entrenching these inequalities or spreading ideological fog. As these specific human rights presuppose definitions of disadvantage or marginalization, they tend to enshrine a status or particular characteristics of special neediness or vulnerability, thus materializing and perpetuating them. In turn, they imply the risk of stigmatizing the targeted groups of people and thus creating new paradoxes (from a feminist perspective, see Brown, 2002; Buckel, 2021).

In the case of children's rights, the question arises how the specific situation of children as legal subjects is conceptualized. They are justified by the assumption that children are particularly vulnerable, immature and dependent compared to adults and thus require additional rights in order to enjoy and exercise them. The CRC is based on this idea. These characteristics of being a child, sometimes referred to as 'generational asymmetry', are considered anthropological universals in the dominant understanding of children's rights. In the CRC, the consequence is that the focus is on protection and provision rights, and the fulfilment of participation rights is linked to certain conditions such as age, maturity and capacity for judgement. They also have the effect of not only creating special rights for children, but also of denying them rights, in particular certain political rights (for example, universal suffrage) or economic and labour rights (for example, right to work, rights at work, or the right to form trade unions).

The codification of special children's rights contains the inherent contradiction of naming specific vulnerabilities children are exposed to in particular, but losing sight of the fundamental disadvantages of being a child. This applies, for example, to the right to non-discrimination as enshrined in Article 2 of the CRC. It may itself result in discrimination, as it ignores (lower) age as a possible ground for discrimination, as if the very existence of the CRC already guarantees that children's particularities will be taken into account. This is referred to by Aoife Daly et al (2022) as the 'CRC paradox'. Another example is the protection against economic exploitation granted in Article 32 and the requirement to set minimum age limits for work. Here, children are excluded from economic activity solely on the basis of their young age, without taking into account the specific circumstances of the children's lives, the conditions of the work and, above all, the children's own will. This way of thinking, fixated on exclusion and prohibition, excludes the possibility of imagining children as actors who want to assume co-responsibility, for example for their families and communities, and for whom work experiences can represent a contribution to the development of vital skills. With such specifications, it is also accepted that children are disenfranchised and prevented from defending themselves against life circumstances that harm them and that they do not want to accept, simply by referring to their young age. Such an understanding of children's rights could be described as *adultist*, since it denies children the right to participate in the determination of their own lives solely on the basis of their age. This also undermines the participation rights formally granted to children and makes them absurd.

A central question is how the differences between children and adults and the special characteristics of children are understood and legally defined. In defining children's rights as specific rights, the alternative is to understand the disadvantage and vulnerability attributed to children as a permanent feature of childhood or as a condition to be overcome. If the special nature of childhood is understood as an anthropological universal, it is obvious that states of disadvantage and vulnerability are made permanent. If, on the other hand, these are understood as socially generated results of unequal power relations, the perspective arises to conceive rights as a possible means of overcoming disadvantage and vulnerability. Understood in the latter sense, the use of rights would tend to make them superfluous for the children directly affected. Such an understanding of children's rights, which I call transformational or emancipatory, is the baseline argumentation in this book.

What does this mean for the different categories of children's rights? Protection rights would be understood as enabling and facilitating children to protect themselves and to have a decisive say in measures taken for their protection. Provision rights would be understood in such a way that their implementation does not primarily take place through measures taken by state or adult authorities, but that the entire society is transformed in such a way that all people of different ages become acting subjects of these rights, taking into account their respective starting conditions. Participation rights would be understood in such a way that they make the unequal distribution of power between adults and children disappear, that is, they become political rights that children can use in their own individual and collective interests just as adults do, always with due regard for their different starting conditions.

This understanding of children's rights turns them into *counter-rights* that can be used by children individually as well as collectively. They are aimed at strengthening the social position of children and counteracting any kind of social and generational disadvantage, subordination and discrimination. In this way, they also contribute on one hand to making social conditions more egalitarian and democratic and, on the other, in particular, to challenging any kind of unequal power. As counter-rights, children's rights have special significance for those children who are particularly socially disadvantaged, marginalized and oppressed. These children are found in all parts of the world, but especially in the regions affected by the inequality of the postcolonial world order, which I refer to in this book as the Global South. I refer to these children as children of the Global South or see them as part of the popular sectors or classes.

What is the meaning of 'the popular'?

The term popular can have different meanings. In communication sciences it has been and is used in relation to culture and denotes expressions that are widely used ('popular') under the influence of mass media and which are different from forms of 'higher' or 'elitist' culture (for instance, 'pop' or 'popular music'). In other fields of science, especially in anthropology or ethnology, the term popular, on the other hand, is understood as a supposedly original or traditional culture represented by people and social groups that have not yet been captured by modernity or enlightenment. This can be expressed, for example, in certain 'archaic' customs or production modes that have survived beyond the 'modernized' world. According to anthropologist Néstor García Canclini (1990; 2002), this approach doesn't take into account the fact that these customs and modes of production have become a general part of capitalist exploitation processes (such as folklore or handicrafts) or are 'popularized' by the mass media or in the framework of mass tourism. They have thus not only lost their originality or traditional distinctiveness, but have become 'hybrid' and ultimately arbitrarily producible and marketable products.

However, in Latin America in particular, the term popular has acquired a different meaning. While this interpretation is linked to the traditional and its particularity, it emphasizes their contrasts and disparities with those who hold power in a given society. This distinction, which highlights the relationship between 'below' and 'above' in societies based on domination, has been expressed in combinations of words such as '*movimiento popular/* popular movement', '*economía popular/*popular economy' or '*educación popular/* popular education'.

Popular movements are usually understood as social movements in which different population groups subjected to power, for example, urban slum and shantytown dwellers or members of Indigenous communities, act to improve living conditions.

Among the variety of claims and demands that were deployed in the region, stand out those of indigenous movements, peasant organizations and Afro-descendant groups, fighting against neo-colonial voracity, accumulation by dispossession, the subjugation of territories and the privatization of common goods and ancestral knowledge. Those of the movements of the unemployed and inhabitants of the peripheral neighbourhoods located in the very heart of the big cities, who deploy repertoires of action and self-organized initiatives of cooperative work, community networks and popular economy, against the processes of gentrification, mercantilization and socio-spatial segregation. As well as the tenacious resistance of sectors of the employed working class, against the precariousness of work and life itself. (Ouviña, 2020: 443)

The term *popular economy* is used, when these population groups (have to) take responsibility for their everyday needs and activities. These activities often arise from particularly precarious social emergencies when there is no other way out. They can express themselves in forms of subsistence economy in rural areas often rooted in Indigenous customs, as an informal survival economy within urban neighbourhoods, but also in factory takeovers or in the formation of self-governed cooperatives. They do not always see themselves as an organized alternative to the capitalist economy, but at their core, they contain many elements of a communitarian or solidarity economy that can form the basis of a 'different' form of social organization vis-à-vis the dominant society. In this respect, they can also contribute to the creation of collective identities that are explicitly directed against the capitalist economy and state policies designed to try to maintain it.

Popular education is understood as an educational concept and practice that equips dominated population groups with the knowledge necessary to resist oppression and exploitation and to achieve socially just living conditions.

The dominant position in relation to popular education is that which links it to the people, the oppressed, the poor, the proletariat, the peasants, the left or alternative groups. Popular education as the opposite of the elite, the oppressors, the rich, the bourgeoisie, the landowners, the right or conservative groups. (Jiménez García, 2015: 35)

This educational concept, which can largely be traced back to the Brazilian pedagogue and philosopher Paulo Freire ([1968] 2000), was originally conceived as adult education, but for more than three decades has also been applied in social and educational work with young people. It is closely related to popular movements and often part of a practice of self-empowerment (see, for example, the *Pedagogy of Tenderness* brought forward by the Peruvian pedagogue Alejandro Cussiánovich, 2010; 2022).

García Canclini (2002) attributes the public success of the term popular to the fact that it unites different social groups, whose common situation of subalternity is not sufficiently named by ethnicity ('Indian'), nor by place in the relations of production (worker), nor by geographical area (peasant or urban culture). The popular allows us to synthetically encompass all these situations of subordination and to give a shared identity to the groups that coincide in this project of solidarity. For this reason, the term popular has become widespread as a name for political parties, revolutions and social movements. However, there is a certain weakness to this polysemy. The popular does not correspond precisely to an empirical referent, to subjects or social situations that are clearly identifiable in reality. It is a political construct, whose theoretical consistency has yet to be achieved (see Kusch, 1977; Laclau, 2005). In this sense, Mexican sociologist José Manuel Valenzuela Arce points out that the popular is the subject of much controversy:

> The definition of what is popular has been the subject of wide-ranging debates, mainly referring to the definition of the concept of the people, the delimitation of its thresholds with the cultured and elitist, or the contestation of the concept for its supposed homogenizing character of a wide range of cultural expressions. The relational connotation of the concept obliges us to avoid essentialist or merely descriptive allusions and to locate the discussion in the sphere of relations where the limits of ascription/differentiation between popular groups and dominant or official groups are defined and redefined. (Valenzuela Arce, 2020: 72)

The discourse of the popular emerged when it became clear that the traditional division of society into bourgeoisie and working class, which goes back to Marx's thinking, was too crude and based on a model that referred only to the industrialized capitalist societies of the North.

Even in the analyses that the Italian philosopher and political activist Antonio Gramsci (2011) undertook almost a hundred years ago, an attempt was made to portray a more dynamic and differentiated picture of this society. When Gramsci spoke of the 'subaltern classes', he not only wanted to describe a social structure, but he was also looking for forces that could challenge the power relations of that society. For him it was clear that these forces were not only the people who were in a direct labour relation and characterized by exploitation. Private owners' production means (factories, companies) were involved as well as many other people who, beyond industrial labour, were subject to the ruling class and suffered from it. What comes to mind, for example, are the women of these workers, whose unpaid domestic work allowed families to survive. Also, the people who did not do any work in the classical sense of wage labour, who kept themselves alive with all kinds of activities, from small traders to people who today are called precarious or 'new entrepreneurs'. Gramsci was also aware that capitalist rule is not based solely on the direct exploitation of workers, but is maintained in a mediated way through the internalization of ideologies about the supposedly different value of different activities and population groups. Here discriminatory ideologies (mainly racism and sexism) play a special role (see Wells, 2018: 28–80), but also, as I would like to add with regard to children and young people, adultism or adultcentrism.

Therefore, it is important not to use the term popular in a homogenizing way, but to take care that within the popular sectors there are quite polyphonic living conditions, social positions and corresponding interests and identities. It is equally important not to lose sight of the fact that 'class demarcations play an important role in shaping the boundaries between the official and the popular' (Valenzuela Arce, 2020: 72). Only in this way is it possible to recognize how processes of resistance and the corresponding movements and organizations take shape.

> The popular refers to situational conditions that define the subaltern sectors' own socio-cultural appropriated, negotiated or recreated practices. They take shape and make sense in networks of social habituation where those referring to intimate or everyday spheres such as the family, the neighbourhood and networks of intense relationships (family and affective), which are often in dispute with institutional or official socialization processes, stand out. (Valenzuela Arce, 2020: 72)

When the popular is seen as a social locus from which a society's relations of domination are challenged in action, one generally speaks of *popular cultures*. It is assumed that the collective identities of self-confidence and resistance crystallize equally.

> Popular cultures refer to significant socio-cultural practices that participate in the construction of the meaning and significance of the lives of subaltern sectors and their resistance to hegemonic and dominant social forms. One of the defining aspects of the popular is the indispensable situated condition of the concept of people in relation to the economic and cultural elites and institutionalized' spheres, as well as their imaginaries, their representations, their knowledge, their religiosity and their everyday practices. (Valenzuela Arce, 2020: 51)

Stuart Hall, an Afro-Caribbean cultural researcher, suggests that we ought always to begin the study of popular culture with the double plea of popular culture, the double movement of containment and resistance, which is inevitably inherent to it. According to Hall:

> [T]here is a continuous and necessarily uneven and unequal struggle, by the dominant culture, constantly to disorganize and reorganize popular culture; to enclose and confine its definitions and forms within a more inclusive range of dominant forms. There are points of resistance;

there are also moments of supersession. This is the dialectic of cultural struggle. In our times, it goes on continuously, in the complex lines of resistance and acceptance, refusal and capitulation, which make the field of culture a sort of constant battlefield. A battlefield where no once-for-all victories are obtained, but where there are always strategic positions to be won and lost. (Hall, 1981: 233)

We have to keep in mind this dialectic of confrontation in the field of culture between powerful and dominated social groups if we want to fathom the potentials and possibilities of resistance (see also Storey, 2006; Harsin and Hayward, 2013).

Legacies of colonialism

The popular is a heterogeneous place full of contradictions. It includes people who, as '*mestizos*', are steeped in the colonial past and are tempted to distance themselves from those who see themselves as native peoples or as descendants of slaves deported from Africa. These are those most affected by colonization and its continuing effects, especially the racism of European descended 'White' power elites. Some popular sectors may hope to mitigate the discrimination they themselves experienced as so-called '*pibes*' (Argentina), '*cholos*', '*chibolos*' (Peru), '*patojos*' (Guatemala), '*pachucos*' or '*morras*' (Mexico) or '*cabros*' (Chile), by dissociating themselves from these groups and seeing themselves as a moderately integrated part of the postcolonial nation-state, which today dresses as being multicultural. This also applies to the manifestations of *machismo* and *caudillismo*, or adultcentrism, which are equally rooted in the popular sectors.

In this sense, one of the great challenges the population of the popular sectors is facing is not to understand their opposing relations with the 'White' power elites at the expense of even more humiliated and discriminated population groups. This is true today not only for the relationship between urban and rural populations, but also for relationships with migrants from other Latin American countries. However, there is a tendency that new subaltern identities emerge in the working-class city neighbourhoods. In the course of migration processes, people of Indigenous or African origin join the *mestizo* population and discover common interests, for example the development of the '*chicha* culture' in the slums in Peru. At least when popular movements that are directed against social inequality and the threat to their own material existence emerge, the differences between people of different origins can dissolve greatly in a subjective sense. However, it must also be borne in mind that racist, sexist and/or adultist attitudes are power-preserving and as such repeatedly revived and instrumentalized by power elites.

Particularly in the case of younger members of the popular sectors, it should be considered that neither urban nor rural popular sectors exist in an isolated space that only feeds on or tries to converse with 'tradition'. Young people's self-understanding and their forms of actions are strongly influenced by technological changes, especially by digital media. This should not only be understood as external influence, the logic of actively using the opportunities that arise to make one's own messages and demands visible must also be considered.

> Technological changes and the uses of new technologies have an important impact on all social sectors. We cannot think of the definition of what is popular in isolation from the influence of the mass media and new technological devices, such as the internet or social networks or the advance of scientific and non-scientific knowledge, since popular sectors make extensive use of these devices and in many cases incorporate them in the reinforcement of their traditional cultures. We can even highlight the use of these technologies for the maintenance of collective memory and as a record, recovery, and strengthening of their own traditions, including language, rites, festivals and other community practices. ... Popular cultures are blurred, recreated or strengthened by emerging cultures, understood as social practices and forms of collective construction of the meaning and significance of life that emerge in the subaltern strata that differentiate themselves from and question the hegemonic cultural logic. (Valenzuela Arce, 2020: 52–53)

At the latest when social movements emerge from the daily struggle for survival as well as spontaneous expressions of dissatisfaction and frustration, it is clear to those involved that they are on the other side of a dividing line and fundamentally oppose the Creole elites. It is not only about disputes over different points of view, but also about an ongoing class antagonism.

> Dominant hegemonic cultures and so-called universal cultures are also class cultures and reflect interests and values that the culture of the subaltern classes is confronted with. Popular cultures refer to cultural fields that challenge the alleged universal character of official cultures, regardless of whether they incorporate elements from the dominant classes. Subalternity is shaped in the economic, social and power relationship with the dominant classes, which is why, beyond the differences between subaltern cultures, shared subalternity forms a common or articulated element, since cultural products are also signified from class positions and situations. (Valenzuela Arce, 2020: 56)

This is particularly evident in the social movements of Indigenous peoples (see López and García Guerrero, 2018). In all Latin American countries they experience that their protests and demands become a matter of 'national security' and are met by the nation-state authorities with violence. When people are not content to be tolerated as a 'cultural minority' and are cajoled with gracious offers of 'intercultural education' (see Tubino, 2005; López, 2009; Walsh, 2012) or 'intercultural health' (Bolados García, 2017) this is particularly apparent. The contrast with 'White' power elites becomes evident when addressing social inequality and demanding the right to land ownership and an economic system of collective self-determination. This may also express an awareness of the colonial roots of their own humiliation and exclusion.

> In colonial relations, defined by profound inequality and polarization in the distribution of income and wealth, as well as by an ancestral racism that reduced the vast majority of the original populations to poverty, Latin American popular cultures have a strong Afro-indigenous imprint. They are defined from the coordinates of class, ethnicity, poverty, coloniality and cultural expressions where religious persistence and traditional knowledge stand out, although these features do not exhaust their definition. (Valenzuela Arce, 2020: 51)

Latin America is still deeply marked by European colonization. This is expressed in this very term, which to this day has hardly been problematized, as well as in the fact that the former colonial languages are still dominant in practically all countries. Very few countries still recognize Indigenous languages as official languages, even in schools. However, there are still hundreds of other languages on this subcontinent that bear witness to the pre-colonial period and are often revived today. It is not a question of going back to the past, but of forming new decolonial identities in the local peoples. This is further aided by attempts to establish a critical interculturality that is not limited to a gracious tolerance of 'traditional' cultures. Rather, it questions the dominant ways of thinking and values imported from Europe and later from North America, including, inter alia, the idea that there are different human races of superior and inferior rank (see, for example, Walsh, 2013).

The continuity of colonial and racial heritage is also expressed in numerous monuments, in the naming of streets and squares and in public holidays. Thus, in almost all Latin American countries, 12 October, when Columbus supposedly 'discovered' America, has been an official holiday as *Día de la Raza* (Day of the Race, until very recently) now often called *Día de la Hispanidad* (Hispanic Heritage Day). Other names that were supposed to express the presence of Europe in America and the *mestizaje* or fusion of races were *Discovery Day, Day of the Encounter of Two Worlds, Pan-American*

Day, *Columbus Day* or the *National Day of Spain*, which in many contexts is still known as '*la madre patria*' (the mother country). During the present century, several countries have questioned the colonial imprint of these names and have changed them for others that express decolonial positions. This happened in Venezuela (*Day of Indigenous Resistance*, 2002), Nicaragua (*Day of Indigenous, Black and Popular Resistance*, 2007), Peru (*Day of Indigenous Peoples and Intercultural Dialogue*, 2009), Argentina (*Day of Respect for Cultural Diversity*, 2010), Bolivia (*Day of Decolonization*, 2011) or Ecuador (*Day of Interculturality and Plurinationality*, 2011). These new denominations do not mean that the policies of these states have since been guided by a decolonial perspective or that racism has been overcome in these countries, but they testify that pressure from below has increased and that the strengthening of Indigenous movements has contributed to this.

Approaching popular childhoods

There are many labels for popular childhood or popular childhoods. Usually they have a stigmatizing connotation. When, for example, the expression 'poor children' or 'children without childhood' is used, social disadvantage is what comes to mind, and the terminology suggests that these children are somehow 'limited' or 'uneducated'. At times, they are even considered 'anti-social' or 'dangerous'. They represent 'a state of minority, weakness, lack, defect, imperfection' (Schibotto, 1990: 313). This is true also for other terms used to highlight the characteristics of specific groups of these children, such as, for example, 'street children', 'orphaned children', 'disabled children', 'child soldiers', 'child labourers'. These are a common part of mainstream and even humanitarian discourses, emphasizing the misery and the need for help and rescue. However, at the same time, and often unintentionally, these terms entrench or even multiply the discrimination against and marginalization of children.

When my co-authors and I speak of popular childhoods or children from popular sectors in this book, we want to express that these are children, who are socially and structurally at the (hierarchical) bottom of society. On one hand, because they belong to social classes that are at the bottom of the power structure of a society, on the other, they are also in a subordinate position as children compared with adults. However, in this book, we do not only emphasize that children are in a socially disadvantaged position, but also that they are part of a class, village or broad social group. They have a social place in life where common interests emerge that can guide and stimulate their own agency. By this we also emphasize that children are not only disadvantaged individually and certainly not by chance, but that they can also draw strength from the experience of being part of a larger whole, that they are not alone. In view of this, we would also like to emphasize that they have a specific childhood which is different depending on gender, age, geographic location, and so on.

These other childhoods are not a homogeneous unit. They have many characteristics which are sometimes described with specific terms. For example, working children, Indigenous children, Afro-descendant children, migrant children, peasant children, or children from specific neighbourhoods or slums or urban-marginalized populations. These categories overlap. Migrant children, for example, may be members of Indigenous or African-descendant communities who have been forced to flee their homes to cities because of poverty in search of wealth or due to violence by powerful groups. Often, peasant children work, although their work is different from that of children in urban neighbourhoods. All of these children also differ in age and gender, which can have a considerable impact on their living situation, the type of work they do and their daily experiences of violence and discrimination, for example.

Since the vast majority of children from working-class backgrounds contribute to their livelihoods in some way through their own work, they are often referred to as working children. This designation not only expresses that children work, but also underlines that these children have a specific type of childhood in which not only their age, but also their economic co-responsibility and work experience influence the construction of their identities (Schibotto, 1990; Liebel, 1994; 2000; 2004).

To the extent that children see themselves as working children, as in the case of the social movements of working children and adolescents (NNATs[1]), this term seems appropriate and important. It emphasizes the specific characteristics of these children and contains a demand for their recognition. Working children as terminology is always associated with criticism of the capitalist economy and the exploitation and degradation it entails, and is therefore by no means a justification for so-called child labour. However, not all children we consider to be members of popular childhoods are or see themselves as working children. In the case of Indigenous peoples living in rural areas, for example, children's cooperation and co-responsibility is not called 'work'. Even in urban neighbourhoods, not all children see their own work as an essential part of their identity.

Given the tendency of the policies of states and various international organizations to stigmatize and even criminalize working children for their work, it seems important to us to insist on the right of children to work with dignity. Although this right has not yet been codified anywhere legally and is therefore an unwritten right, it is always rightly demanded by working children's movements (Liebel, 2004; Liebel and Martínez Muñoz, 2009). It remains important to make it visible and to liberate the children from illegality and stigmatization, wherever it takes place. The prohibition of and combat against child labour has resulted in working children having largely disappeared from public view at least in urban centres and that they are forced to work in hidden places or at night. This scandal must be countered politically, but this cannot be achieved by inventing other labels for their doings.

As I look to the future, I also think it to be important to remember that the forms of work that children do have changed and continue to change. As with adults, work can no longer be strictly distinguished from other activities. The separation of periods of work and non-work has always been typical of capitalist societies, where only dependent and paid work is recognized as such. This separation has always been problematic with regard to so-called reproductive work, which is mostly carried out by women and girls in their own homes and is neither remunerated in money nor taken into account in labour statistics and policies. Today, in addition, especially young people are often engaged in work, which, although it is paid, is not seen as work but as an activity that they have consciously chosen with specific intentions. This is especially true in the field of digital media, where even children, for example, create their own blog or act as 'influencers' or co-creators of computer games. This is not always done in order to make money, but can become an important part of their own identity.

Having said this, I would like to point out and advocate not to view children of the popular sectors as working children only, but to always understand them as active children in some way. This applies especially if these activities are important for their self-perception as persons, for the recovery of their dignity and the recognition that what they do is important in their living environments.

Creating identities of resistance

Every classification of people is an abstraction that contains the danger of making their peculiarities disappear or of distorting them in a one-sided way. This danger also exists with the terms *popular childhoods* and *childhoods of the Global South*. Therefore it is necessary to try to use them in an open, non-essentialist way, bearing in mind that the children subsumed under these terms are always, as all children, children with their own distinct characteristics and images. These, in turn, must be expressed in such a way as to highlight not only what is happening to these children, but also how they themselves act or their capability of acting as protagonists. This action is guided and stimulated by interests arising from specific social experiences.

When I talk of popular childhoods or childhoods of the Global South, I also assume that their interests arise from the experience of social disadvantage or social exclusion on the one hand, but also from the experience of social belonging on the other. Thus, if children are seen through an intersectional lens, a child is never just a child who can be characterized by age, for example, but is always part of a social group, a community or territory, a family, a country, a linguistic community or culture and a generational group, historically speaking. Since children always have more or less close relations with different groups, it would be a great simplification, an essentialization, to identify them with one of these groups only. Every child has several identities, which also contain the potential for conflicts that manifest themselves in a context-specific way. A child is not a mere reflection of one or more of these collectives, but always embodies individual and group characteristics and subjectivities. Moreover, the situation and subjectivities change in the course of life or due to incisive events and experiences.

Even in popular sectors, childhood does not automatically mean that children are recognized or treated in a way that respects their subjectivity and their status as morally equal persons to adults. Here too, they experience social silencing, abuse, humiliation, violence, disrespect. These actions can take place in their own family or come from their neighbourhood or from local authorities. As I noted earlier, this treatment is sometimes called adultism. It is caused, among other things, by the prevailing injustice, by the hardships in which members of the popular sectors find themselves. They are also partly influenced by the dominant ideology of childhood in society, which regards children as 'minors', as people of lesser value. Patriarchal ideologies based on the supposed natural superiority of men also play a role, and sometimes lead to forms of discrimination and sexual violence mainly against girls and young women. All this shows that people who are exposed to the injustices of capitalist society are additionally affected by the prevailing societal ideologies.

In popular sectors, there have always been creative expressions of resistance to oppression and violence. Today, these resistances come more than ever from young people who are no longer willing to accept their subordination and humiliation and who are activating new political narratives, as has been seen in 2018 in Nicaragua, 2019 in Chile, or 2020 in Peru and Colombia, for example. These narratives confront a political class that they feel no longer represents them.

With this book, I want to contribute to making visible, understanding and sustaining these processes of resistance that challenge authoritarian or adultist power through the defence of the *children of the people* in the construction of their organizations and the demands of a society and social conditions that deserve to be called democratic, inclusive and just. It is important to keep in mind that there is 'a certain disjunction between the political form of democracy and the principle of popular sovereignty, since the two are not the same' (Butler, 2015: 2). These are real processes, existing practices that re-signify the history of the popular, and making it, in a certain way, more intergenerational. With this book, I also want to make clear the role that children and adolescents themselves, as protagonists of the popular sectors in resistance, can play in the appropriation, vindication and reinvention of their rights. In the words of Alejandro Cussiánovich in the closing of Schibotto's book (1990), referring to the NNATs, 'these popular militants who are on a path of renewal of options, convictions and dreams'. Furthermore, he remarked, 'when they discover the vein of utopia by conquering their self-esteem, they initiate a process of dream and reality, of daily routine and novelty, of aggressiveness and tenderness, of imitation and creativity. That is where we must persist and affirm' (Cussiánovich, 1990: 413–414).

With this book, I want to continue to contribute to this by making emancipatory practices visible in compiling diverse expressions from the popular childhoods of the Global South.

The content of the book

The book has two parts. In Part I, which focuses on the question of children's rights, some developments in Europe are discussed and their history in other parts of the world is traced. I am mainly interested in reconstructing the debates about an emancipatory and liberating history of these rights. Until now, they have received only little attention. However they have recently found their own expression with new accents in the Southern regions of the world resulting in a reverse influence in the North. I want to make clear that in this history, children whom I summarize under the term *popular childhoods* had already provoked such reflections on children's rights more than a hundred years ago.

At the beginning, I examine some humiliating traces the colonization process has left in the postcolonial childhoods of the Global South, and ask what challenges for decolonization arise (Chapter 1). After an overview of the hidden history of those currents that conceived of children's rights as a means to children's self-empowerment (Chapter 2), Rebecca Budde and I reconstruct the international debates on the aims and approaches of recent and particular studies on children's rights (Chapter 3). In the following chapter, Urszula Markowska-Manista and I explore some of the ethical challenges and dilemmas facing childhood and children's rights studies (Chapter 4). In the final chapter of this part, Philip Meade and I discuss how children's rights, in particular their right to vote and political participation, can counter adultism as a form of colonization of childhoods, and contribute to the realization of intergenerational justice (Chapter 5).

Part II focuses on the question of how popular children or popular childhoods are affected by the unequal postcolonial world order and how they can contribute to influencing processes of decolonization, which remains an urgent challenge. In this context, I also discuss some theories relevant to this question.

First, I explore the question how the experiences children of the popular sectors have in their daily lives contribute to the development of their political subjectivities (Chapter 6). I then address the concept of resilience, which has become fashionable in recent decades, and discuss possible alternatives (Chapter 7). In the following chapter, I reconstruct a debate that has been going on in Latin America since the 1970s, which revolves around the idea of *protagonismo infantil*, and discuss how this action-guiding concept can be specified and concretized today (Chapter 8). In the last chapter of the book, I outline possible perspectives for insurgent research with popular childhoods in light of children's rights (Chapter 9). I do this in the hope that they may be useful for practices of solidarity with children and their rights.

PART I

Children's rights from below

Submission and humiliation of childhoods from a decolonial perspective

Introduction

In this chapter, I explore how the lived childhoods of the Global South result from colonization and how children from popular sectors are affected by its aftermath in the postcolonial era marked by the coloniality of power. For children, being affected means being subjugated and humiliated in various ways, but it also ignites their resistance. The basic thesis is that the modern pattern of childhood is a colonial construction in the triple sense: it is inspired by the colonial relationship, it serves to justify colonial conquest, and in the postcolonial era, it serves to render invisible other childhoods that do not conform to the Western norm or to make them appear deviant and backward. After explaining the multiple forms of subjugation and humiliation of childhoods under conditions of coloniality, I explain the need for and possible ways of decolonizing childhoods and the practice of children's rights. I begin by highlighting some of the ideological underpinnings that, in my view, foster the subjugation and humiliation of children in colonial and postcolonial contexts.

Binary thinking as an ideological basis for humiliation

The subjugation and humiliation of children, to which I refer here from a decolonial perspective, finds its ideological basis in binary categories constructed in a hierarchical and pejorative manner, in which a distinction is made between 'us' (belonging, normalized) and 'others' (excluded, deviant), according to Edward Said ([1978] 2013), called 'othering' or 'otherness'. This binary coding has its origins in the thoughts of philosopher René Descartes and continues to have an effect today. It refers to territories as well as to people and populations. I will now name some of these binary codes:

- developed *versus* underdeveloped (technically, socially and culturally);
- modern or progressive *versus* backward;
- civilized *versus* barbaric;
- cultivated *versus* nature-bound;

- rational *versus* irrational;
- self-controlled *versus* emotion-driven;
- educated and conscious *versus* ignorant and stupid (mastery of a certain knowledge, a certain way of thinking, includes mastery of a certain language – discursive power);
- ability or power to act *versus* inability or powerlessness to act (as a personal characteristic); and
- superior *versus* inferior (in the sense of 'power over' and devaluing people).

With reference to similar binaries, Michael Bourdillon, Sylvia Meichsner and Afua Twum-Danso Imoh refer to the category of childhood as follows:

> These binary pairs are associated and can easily result in the stereotypical categorisation of 'good childhood' as opposed to 'bad childhood'. ... The evaluative connotation of some of these pairs are compounded by the colonial history of political domination and the imposition of colonial ideologies on subordinate nations. While it is important and constructive to take account of differences in access to material resources or to technical knowledge, it is misleading to build these differences into a stereotypical categorization of acceptable childhoods versus those that are not acceptable. (Bourdillon et al, 2019: 256–257)

Deviant childhoods are often labelled, for example by UNICEF and some development agencies, as 'children without childhood', or in politics and studies on migration as 'left-behind children' (Gu, 2022), which may be done with the best of intentions but in fact contribute to their subjugation (Liebel, 2017; Crawley and Skleparis, 2018). I refer in particular to children of the Global South, while understanding this term not in a geographical but in a geopolitical sense. It includes all children affected by colonization, its aftermath and forms of 'coloniality of power' (Quijano, 2008; 2019) or 'informal colonialism' (Goldsmith, 2002):

- Children living in former colonized areas who are particularly affected by the social inequality of the current world order with the consequence of being excluded and invisibilized.
- Migrant and refugee children from former colonized areas and socially disadvantaged and marginalized children in former colonial countries, including members of minorities (see Markowska-Manista and Liebel, 2023). Here I will only refer to the first group mentioned.

As a decolonial point of view, I understand a critical analysis of the reasons for the subjugation of children of the Global South and possible ways to overcome these reasons, taking into account the perspectives, subjectivity and human rights of the affected children. This means that I understand children of the Global South not only as helpless victims, but also as (at least potential) actors of their decolonization. The children of the Global South are not a homogeneous group, but they share the experience of being humiliated and degraded. Through mutual support, the recognition of common interests and the appreciation of their individual and collective rights, they can become actors in the decolonization of their way of existence. In this context, adults in general and researchers in particular can play an important role. They can hinder or contribute to making children of the Global South visible and empower them to resist their subjugation. This includes questioning the Western pattern of childhood that has spread around the world from above through capitalist globalization. According to it, childhood is a phase of life that is not only strictly separated from adult life, but has a social status subordinate to that of adults. The ideological basis is the assumption that children, unlike adults, do not have the rationality and capacity to make their own decisions, especially if the latter affect the lives of adults. Therefore, children must be protected and prepared first and foremost, while adults are presented as whole, rational and competent people.

My basic thesis is that the modern, Western model of childhood is a colonial construction in the triple sense:

- It is inspired by the colonial relationship.
- It serves to justify colonial conquest.
- In the postcolonial era or coloniality, it serves to render invisible other childhoods that deviate from the Western norm or to make them appear 'deviant' and 'backward'.

The Western childhood pattern has repressive and humiliating consequences because it is based on a hierarchical and separating construction between adults and children (adultism or adultcentrism). The humiliating consequences are reinforced by the fact that it is based on the dominance of the 'White' adult male, presented as rational and civilized, over people with different (visible and/or attributed) characteristics. I will illustrate my thesis with a view upon the historical epochs of colonialism, coloniality and the processes of decolonization.

Humiliation under colonialism

Colonialism has existed in various forms throughout history. For example, the ancient Romans colonized parts of Europe, Asia and Africa in order to build an empire, raise armies and increase wealth. The Romans and ancient Greeks subordinated slaves (some of whom were children) who formed an underclass within the polis. However, when people speak of colonialism today, they often refer to the modern era of colonialism from the 15th to the 19th centuries. This era included the slave trade from Africa, the enrichment of the 'mother countries' of Western Europe through the exploitation of southern and eastern territories and their populations, and the establishment of settlement colonies in the Americas, Africa, Australia and New Zealand.

As the two most common forms and outcomes of colonialism, historian Jürgen Osterhammel (2005) distinguishes between *exploitation colonies* and *settler colonies*. Settler colonialism consists of the occupation of other countries for the purpose of settlement. Satellite domains are established, which are connected to the metropolis. The basic purpose of occupation in exploitation colonialism, on the other hand, is to extract resources and/ or people in order to increase imperial wealth. The role given to children is different in each of these forms. Exploitation colonialism expelled children from their lands and families, either by integrating them into a slave economy (in the case of Africans, for example) or by expelling them and sacrificing them to use their lands for the production of valuable crops and mineral resources (as in the case of children in the Americas and parts of the Pacific). While in the context of exploitation colonialism, the enslaved population was deliberately filled with children, the presence of children 'as such' in this system was not specifically considered, perhaps because of the dissonance between this practice and modern Western ideals of childhood. Settlement colonialism, on the other hand, is characterized by a particular concern with notions of childhood and the regulation of children according to this ideal.

In each of these cases, colonialism can be understood as a highly organized and complex system of expansion, encompassing a range of interconnected technologies and spheres of life: from militarism to trade, government, science and law, agriculture, industry, housing, religion and the arts. Colonialism not only extends the land available to an empire, but also the power and wealth of its government and some of its inhabitants. Colonialism materially enriches the colonizer through the cultivation and appropriation of goods such as sugar, tobacco, silver and gold and, in the case of settlement colonialism, the land on which they build their settlements. Culturally, colonialism increases the power and freedom of (part of) its own population by erasing or reducing the power and freedom of others.

For this reason, colonialism is not only a crude assertion of power, but also a psychological and ideological formation that produces colonial subjects, especially colonizer-occupiers who believe in their right to colonization. As Albert Memmi ([1957] 2016), Edward W. Said ([1978] 2013) and Ashis Nandy (1983) show, the key to increasing colonial power is the production of a seemingly complete knowledge system. It establishes a hierarchical relationship in which the colonizer is elevated to the position of 'knower' and the colonized is demoted to 'object of knowledge'. Through various media (literature, scientific texts, art, cartography, museums, film and television) the colonized 'other' becomes a caricature that embodies the reflection of the colonizer's self-perception. Thus, the colonized subject is represented as 'irrational', 'capricious', 'savage', 'primitive' and 'carnal', in contrast to the rationality and rational capacity of the colonizer. If the colonized does not meet the colonizer's expectations or does not correspond to his caricatures, the colonizers describe him/her as 'inscrutable' and 'unreliable'. This process of objectification includes the epistemological dimension of colonial power. Producing the colonized 'other' as 'what is known' is a technique used to maintain control over him/her.

Reflections on this epistemological dimension of colonialism help to understand the meaning of 'childhood' in this system. Colonialism was conceived by the colonizers according to the European family pattern that emerged during this period. The metropolis 'reproduces' itself in the form of colonies, which in turn are administratively linked to the 'parental' homeland. For example, in his major work *Leviathan*, philosopher Thomas Hobbes (1651) described the colonies and plantations as 'children of the Commonwealth'. This pictorial reference to the colonies as children is an indication of both the state of the colonies and the state of children at the time. Children were subordinate to adults, just as the colonies existed in relations of subjugation to the metropole or 'mother country'.

Colonized peoples were characterized in the most derogatory terms as incorrigibly infantile. Historically, Indigenous peoples have been depicted as incapable of autonomy, irresponsible, reckless and resistant to education or improvement. This caricature profoundly influenced the 'administration' of the colonies and the relations between colonized peoples and colonizers. The infantilization of Indigenous peoples is ideologically consistent with cultural chauvinism and White supremacy, as well as with Western assumptions of patriarchal authority over children. The understanding of childhood as inherently uncivilized and in need of correction conditions the colonial relationship by justifying violence. The brutal (often lethal) methods of colonialists are justified, as are contemporary discourses of disciplining children with their 'civilizing' function, that is, ultimately, for the supposed good of the 'natives' themselves (Rollo, 2018; Faulkner, 2020).

There is a negative dialectic between the invention of the Western model of childhood and the European colonialization of non-European territories and populations. The Western pattern of childhood develops in parallel with colonization. It is constructed as a form of conquest of a foreign, unknown, empty, natural and uncivilized territory. In this sense, childhood was conceived by the liberal philosopher John Locke ([1690] 1995) as a '*tabula rasa*' or blank slate, and almost a hundred years later by the Enlightenment philosopher Jean-Jacques Rousseau ([1755] 2016) as 'pure nature' in the sense of the '*homme naturel*', the original natural man. These constructions were preceded by the fantasies of the 'noble savage' that accompanied the 'discovery' of the 'New World' called America.

The colonial view also shaped the beginnings of sociology, psychology and the educational sciences in general, as well as childhood studies in particular in the 19th and early 20th centuries. In his lectures at the Sorbonne in Paris in the early 20th century, Emile Durkheim, one of the fathers of positivist sociology, compared children to 'primitive man'; the 'intractability' of their 'primitive passions' corresponded to that of 'savages'. In order not to endanger the cohesion of civilized society, they would have to be subjected to a 'prevailing' moral education, to 'discipline' and to 'self-control', in particular by the school (Durkheim, 1934). In his magnum opus *The Social System*, the influential US-American sociologist Talcott Parsons ([1951] 1991) also equates the development of societies with the development of the individual personality. Thus, he thinks of certain social groups or societies as immature, primitive or backward with respect to others, 'like children', without perceiving their specific distinctive characteristics. With regard to children, Parsons speaks of a 'barbarian invasion' ([1951] 1991: 143) in the sense of the incessant influx of new members born into it. This pattern of childhood has two material and historical prerequisites:

- The exploitation of colonized territories and peoples created the material resources for relegating children to a separate social space, while denying them responsibility for the production and reproduction of human life. This social space was privatized within the framework of the bourgeois family ('family childhood'), while children were also institutionalized and pedagogized within the framework of bourgeois society ('school childhood').
- The emergence of the capitalist mode of production, with its destructive tendencies, made it necessary to protect children from premature harm and to prepare them as future workers and soldiers. This went hand in hand with the emergence of nation-states, which consider their next generations as a potential for 'national development' and, accordingly, institutionalize them in a developmental form through compulsory schooling.

The ideal background for this is the bourgeois notion, objectified in civil law, of the self-responsible, autonomous and rational individual who exists by himself and who controls and dominates himself, according to liberal philosopher John Stuart Mill ([1861] 2001: 50) 'the first lesson of civilisation'. This notion is fundamentally different from the notion that all individuals are born as social beings who are mutually and intersubjectively dependent on and co-responsible for other human beings. For its part, the Western model of childhood is instrumentalized to justify colonial conquest. Conquered peoples of all ages are declared children, ergo 'infantilized'. This allowed

European colonial powers to present themselves as saviours (supported by the Christian doctrine of salvation) who took on 'the white man's burden' (Kipling, 1899) to enlighten and civilize 'primitive people'. In this sense, colonialism was advocated as 'educational colonialism' (Osterhammel, 2005: 110).

This staging of colonialism conceals that it is about domination, control and exploitation. The category of childhood was applied to colonized peoples in the sense that they were separated from the colonial rulers in reservations and given a life of misery, which in turn facilitated their exploitation as labourers. By labelling them as childlike, there was no need for special consideration of their children, who would otherwise be entitled to a childhood according to the Western model. These children were exploited as much as their adult counterparts under the guise of inclusion in 'shared responsibility' processes that is common in many non-Western cultures. Western childhood is only applied to them at the stage of coloniality and becomes the standard for their developmental status.

However, special and humiliating treatment was accorded to children who did not conform to the standards of normality set by the colonial powers. In Latin America, this applied particularly to Indigenous children. It also applied to those who emerged as a kind of collateral damage from the encounter of the conquistadors (White men, including priests and other figures in the Catholic Church) with Indigenous and Afro-descendant women. Even the colonizing countries' own children, who were considered useless because they deviated too much from the normal standards of Western bourgeois childhood, were simply deported to the colonial territories, exploited there (sometimes with the help of charitable organizations) as cheap labour and, at the same time, used as a 'White' population reserve for the Europeanization of the colonial territories. Colonialism involved the destruction and humiliation of children of all kinds: violent acts of extermination (genocide), segregation, and assimilation due to the construction of their otherness and their non-recognition as morally equal human beings.

Humiliation under coloniality

In so-called postcolonial theories, the period following colonialism is often referred to as postcolonial. Indian social researcher Sarada Balagopalan (2019: 20) sees this period as 'colonial past in the present'. The colonial past leaves many traces in the former colonial territories and continues in various forms in the inequality of power between North and South. In relation to this, the decolonial perspective means uncovering and opposing these traces and forms, both in theory and in practice. To understand the forms of humiliation in this period of history that continues to this day, I refer primarily to the decolonial approaches that have emerged in Latin America since the 1990s (see Liebel, 2020: 63–68). One of the most important approaches goes back to the Peruvian sociologist Anibal Quijano (2008; 2019). However, Quijano is deliberately not talking about the postcolonial but about *coloniality*, because colonialism does not end with the formal independence of former colonial territories as nation-states, but continues in other forms. The author describes this state as the *coloniality of power* and considers it to be closely linked to what he and others (for example, Lander, 2000) call the *coloniality of knowledge*. The coloniality of power thus has both a material and an epistemic dimension.

The material dimension is reflected in the fact that, even after the end of colonialism, the power differential and material inequality between the former colonizing nations and the colonized territories has not been broken. Inequality has taken other, less visible forms, but it has not diminished. According to available economic data, material inequality between different parts of the world's population has never in human history been as great as it is today. Although poverty has relatively decreased and infant mortality has decreased, the absolute number of people in precarious situations has increased (see World Inequality Lab, 2018; Kaltmeier, 2019; UNDP, 2019; Piketty, 2020). The consequences of climate change, caused by the extractivist capitalist economy and the imperial lifestyle, also affect people of the Global South much more than of the Global North. Finally, if we consider that in the countries of the South the proportion of children is much higher than in the Northern regions of the world, it can be assumed that children are even more affected by material inequality and power imbalance. The humiliating effects can be seen in the fact that for the majority of children:

- Their lives are less valid, less valuable.
- Their livelihoods are destroyed (condemned to material poverty, exacerbated by climate catastrophe and more recently the COVID-19 pandemic).
- They are exposed to greater economic exploitation.
- Their life expectancy and life chances are reduced.
- Their mobility is severely restricted (passports are less valid, if accessible at all) or they are forced to flee in mortal danger.
- They are hostile, discredited and excluded because of their social or ethnic origin and the colour of their skin.

However, these humiliations cannot be understood without the *coloniality of knowledge*. It consists in the fact that certain ways of thinking and knowing, which were developed during the colonial period in Europe, are considered the only true and valid ones and are imbued with power over the population of the former colonized areas. Some authors speak of 'epistemic violence'

(Spivak, 1988; Cannella and Viruru, 2004) or 'epistemicide' (De Sousa Santos, 2014[1]) in this regard. These include the binary and hierarchical categories mentioned earlier, such as between progressive, or modern and backward, developed and underdeveloped, rational and irrational, and so on. They are associated with certain ideas about valuing people differently according to their origin, skin colour and way of life. People of Indigenous origin are considered backward and an obstacle to progress in terms of their way of life and way of thinking. Devaluation is often, but not always, associated with visible characteristics such as skin colour. It has long been explicitly and still is implicitly legitimized by the supposed existence of different human races.

Using four examples, I will show how the coloniality of power leads to the humiliation of children. First, I refer to the post-independence treatment of children in Latin American states. Second, to humiliating practices in the United States, Canada and Australia. Third, to the humiliating impacts of a dogmatic implementation of the UN Convention on the Rights of the Child (CRC) in Africa. Fourth, to the humiliating consequences of a paternalistic practice of aid to children by Northern-based humanitarian and child rights organizations.

Humiliation of 'illegitimate' and 'bastard' children in Latin America

Whereas in colonial times children of poverty-stricken native peoples were received with an attitude of charity, with the emergence of the newly independent states in Latin America the tendency to 'improve' children gradually increased. In particular, it focused on children of Indigenous, African origin (heirs of slavery), and those who had arisen from extramarital relations between White men of Spanish or Portuguese origin and Indigenous or Black women. They were considered 'illegitimate' or 'bastard children', those descended from priests were called 'children of the Church' (see Liebel, 2020: 91–92; on illegitimate children called 'huachos' in Chile see Rojas, 2010; Salazar, 2012; Dias et al, 2016). Among them, above all, children were believed to be found 'wandering' the streets of fast-growing cities, where they engaged in a wide range of activities to support themselves and often their families provided they had one. For children who were picked up from the streets, new types of 'houses of correction' or 'reformatories' were created with the aim of 'eradicating vagrancy and the forms of life it entailed (theft, begging, and so on), as well as instilling them with work discipline and respect for authority' (Sánchez Santoyo, 2003: 43). In particular, girls were condemned when they went out alone dancing or to the cinema, instead of doing housework. The most suspect were unmarried mothers, who were denied any moral quality for the education of their children.

A woman who did not marry was considered 'very harmful' to society (Sánchez Santoyo, 2003: 53; on a reformatory called '*escuela correccional*' in Mexico see Bailón Vásquez, 2012).

Children were perceived as 'juvenile offenders' or 'abnormal individuals' who 'had received from their parents the natural tendency towards crime and would inevitably pass it on to their descendants' (Sánchez Santoyo, 2003: 55). It was surely no coincidence, therefore, that in the 1920s programmes to sterilize children who had been picked up and trapped emerged to prevent the further spread of what were often called 'bad racial qualities'. This discriminating view was based on positivist discourse that interpreted misery and poverty in society as the result of 'genetic' differences between social classes. A racist discourse was used with the pretence of 'combating and correcting the defects inherent in the "nature" of boys and girls through eugenics, hygienic discipline through medicine and biology, as well as through the sciences of personality' (Corona Caraveo, 2003: 16).[2]

In Chile, for example, at the turn of the 20th century, after victorious wars against the Mapuche and other Indigenous peoples in the South as well as against the neighbouring states of Bolivia and Peru, the view prevailed among the ruling power elites 'that indigenous blood was a racial burden that explained Chilean everlasting underdevelopment' (Araneda-Urrutia, 2022: 2). They fantasized about a 'Chilean race' that they saw endangered by 'miscegenation'. They used as evidence the rampant alcoholism, criminality, children born out of wedlock, morbidity and high infant mortality among those driven into poverty. The 'imperial sanity' gained by Chilean power elites after Chile's geopolitical repositioning in previous decades led them not only to believe themselves superior to other Latin American peoples (Beckman, 2009). They also advocated in a Social Darwinist manner for a nation in which Indigenous and *mestizo* people and their children, considered genetically inferior, were sorted out and subjected to special treatment (Walsh, 2019). These people were to be saved from themselves. Not only did the supposedly wayward children become targets of bio-political surveillance and control, furthermore, their membership in humanity was called into question in the first place. 'The monstrous child who should not be born nor propagate the defects and sins of his degenerate parents was not an "Other" still recognizable as human but an unintelligible outsider creature' (Araneda-Urrutia, 2022: 3).

For obvious reasons, after the Nazi experience in Germany, a programme that spoke of the 'superiority of the race' could not be maintained. Thus, from 1942 onwards it was replaced by the notion of the dangerous or antisocial child, focused on the need to establish programmes to correct antisocial behaviour (visible in the Pan-American Children's Congresses held since 1916).

In countries such as Brazil, Colombia or Guatemala, the desire to 'save' children has not only generated efforts to 'improve' children considered inferior through drastic educational measures, but also through severe repressive practices. The various measures of persecution are painted as acts of 'social cleansing' ranging from violent displacement of children and youths from public spaces, to 'disappearance', to ostentatiously staged acts of physical extermination.

Until the 1980s, a specific form of humiliation also consisted of Indigenous children from poor families being rented to rich families, as Jaime Antimil Caniupan describes using the example of the Mapuche in Chile. The rented child was degraded as an 'Indian animal' (Antimil Caniupan, 2015: 171). The humiliation of Indigenous children is also reflected in the fact that in almost all Latin American countries they are confronted at school with a history that glorifies colonization as a civilizing achievement, that they are often forbidden to speak in their mother tongue, or that girls are not allowed to wear traditional clothes. Although there are now also primary schools where teaching is conducted bilingually, 'patriotic' indoctrination, often in conjunction with military rituals, further continues in these schools. Moreover, they are only found in regions with a high percentage of Indigenous population and offer hardly any opportunities for further educational qualifications (on Argentina see Novaro and Hecht, 2017).

Racist attitudes continue to this day in several Latin American countries. In some countries, such as Chile and Argentina, suspicion is nowadays particularly directed at migrant children from poor families from other Latin American countries. In reference to their darker skin colour, they are the target of 'positivist discourses of race whitening' (Palominos, 2016: 204). The racist connotation has recently been obscured by a discourse of 'multiculturalism', which, under the cloak of tolerance, exalts and excludes children who are understood not to belong to the 'Nation' and establishes their social disadvantage (Novaro and Hecht, 2017; Enriz et al, 2020). In Chile, conservative elites continue to speak bluntly of the 'Chilean race' with a view to the privileged sectors of the population of European origin. Within the 'postcolonial' state, 'internal colonialism' continues as a 'civilizing enterprise' against the children of Indigenous minorities such as the Mapuche (Nahuelpan Moreno, 2019).

Humiliation of Indigenous and Black children in the United States, Canada and Australia

Many states, including the United States, Canada and Australia, grew out of so-called settler colonies. Settlers violently expelled Indigenous peoples and communities from their lands, claiming them for their own. They stripped them of their means of subsistence and condemned them to a life of poverty and dependency. This practice is justified by the claim that the wretched Indigenous population needs to be 'civilized' and 'protected' from their own destitution. Part of this history is how the children of Indigenous peoples, as well as the sons and daughters of Indigenous women, fathered by White soldiers or settlers, were treated. From the late 19th century onwards, these children were systematically separated from their parents in order to make them 'White'. They were adopted into White foster families and/or forced into special boarding or residential schools, where they were quartered, tortured and ideologically indoctrinated. In this way, the children, according to the official explanation, could be 'civilized' and 'saved' from a life of backwardness and poverty and made 'useful' for modern society. 'Policy makers regarded the surviving Indigenous populations as standing in the way of national unity, modernity and progress and envisioned child removal as a means to complete the colonization of indigenous peoples' (Jacobs, 2009: 26).

While *cultural assimilation* was favoured in the United States and Canada, in Australia the preferred practice was *biological absorption* (sometimes referred to as 'breeding out the colour'). Child abduction was cynically justified and seen as a child 'protection' measure. This practice was presented as a humane alternative to warlike and hostile combat against the Indigenous population. In Australia, a distinction was made in policy between 'full-bloods' and 'half-castes'. The children of the former were strictly segregated and forced to live in conditions that would hasten their extinction, while the latter were to be distributed and absorbed into the 'White' population.

It is no coincidence that the practice of child relocation in the United States and Australia began at a time when these countries were preparing to become modern, industrialized nation-states. Dominant groups strove to create a unified national sentiment, in which Europe – a heritage and dominance of 'White' immigrants – could be secured. Racist ideologies emphasized their foreignness, inadequacy and inferiority, and justified the special treatment of Indigenous children and children of African descent. In Canada, similar procedures were imposed on Indigenous children by the state and the Catholic Church as part of a policy that openly aimed to 'kill the Indian in the child' (Darian Smith, 2013: 171; see also Merasty and Carpenter, 2017).[3]

In the United States, racial discrimination against Black children is still omnipresent today, this can be seen particularly in the higher rate of police persecution against them. The brutal, often deadly behaviour against Black children (and young people) is justified on the grounds that they are not 'real children' who, unlike White children, do not deserve special attention and protection. Under the ideological premise of 'adultification', they are 'pathologized as angry, disrespectful, sassy, deviant, threatening, criminal, sexually precocious and carry adult-like culpability' (Patton, 2022: 169; for empirical evidence on boys and girls, respectively, see Goff et al, 2014; Crenshaw et al, 2015). They are denied empathy and opportunities to find their place and learn from their mistakes like their White peers (Gilmore and Bettis, 2021). In the dominant imaginary, 'Black children are and have always been a threat to the continuity of White supremacy, and consequently have been treated as enemy combatants in the same brutal manner as their elders' (Patton, 2022: 171). They continue to be treated as potential criminals to whom the 'severity of the law' must be applied in all circumstances.

Since the 1990s, thanks to the resistance of the affected population and the idea that children have rights, this pattern of child neglect and humiliation has begun to be considered problematic. However, there is no doubt that there is still a long way to go before all children can grow up in conditions of equality and lead a life of dignity, regardless of their social situation, their origin, their appearance, their gender and their age.

Humiliating enforcement of children's rights in Africa

The idea of children's rights has not only positive implications. Particularly, the implementation of the CRC is also often carried out in a way that has humiliating effects. This happens, for instance, when the Euro-Western standard of childhood on which the CRC is based, serves as a criterion for dealing with socially disadvantaged and marginalized children. One example is campaigns in Africa that scandalize children's migratory movements in sweeping terms as abuse and exploitation, without taking into account the specific circumstances. For example, a study states:

> Institutions across a variety of contexts have come to understand a child's departure from the parental home (whether for care, learning, or labour) as a child protection violation, seemingly representing an involuntary act that stems from adult negligence and exploitation, and leading inexorably to harm for children, their families and their communities. Child movement has thus increasingly become conflated with trafficking, a conceptual confusion that has significant consequences for policy. (Boyden and Howard, 2013: 354)

In this way, mobile, homeless and nomadic children had become a site of widespread institutional moral panic. Similar issues arise with regard to policies that seek to improve the situation of children in urban street situations. Like 'trafficked children', these children are often seen as mere passive and helpless objects of compassion. In a study, Ofosu-Kusi and Mizen (2012; see also Mizen, 2018), based on research with street children in the centre of Accra, the capital of Ghana, found strong social bonds between them. The authors interpret these social ties as 'new ways of life' and 'new modes of childhood'. They do not describe how these bonds emerged, but it can be assumed that memory or experience with traditional cultural forms of reciprocity are reflected in these children and, in the face of the new challenges of urban street life, are reactivated. The forms these traditions take may be contradictory, and their scope limited, in terms of overcoming daily deprivations, risks and humiliations. However, they clearly contain a potential for resistance, in the sense that a social form can emerge, in which people are not judged by their outward appearance or their purchasing power, and their human dignity is unconditionally respected.

Similarly, two South African researchers, with respect to 'tireless advocates, researchers and activists in HIV/AIDS work', call for reflection on the effectiveness of 'their orphan-centred, rhetorically charged appeals to mobilize interventions in a disastrous epidemic compromise' (Meintjes and Giese, 2006: 425). The authors illustrate how the global focus on orphans leads to entrenched stereotypes of children's experiences, and argue that those writing about and responding to children in the context of HIV/AIDS should pay more attention to conceptual and representational issues. They caution against the assumption that children are helpless victims because of their 'orphanhood' and call for more attention to be paid to their similarities with other children living in poverty. When poor children are characterized as passive victims, negative stereotypes attach to them (for further examples, see Chapter 3). In a recent publication, South African legal scholar Julia Sloth-Nielsen and Dutch anthropologist Katrien Klep (2020) introduce the concept of 'independent children' for children who depend on themselves, and ask how children's rights can become a means for their recognition and (self-)empowerment. In addition to children in street situations, they also refer to children living in child-headed households, a new family form that is widespread in Southern Africa.

Where children are dependent on helping themselves, as in the case of migrant, street or orphaned children, their rights and interests are best served if they find recognition and support for the way of life they consider appropriate. Only then can they see the value of children's rights and perhaps use them to achieve a life of dignity.

Humiliation by benevolence

The humiliation of children of the Global South continues today also in actions that purport to help children and improve their situation, what we would like to call a kind of *paternalistic postcolonial benevolence*. Aid organizations based in the North largely fund their work through donations, mainly through advertising campaigns or the offer of sponsorships for children. Despite the claim to understand children as subjects of rights and to treat them in a spirit of partnership, almost all of these organizations repeatedly resort to language and images that demean and humiliate the children they purport to help. Despite the best intentions to give these children a better life, their livelihoods are devalued as deficient or underdeveloped. Children often appear on donation posters and advertisements as victims in need of help and are the target of the relief efforts of those who supposedly have a better understanding of what children need and what is good for them. They give the impression that they need to be *rescued*.

For many years, donation posters showed supposedly poor, sick, hungry or physically disabled children looking at the camera with a facial expression that appears to be suffering, sad or empty. In this context, the term 'misery pornography' has been correctly used (Caparrós, 2020). For some years now, children have also been portrayed laughing or smiling. But it is only at first glance that children's dignity is preserved and they appear as subjects of their own actions. The context, the reality of children and their life situation remain hidden. These positive images of children are used to show donors how their donation has worked and changed their lives.

In donation posters, children from rural and impoverished areas are often depicted. In one poster, for example, the slogan 'Closing Education Gaps' is combined with an image that visualizes the entire African continent as a black 'education gap' in an otherwise white Lego environment. In this way, the childhoods of the Global South are homogenized 'within a language of "lack"' (Balagopalan, 2019: 14). The idea of the poor and uneducated subjects of the South is opposed in ever new images to the rich, educated and modern people of the North.

Another central motif is the construction of the 'self' – in the form of the organization and donors from the North – as active, and the 'other' – in the form of children and people from the South – as passive. Consequently, the word 'aid' often appears on posters. Formulations such as 'Help now', 'Please help', 'We help children in need' or 'Help us save lives' are just a few examples of how various humanitarian organizations use the word 'aid' on posters. Such formulations, however, not only construct the 'others' as passive and in need of help, but also suggest who are the only ones who can help poor children: 'they', the competent donors from the North, and 'we', the competent organization actively providing aid.

One example is a campaign by the Nike and NoYo foundations in the United States, which asked 'American girls' to help girls in Southern countries under the slogan 'Girls Power'. In it, girls in the United States are portrayed as 'self-reliant' and 'strong', while girls in the South are portrayed as vulnerable and in need of help. Northern girls are flattered that they have what it takes to 'save', 'empower' and 'liberate' Southern girls by helping them get a better education. This dichotomy between two fundamentally different childhoods reproduces the colonial relationship pattern that Western people, in this case girls, have more developed abilities than their age and gender peers in regions of the world where development is still pending. The criterion for this distinction is the presence or absence of autonomy and strength. At the centre of the campaign are 'the devastating impacts of Third World patriarchy, dominance, and inequality, while simultaneously experiencing the benevolent rescue of Third World girls by the Western subject' (Bent, 2013: 9). Western girls are taken into service as 'philanthro-teens' (Bent, 2013: 15).

To counter these humiliating practices, a decolonizing perspective in childhood and children's rights studies is needed, which we will outline in Chapters 3, 4 and 9.

Decolonization as liberation from humiliation

I understand decolonization as countering the coloniality of power in both its material and discursive manifestations. This includes recognizing that there are no 'children without childhood' in the world, but a great variety of childhoods. By ignoring this variety or rendering it invisible through a Eurocentric bias, many children are created *out of place*, with multiple humiliating consequences.

The colonization of childhoods is a multidimensional process that encompasses the unequal balance of power between different age groups, as well as other aspects of social inequality that also apply to and between adults, and between boys and girls from different circumstances. From a decolonial perspective, it is primarily about the unequal North–South relationship, which unequally distributes life chances and is reinforced by disadvantages due to racist and sexist stereotypes. Disadvantages have material and ideological reasons, which in turn are linked in real life and can reinforce each other.

It is also important, in our view, to recognize that different childhoods do not exist in isolation from each other, and that they are not absolutely distinct and cannot be delimited from each other. They are the long-term result of economic, political and cultural processes and change over time. These changes and mutual influences have intensified with economic and cultural globalization. But they have not led to a unified global childhood, but to many globalized, 'hybrid' childhoods, which are themselves constantly changing. However, these changes take place under unequal premises that need to be taken into account in the decolonization of childhoods. Decolonization therefore requires at least two aims:

- Overcoming the material preconditions for social inequality, disadvantage and exclusion of children based on unequal economic and political power.
- Replacing the dominance of the Euro-Western childhood standard as a measure of the 'right' or 'good' childhood with an equal recognition of all socio-cultural forms of childhood. This recognition, however,

should not be understood as a mere tolerant concession to the plurality of childhoods, but as the result of intercultural exchange and mutual learning on an equal footing.

Furthermore, this raises the question of who the potential subjects of the decolonization of childhoods are. If decolonization is not merely a 'tolerant' concession of the colonizers to the colonized, then children themselves should have a central role in this process. This is not just a speculative wish, but one supported by social reality. Since children in non-Western cultures already assume co-responsibility at a young age, they are confronted with 'adult' reality earlier than children in Western societies, and, therefore, find themselves compelled to play an active role in society. This is exemplified by the social movements in which children are important and often leading actors. They can thus also become role models for children beyond the Global South and contribute to the 'provincialization' of the dominant, Euro-Western model of childhood.

Today, the international practice of children's rights and children's policies is itself a component of the colonization of childhoods. Despite its claim to counter the social disadvantage and humiliation of children in the Global South, it helps to establish absolutely its standards of a 'good' childhood through the supremacy of its organized actors (governments, UNICEF, the International Labour Organization, international non-governmental organizations), which are based in the North and possess the greatest material resources. This often leads to the humiliation of children from the Global South itself (for example, in campaigns to 'eradicate child labour'). Children's rights are often understood in a way that leaves little room for interpretation by 'cooperation partners' and especially by the children concerned. For this reason, children's rights, especially participation rights, are often understood in the regions of the South as an imposed import and are only reluctantly taken up, if at all. The fact that the Western childhood pattern dominates in the CRC contributes to this (Cordero Arce, 2015b). Certainly not all actors can be blended, and processes of learning and change are also emerging in the North, but the dominance of Western actors in international child rights practice and child policy remains.

Like the decolonization of childhoods, the decolonization of child rights practice and children's policies requires questioning one's own supremacy and norms. This can only be done by subjecting them to intercultural dialogue that is respectful of children's perspectives. In this sense, children's rights must be understood in a context-specific and culturally sensitive manner (see recently Faulkner and Nyamutata, 2020; Vandenhole, 2020). The children of the Global South, then, should not be treated as helpless recipients in need of paternalistic interventions, as is still the prevailing view in the West. Instead, their specific experiences and competencies must be taken seriously, and they must be given the opportunity to exert a decisive influence on the policies and actions of governments and international organizations alike. It is no less important to work with children to address the structural conditions and policies responsible for their disadvantage and subjugation. This would help strengthen the social position of Global South children, supporting them in their struggle for a dignified life in a collective and organized manner.

2

Children's rights movements and the hidden history of children's rights

Introduction

If we understand children's rights as a specific form of human rights, their beginning would be dated in the European Enlightenment or in the 18th century. However, when we take a closer look at the different aspects of children's rights, it is not possible to limit them to a purely European achievement nor to the past 250 years. Human rights and children's rights are not only the fruit of the illustrious ideas of some philosophers and pedagogues, they also emerge from social struggles for a better life, understood as humane, which could no longer be withheld from children. Children, especially those from the subaltern classes, in former times also participated in this struggle. Today, major impulses for the reconceptualization of children's rights come from young people of the Global South.

In the history of children's rights, two main strands can be distinguished: on one hand, those who emphasize the protection of children and later the guarantee of their dignified living conditions, and on the other hand, those who strive for the equality and active participation of children in society (see Renaut, 2002).[1] The two strands are not entirely opposed to each other, although they have each developed separately until very recently. Internationally, one strand is represented by the Geneva Declaration on the Rights of the Child, which was adopted by the League of Nations in 1924. As this history of children's rights has already been described extensively,[2] it will not be part of our elaborations here. Rather, we look to the other, less known development, in which children's rights are foremost seen as an expression and means of the emancipation and equality of children (as human beings). As they generally go hand in hand with social movements, which aim at changing social and political conditions, we call them children's rights movements.

Children's rights movements are sometimes distinguished as 'radical' compared to 'reformist' and 'pragmatic' movements (Verhellen, 1994: 59–60). Here, we refer mostly to the 'radical' ones. We see the distinction between 'children's rights movements' and 'children liberation movements' made by Veerman (1992) as problematic, because there is a particular understanding of children's rights in both movements. As Reynaert et al (2009: 521), we understand children's rights movements as 'counter-movements' against movements mainly centred in paternalistic notions of child saving and child protection.

In this chapter, I give an insight into the less known history of children's rights and their origins. This hidden history is threefold: first, it has received little attention; second, it has hardly been represented in international law; third, we know little about the extent to which and the ways in which young people have contributed to it. The last point in particular is an enduring challenge for historical research. I can only give some hints here and hope that they will be taken up in further research. At the end of the chapter, I will make clear why children's rights must not be understood abstractly, but must be related to the concrete life contexts of children and must be developed further with relevant participation of children. This also amounts to combining the practice of children's rights not only with pedagogical but also with political action.

The emergence of children's rights

With regard to the United Nations Convention on the Rights of the Child (hereafter CRC), a differentiation between *protection, provision* and *participation* rights (the 'three Ps') or rights to freedom is often made. I take up this distinction to illustrate the respective emergence of different children's rights.

Rights to *protect* children probably have the longest and most widespread history. They emerged from the conviction that the life of a newborn deserves protection; that children are not equal to a thing that can be handled discretionally. This can be seen particularly well in regulations prohibiting the killing of children. The reasoning behind this attitude towards children can be found in the common belief held by all of the world's big religions that children do not belong to individual persons who have power over them but that they are god's creations. In Europe in 1530, Martin Luther (1483–1546) was probably the first person to voice that children do not belong to their parents but to God and to the community (Alaimo, 2002: 6). About 150 years later, at the end of the 17th century, English philosopher John Locke (1632–1704) also questioned parents' right of disposition over their children (see Archard, 2015). The Scottish moral philosopher Francis Hutcheson (1694–1746) also stressed that children are not the property of their parents, but are 'rational agents' who can claim their own rights, and that they must be respected (Hutcheson, 1755: 192).

However, even into the 19th century this applied only to male descendants. In those days, farmers in France, for example, would say: 'I don't have any children, only girls.' In Naples, Italy, it was very usual to fly a black flag when a girl was born as a signal to everyone that congratulations were not appropriate (Verhellen, 1994: 12). In some parts of the world, for instance in China or India, similar customs are still practised today and sometimes lead to abortion or avoidance of girl births using modern reproductive medicine. However, it should also be borne in mind that, until the 20th century, children's rights, like human rights in general, had no validity whatsoever in the world regions colonized by the European powers. The children of the colonized peoples or the slaves recruited from them were not considered as people with own rights, nor were their parents. This status continues today with the widespread racist discrimination these descendants face.[3]

Provision and *participation* rights are newer, although there is a notable exception in Thomas Spence (1750–1814), who defended the right to common property in England against private, consistently violent appropriation of land.[4] In his booklet *The Rights of Infants* (Spence, 1796; documented by Freeman, 2020: 425–436), he explicitly attributed the 'natural right' to children 'to a full participation of the fruits of the earth'.

In many non-Western cultures a centuries-old custom is to acknowledge the capacities of children and to assign certain tasks to them, which, according to Western understanding, are reserved for adults that have reached 'legal age'. In some African and South American regions, children are assigned a piece of land or cattle at a very young age, which they handle and have the responsibility to care for. To some extent, these practices serve to learn necessary life-skills at an early age, yet they also express the belief that children already have their own qualities, which are to be respected and promoted. In the highlands of Bolivia and Peru a tradition is upheld until today in which so-called 'curious children' at the age of 10 or 12 are elected to be a traditional authority, as the belief is that children can give specific impulses for community life that adults may not (for an overview see Liebel, 2004: 77–99; Bolin, 2006; PRATEC, 2020: 36–37, 70). Nobody in these villages would think that the children lack the necessary competencies for this task let alone the legal measures to vote and to be elected. Generally, children of the same villages also do fieldwork, and no one would think that they have to go to school first to do so or to have reached a certain minimum age.

In the Indigenous cultures of South and Mesoamerica, as in other ancient cultures on other continents, it is not common to separate children and adults by age; both are seen as an integral part of the community, each with their specific characteristics. Children are seen as 'small persons', who are to be taken seriously just like 'adults'. They are ascribed different capacities that are important for communal life and which 'adults' may not have (anymore) to the same extent. Since they are 'small' they are also looked after and normally no tasks are assigned to them that would overwhelm or harm them. Nonetheless, these customs are not seen as 'individual rights' of children they can refer to in case of conflict. They are also not codified in legal texts that are renewed by formalized legislative procedures. Rather, they are embedded informally in centuries-old traditions, which are kept alive in a ritualized way.

In Europe, the idea of provision rights is based on the common belief from the Enlightenment days in the 18th century (similar to the idea of child protection), that children are different to adults in basic needs and that these needs are to be taken into special consideration. Another idea that fuelled this was that children must first 'develop' to become a fully fledged adult and that they had to be prepared for this in special institutions. Generally, at this stage, there was (and still is today) an 'investment motive' behind the understanding of children's rights: 'Society's concern for the child is seen very much in terms of the child's usefulness to society. Children are objects of invention rather than legal subjects' (Freeman, 1992: 30). Understood as such, the child's right to education was for example not formulated as the right of the child to choose an education but as a responsibility of the parents to send their children to school, which the state had established for their (obedient) education.[5]

The belief that children should have more independence is intertwined with the idea that the community – represented by the state – ought to care for their wellbeing and their development to become an adult who is capable of working. Whereas the history of general human rights – at least in Europe and North America – started with freedom rights, the beginnings of children's rights were marked by *protection* of children, not by their freedom (Quennerstedt, 2010). This can be seen clearly in the history of legislation on child labour, which was (and still is) focused on the prohibition of children working for money. It did not bring the children rights that they could claim or use as they wished, but rather put the duty on factory owners and parents to safeguard children from situations and actions that could harm their health or development.

If, by contrast, we understand the quintessence of children's rights to be that they are rights of *children*, that is, rights that children can enforce and claim themselves (or the guarantee that nothing may happen against their will) then their history is still at its beginning (Ferguson, 2013). It remains a challenge for historical research to what extent and in what ways children and young people have claimed rights for themselves. Of course, there are almost no written documents by children to attest this. One such testimony is a petition that children employed in Manchester's textile industry presented to the House of Commons in 1836. It states:

We respect our masters and are willing to work for our living and that of our parents, but we want more time to rest, to play a little, and to learn reading and writing. We do not think it right that we have to work and suffer from Monday early to Saturday night to make others rich. Honourable Gentlemen, enquire carefully into our situation![6]

From this period until the outbreak of the First World War, there are also reports from other countries including Denmark, Belgium, Germany and the United States of strikes and street demonstrations in which working children demanded rights (see Bartoletti, 1999; Liebel, 2004: 216–221; Woodhouse, 2008: 234–256; DiGirolamo, 2022).[7] It is probably not a coincidence that it was working children, first, who actively claimed their own rights. Not only did they see themselves as children, but they had learned to stand up for social and political rights as part of the labour and trade union movement that emerged in the 19th century. This is also an indication that children's rights should not be understood as special rights of an age group but as part of human rights.

Although there have been several initiatives since the First World War to give children these rights, under state law they did not surpass declarative intentions or had validity only intermittently in limited ways. Only in 1989, with the CRC, were children granted such rights in a legally binding way under international law. Yet even here we should keep in mind that the rights in the CRC were not formulated by children, but by adults *for* children and that they are specked with reservations. 'There is no evidence that children or children's groups as such, participated in drafting or had any real influence in preliminary discussions' (Freeman, 2009: 383; see also Freeman, 2020: 6). Moreover, there is still a large gap between the legal claims including the image of a 'good childhood' and the social reality and self-understanding of the vast majority of children in the world.

What are children's rights based on?

The history of children's rights is closely linked to the history of human rights. In its preamble, the CRC refers explicitly to the Universal Declaration of Human Rights of 1948, which begins in Article 1 with the words: 'All human beings are born free and equal in dignity and rights.' This suggests that the children's rights enshrined in the CRC are to be understood as 'natural rights' which belong to children by birth or to which they are entitled by virtue of their natural characteristics. But children's rights, like human rights in general, are historical products that emerge from and are understood by social movements and struggles as well as greater awareness of the needs of children. The CRC is proof of this.

The assumption that human rights have a natural basis goes back to the liberal philosopher John Locke, who in his treaties on 'good government' (Locke, 1689–1690) assumed that people are by nature free and equal. This assumption contrasted with the feudal society of estates, which had assigned people their place as birth-related members of an estate, which in turn had been sanctified as an expression of 'divine will' and had been asserted as irreversible. Hardly a hundred years later, on the eve of the French Revolution, Jean-Jacques Rousseau (1712–1778) in his writing on the social contract (Rousseau, [1762] 2017) affirmed the natural origin of human rights, but at the same time also questioned it: 'Man is born free, and everywhere he is in chains.' In this remark by Rousseau, legal philosopher Norberto Bobbio (1996) suggests that freedom and equality of human beings are not a fact, but an ideal to be pursued, nothing existing, but a value, an obligation. In the emergence of human rights in the days of the European Enlightenment, Bobbio sees the reference to nature as a purely theoretical model, the sole purpose of which was to justify the demands for freedom of those who fought against the churches' dogmatism and authoritarian states. In this way, these rights were regarded as inherent in human nature, and as such they could not be violated by political rulers or even abandoned by the holders of these rights themselves.

According to Bobbio, the emergence of new legal claims is thus based on the social reality of his time, on its contrasts and on the changes that were gradually set in motion by these contrasts. If we follow this interpretation, the hypothesis of a simple and abstract state of nature today no longer fulfils any practical or theoretical purpose. This can already be seen in the fact that the list of human rights has become longer and more diverse. New rights are demanded and created because people rebel against living conditions that no longer seem reasonable to them, and because their ideas of a life worth living expand. In addition to civil liberties, there are social, economic and cultural rights that go far beyond the satisfaction of basic needs. In addition to general human rights, which apply equally to all human beings, specific rights have been added which affect particularly disadvantaged groups of people, both individual as well as collective rights. New rights concerning the dignity of non-human beings, the preservation of natural resources (ecological rights or rights of nature) or the interests of future generations are emerging.

Children's rights combine general rights with specific human rights. Just like the rights adults claim for themselves, they cannot be traced back to the 'childlike nature'. Even the assumed greater vulnerability of children, which has led to special protective rights, has both natural and social reasons. And the idea that children's rights are not only to be understood as rights practised by adults for the benefit of children, but also as rights exercised by children themselves, is based on changing ideas of what children are entitled to and can be trusted to do. Even though children's rights have so far mainly been invented by adults, children today are becoming increasingly aware of their own rights and are demanding rights that adults could not or would not have thought of. At the same time, this means that the rights enshrined in the CRC should not be understood as the last, sufficient and wisest convention, which now only needs implementation. We have to think further. We must ask about the historical preconditions for the emergence of children's rights, the role of children in this process, how the rights are understood by the children themselves and how they can be further developed together with them.[8] In my opinion, this is a genuine challenge for research on children's rights.

Children's rights movements since the beginning of the 20th century

Parallel to the efforts to establish international treaties for the protection of children, in some countries, movements emerged at the beginning of the 20th century that expressly promoted rights of children to self-determination. They became the basis of endeavours to achieve more (political) participation of children and to recognize them as equal citizens in society. These endeavours were not limited to so-called freedom rights, rather, they were at times also extended to social and political rights of children. They emerged either in the context of political revolutions and reformist attempts or had social movements of disadvantaged population groups as role models.

One of the first written manifestations of emancipatory children's rights movements was the Moscow Declaration on the Rights of the Child. It was the result of a group of committed educators who advocated for the 'Free Education of Children'. At times, they worked within the so-called Proletcult Movement that had come into being with the Russian Revolution of 1917/1918 (see Liebel, 2016). With their proposal, the group had taken up ideas that had been circulating in several European countries and in North America since the turn of the 19th to the 20th century. They had developed mainly from the critique of authoritarian repressive schools, which was partly driven by young people themselves and that manifested itself in various alternative school foundations as well as socialist and anarchist education concepts.

Generally, the book *Century of Childhood* is seen as the first manifestation of this new thinking that focused on children's needs and aimed at a 'pedagogy from the child'. It was written by the Swedish pedagogue and feminist Ellen Key (1849–1926), published first in 1900 and translated into many languages, including Russian (first into English in 1909), and attracted a lot of attention.[9]

Although Ellen Key stuck to the romantic childhood myth mostly, in which children are idealized as innocent, 'good' creatures by nature and in which childhood is viewed as an ideal world (see Dekker, 2000), she also demanded rights for the children that result from their living situation. These are for instance, equal rights for children born out of wedlock and the right of the child to physical integrity and respectful treatment. According to Key, children also had the right to be 'bad' or in other words didn't have to be only 'good' all the time. They had the right to think for themselves, to have their own will, their own opinion and own feelings. The aims of Ellen Key and most other reformist pedagogues revolved around the thoughts on how the behaviour of educators may be influenced and how the pedagogical institutions could be reformed to include children's views and how better learning conditions could be achieved for them.

The Polish paediatrician, writer and pedagogue Janusz Korczak (1878–1942)[10] went a step further. As director of a Jewish orphanage in Warsaw, he actively promoted the independent and active role of the children he cared for, but he also explicitly fought for more individual rights and a stronger position of children in social life. As early as 1919, in his first big pedagogical work *How to Love a Child*, Korczak (2018: 30) proclaimed in a 'Magna Charta Libertatis' three elementary rights for children: the 'child's right to die', the 'child's right to the present day' and the 'child's right to be what a child is'. The right to die sounds strange at first glance, however from the remarks and explanations, it becomes very clear what Korczak meant: it is the demand for self-determination and self-experience which is often cut short by excessive care, over-protection and restrictions by many parents. With the other two rights, Korczak underlines his belief that children do not become persons but already are persons and have the right to their *own* life.[11]

Based on this belief, Korczak criticized the 'Geneva law makers'[12] a few years later in his essay 'The child's right to respect' (Polish original: 1929; English edition: 2009), arguing that they had 'confused duties with rights; the tone of the declaration is one of persuasion not insistence: an appeal to goodwill, a plea for kindness' (Korczak, 2009: 34). The child is neither given nor trusted to be able to act on its own: 'The child – nothing. We – everything' (Korczak, 2009: 25). The relationship between adults and children is 'demoralised by the child's poverty and material dependency' (Korczak, 2009: 25).

> A beggar can dispose of his alms at will. The child has nothing of his own and must account for every object freely received for his own use. He is forbidden to tear, break, or soil; he is forbidden to give anything away as a present; nor is he allowed to refuse anything with a sign of displeasure. The child has to accept things and be satisfied. Everything must be in the right place at the right time according to his regimen. ... Since he has no vote, why go to the trouble to gain his good opinion of you? He doesn't threaten, demand, say anything. Weak, little, poor, dependent – a citizen-to-be only. ... The brat. Only a child, a future person, but not yet, not today. He's just going to be. (Korczak, 2009: 25–27)

With this understanding, Korczak vehemently demanded a comprehensive participation of children whose 'democratism' in his eyes does not know any hierarchy (Korczak, 2009: 26). They ought to be trusted and allowed to 'organize' as 'the expert is the child' (Korczak, 2009: 33; see also Eichsteller, 2009; Liebel, 2018a).

At the end of the 1920s, the Chilean poet Gabriela Mistral (1889–1957) had also demanded fundamental rights for the 'South American child'. In her declaration, which she had drafted in December 1927 during a stay in Paris (first published in the magazine *Amauta* in February 1929), she represented an understanding of children's rights that was obviously influenced by Ellen Key's romanticizing childhood image, but also came close to what was later called 'children's protagonism' (*protagonismo infantil*) in Latin America. 'Each child brings a powerful and mysterious hope for the frail communities that animate our America. There is no adult institution that contains a similar inspiration to that of childhood for a better life. And no one is more inspiring to reorganize the world' (Mistral, [1927] 1979: 62).

Children's rights movements in the 1970s and 1980s

The thoughts and demands of Janusz Korczak or the Russian association 'Free Education of Children' were not considered or taken into account in children's rights debates of the following decades. With the early exception of Alexander Neill (1953) in Britain, they were only taken up again in the 1970s, initially in the United States with the so-called *Children's Liberation Movement*.[13]

Richard Farson, one of its public mentors, who in 1974 published the polemic book *Birthrights*, was inspired by the civil rights movement. Beyond the oppression of Blacks, the movement 'alerted us to the many forms oppression takes in our society' (Farson, 1974: 2). After various ethnic minorities and not lastly women claimed their equal rights in US society, children are understood as the 'last minority', whose emancipation is still outstanding. The rights demanded for the children are to guarantee that children are no longer treated as a special group but can become an accepted and integrated part of a democratically constituted society. 'In a free and democratic society, there is no valid basis to exclude children from the decision-making process' (Farson, 1974: 178). They should have the same rights to freedom and democracy as adults.

The Children's Liberation Movement in the United States judged that the traditional practice of child protection reinforces a 'paternalistic view' (Farson, 1974) and harms the children more than being useful to them. It would be a better support to children if their full civil rights were guaranteed by persistent and insistent work instead of always interfering for their protection. Instead of always looking at what the children are not (yet) able to do, one should look for the 'children's potential' with intuition and empathy. In addition, conditions are to be established that allow children to identify and to express themselves. Adults can only get to know children in all their facets if they 'develop a new appreciation for their rights and a new respect for their potential' (Farson, 1974: 13).

Thus, this children's rights movement also opposed any form of 'infantilization' of children, that is, any attempt to make them 'smaller' than they are, and to measure them only by criteria fixed by adults. According to such criteria the 'ideal child is cute (entertaining to adults), well-behaved (doesn't bother adults), and bright (capable of early admission to his parents' favourite college)' (Farson, 1974: 2). This required a new evaluation of children's behaviour which until now had been regarded as problematic. For example, 'we may view differently the incorrigible child, the stubborn child, the runaway child' (Farson, 1974: 194). Instead of only regarding such a child as 'troubled', it must be asked if it is not 'the good, well-adjusted child (who) may be less far along in his own consciousness-raising, in his own development towards maturity' (Farson, 1974: 194).

The children's rights movement in the 1970s was not satisfied with regarding the child in a new light and with proclaiming children's rights. It also asked what had to be done so that children could really claim their rights. First, it was assumed that children's rights only have a chance to finally be put into effect if the children themselves fight for them in an organized way. In a society in which children are at the disposition of adults, it cannot be expected that adults have a special interest in the realization of the rights of children, as it would limit their own right of disposal. Therefore, children are dependent on developing 'greater strength and vision as a group' in order to 'act on their own behalf' (Farson, 1974: 8). Like the members of other less powerful social groups, children cannot emancipate themselves individually, but only 'as a class' (Farson, 1974: 16).

Second, a 'right to economic power' is claimed. According to Farson, only this right gives the children the necessary power to realize the other rights as well. Nowadays, children are so weak and dependent above all because they are kept 'unproductive and out of the economic mainstream of society' (Farson, 1974: 155). Through the income earned for their work, children 'stand to gain not only financial rewards, but the dignity which derives from work and achievement. With it will come a new measure of respect from adults, and more importantly, a new measure of respect for themselves' (Farson, 1974: 155). The child would have better chances 'to make constructive changes in his environment and to pursue self-determined life goals' (Farson, 1974: 109). With this, Farson took up ideas that were widespread in the reformist educational movement of the 1920s and had also been reflected in the Moscow Declaration on the Rights of the Child.

With John Holt, another public representative of the US Children's Liberation Movement who worked as a teacher for a long time, the argumentation for children's rights shifted to a stronger (anti-)pedagogical approach. The target of his critique is the 'institution of childhood' which came into being with bourgeois society. It has 'infantilized' children and locked them into a privatized area where – for better or worse – they became dependent on the goodwill of adults. By separating children from the adult world, it is made 'difficult or impossible for young people to make contact with the larger society around them, and, even more, to play any kind of active, responsible, useful part in it' (Holt, 1974: 26). According to Holt, this is especially clear and vehement in modern school, where the children's abilities are cut back and underestimated. Through observations of everyday life, he demonstrated that a child can clearly 'be able to do what we think of children as being wholly unable to do until they are much older' (Holt, 1974: 100). If three- or four-year-old children were regularly given the opportunity to explore their surroundings on their own, they would be able to draw a mental map and would be able to find their way around independently.

The children's rights movement of the 1970s and 1980s is also criticized by some using the argument that the differences between children and adults are not taken into consideration and that children are treated like adults (for example, Moosa-Mitha, 2005). This critique does not take into account that this movement did not see childhood as a natural category, but – like today's subject-oriented childhood sociology – as a specific, historically created and therefore a changeable social construction.[14] The aim of the movement was not to demolish differences between adults and children, but rather to question the power difference and privileges of adults deriving from this concept of childhood and to insist, despite existing differences, on the equality and equivalence of children (Roose and Bouverne-de Bie, 2007: 432–433).

In Europe, the demands of the US American Children's Liberation Movement were taken up in the 1970s. The protagonists were adults who were critical towards traditional child protection and who rejected any form of education as an 'attack on the growing generation's freedom' (Kupffer, 1974: 25). Most of them were active in alternative and anti-pedagogic initiatives. Their goal was to reform 'all objectively child phobic laws', so that 'children and young people have the unlimited and direct enjoyment of agreed basic and human rights' (Stern, 1995: 16).[15] However, they did not come up with the idea of asking children and did not, like Korczak, develop their ideas from encounters and interaction with children. In contrast to the US children's rights movement, the European initiatives thought little of the preconditions necessary to reach equality for children nor did they ask how children themselves could contribute to this. Instead of asking – as in the US debate and as Janusz Korczak already did – under which 'economic' preconditions the children could (re-)acquire autonomy and play an active, participatory role in society, they limited themselves to appeal to the child-friendliness of adults and to demand a 'rethinking' in relation to children.

Parallel to movements such as the Children's Liberation Movement, which was initiated by adults, adolescent movements also emerged. Although the members were often under the age of 18, they did not consider themselves children and therefore did not understand themselves as children's rights but rather youth rights movements. One of the earliest and best known movements in the United States was the Youth Liberation of Ann Arbor in Michigan. It existed from 1970 to 1979 and was one of the main precursors of several teen movements in the United States, including the Youth Rights Movement, Youth Voice Movement and the Youth Media Movement. The organization was founded by several teenagers in December 1970, when the Youth Liberation Platform was created. The members of this group opposed 'adult chauvinism', which they understood in the sense that young people are denied rights simply because of their young age. The group attacked sexism, racism and compulsory education, insisted on being economically independent of adults and saw itself as part of the common struggle for a peaceful and just world without colonialism (the complete group's manifesto is documented by Gross and Gross, 1977: 329–333, and Boulding, 1979: 146–149, a short version by Freeman, 2020: 440–441). The wording of the manifesto's short version is:

YOUTH LIBERATION PROGRAM LIST OF WANTS – '*We must liberate ourselves from the death trip of corporate America.*'

1. We want the power to determine our own destiny.
2. We want the immediate end of adult chauvinism.
3. We want full civil and human rights.
4. We want the right to form our education according to our needs.
5. We want the freedom to form into communal families.
6. We want the end of male chauvinism and sexism.
7. We want the opportunity to create an authentic culture with institutions of our own making.
8. We want sexual self-determination. We believe all people must have the unhindered right to be heterosexual, homosexual, bisexual, or transsexual.
9. We want the end of class antagonism among young people.
10. We want the end of racism and colonialism in the United States and the world.
11. We want freedom for all unjustly imprisoned people.
12. We want the right to be economically independent of adults.
13. We want the right to live in harmony with nature.
14. We want to re-humanize existence.
15. We want to develop communication and solidarity with the young people of the world in our common struggle for freedom and peace.

In 1972, Sonia Yaco, a 15-year-old student, ran for the Ann Arbor School Board as a member of the local Human Rights Party. The rules stipulated that only adults could run for the school board, but Yaco's demands for a student voice in school governance received 1,300 votes as a write-in candidate, or 8 per cent of the total. Her campaign indirectly influenced the establishment of the experimental, alternative Community High School in Ann Arbor later that year (Hefner, 1979). Furthermore, Elise Boulding (1979: 149) documents a letter directed to a newspaper columnist in which a young person from Las Vegas drafted a 'Kid's own Bill of Rights'.

At the same time, school student movements with similar aims also emerged in several European countries. Mainly, they opposed authoritarian education in their families and schools and advocated for self-determined ways of life. In some cases, they occupied empty buildings and converted them into self-organized youth centres or used them for communal forms of living. As in the United States, children's rights were not an issue for them at the time, as they did not see themselves as children and perceived the children's rights movement as paternalistic action by adults.

On the other hand, since the 1970s, new discourses and movements have emerged in Latin America that link the struggle for children's rights with children's self-organization, and refer explicitly to their social and cultural situation. In contrast to North America and Europe, the focus is more on children of the working or popular classes.[16]

Today's children's rights movements

Today, children's rights movements exist almost everywhere in the world. Even though earlier movements only played a marginal role in the development of the CRC,[17] today's children's rights movements would not exist without it. Most of them explicitly refer to the CRC yet do not see their task as a mere 'implementation' of the convention. Instead, they develop their own ideas on children's rights and the role of children in society, which sometimes go beyond the CRC or contrast it. They emphasize, as did earlier children's rights movements, the necessity for children's equality and oppose any form of discrimination due to not yet having reached legal age. They particularly insist on creating conditions which allow children themselves to effectively make use of their existing rights and if need be create new rights which seem important to them and to receive social and legal recognition for them. However, the emphasis is not put on lobby work but on the attempt to acquire validity for their rights and interests mainly by self-organization. Unlike non-governmental organizations, they are a form of social movements or organizations in which children themselves are active, or which they even direct.

An example is the working children's movements, which arose in the 1970s in Latin America and since the 1990s also in Africa and Asia. Their self-conception is crystallized in the term *protagonismo infantil* (children's protagonism) and influences the children's rights discussion and practice in particular in the Global South (see Chapter 9 and Taft, 2015; 2019). Whereas the children's rights movement was first directed against the persecution and oppression of the so-called street children, today's movements are directed mostly towards the social role of working and Indigenous children. They connect criticism about their economic exploitation and racial discrimination with the demand for recognition and respect for their economic contribution to their families and societies. They promote dignified working conditions and social relations that are not based on the exploitation of mankind.[18]

In Latin America, the children's rights movement that goes beyond the working children's movements has also found an amazing echo in legal debates. The Colombian law professor Ligia Galvis Ortiz remarks:

> The consideration that children are to be understood as active rights holders deserves a profound and radical reflection. Because of this, the necessity could arise to reform the classical institutions of law and to create new approaches, in which cultural pluralism spreads on the recognition of the children's world as a universe with its own characteristics. In this world, we find elements, languages and symbols with which the children express and exercise their rights. (Galvis Ortiz, 2006: 12)

Galvis Ortiz sees the biggest barrier for the recognition of children being active rights holders in the rights discourse in 'being limited to the verbal language(s) mastered by adults and that the distinct articulations of children are not seen as sensible and meaningful forms of language' (Galvis Ortiz, 2006: 33–34). The intelligent lifestyle of children is expressed in the language that matches their life cycle. The problem is not the expression of children but rather the incapacity of adults to understand the messages, which can be read in the looks, the gestures, the movements and sounds they make.[19] Galvis Ortiz requests to overcome the established hegemony of a mindset that judges the world and lifestyle of children solely by the views and in the language of adults:

> Once we have finally freed ourselves from the adult centrism, we enter a colourful world of languages a world of diverse actors and mediators. This leads us to break with the doctrine and the entire philosophical, psychological and legal literature, which turn children into objects and we get to a place where we allow children a psychosocial status as active persons. Only in this way can we recognize their capacities

and messages, by which they reconstruct the world, create, change or resist it. (Galvis Ortiz, 2007: 61)

In the meantime, the thought and the expectation that children (can) play a major role in the creation, formulation and implementation of their rights has gained influence in other parts of the world. In the following section, I will explain what this means for the treatment of the human rights that have been granted to children in the CRC.

For a contextualized understanding of children's rights

According to the CRC, today, children across the globe are understood as legal subjects or legal entities. They therefore have their own rights and are not simply dependent on the goodwill of others whose support they do depend on. Insofar as children are still dependent, this dependence is cushioned by their own rights, which are intended to prevent any arbitrariness towards them and to secure their autonomy to act step by step. According to this concept, children are no longer just 'minors' who have fewer or no rights, but people who have the same, different or additional rights and can claim them.[20] The question is what conditions are needed that children can really exercise these rights. This section will discuss, from different angles, the pitfalls of invoking children's rights and what can or should be done to make rights accessible to children and a useful tool in their eyes. This requires a politically reflected and contextualized understanding of children's rights.

At first, the rights system resulting from liberalism and bourgeois societies only recognized children as 'minors', and because they 'by definition lack the capacity to act, it made it impossible for them to engage in any kind of economic trade relations' (Barranco Avilés, 2007: 16). With the liberalist idea that all men are equal (under law), no distinctions were made between differing circumstances and needs, the only exception being one law stating that you are still not 'legally mature' at a certain age. 'Under the same liberal framework, neither the existence of different people with different needs is taken into account nor are any temporary situations between full capacity and total dependence foreseen. Until the moment in which majority is acquired, the child is seen as unable to enforce his rights' (Barranco Avilés, 2007: 16–17). This framework was revised only with the CRC, which recognizes children in an internationally binding legal way as subjects with their own rights. The prerequisite was that two changes be made in the law, which María del Carmen Barranco Avilés, following Norberto Bobbio (1996), describes as 'generalization' and 'specification':

The process of generalization was based on the extension of dignity with the consequence that now there were subjects who were rights holders, whom one would not have thought of before as such. This process led to the dissolution of the concept of an 'abstract human being' which was connected to the first declarations on human rights and which resulted in not matching any human being. But it also became clear that dangers exist that threaten human dignity, and that cannot be scared away by establishing formal rights on equality and freedom. ... The process of specification starts with the thought that some needs are not shared by all persons. The dignity of some human beings requires satisfying needs which others do not have. The process of specification opened the discourse on vulnerable groups and established instruments by which one could give some – yet not all – human beings specific rights. (Barranco Avilés, 2007: 17)

The distinction in the CRC is based on the assumption that children have different *needs* than adults. These should be satisfied by rights to special protection and provision or rather developmental rights. In legal theory, rights that are deduced from needs (for instance special vulnerability) are generally called *moral* rights (Archard and Macleod, 2002). Regardless of their codification in formal rights systems, the historically developed 'moral' (self-)commitment of society to care for the especially 'needy', 'weak' and so on is manifested. These legal concepts do not foresee that children (or other 'weak' persons) can claim these rights themselves and ensure their implementation. In the CRC, they are voiced as children's rights but as the CRC is an international rights treaty, they are in fact treated as *state obligations*.[21] Therefore in academic legal debates it is sometimes contested that these rights are actually children's rights (Griffin, 2002), or they are called *welfare rights* and are distinguished from *agency rights* (Brighouse, 2002).[22] Similarly, Woodhouse (2008: 34–47) distinguishes between *needs-based* and *capacity-based* rights in relation to children's rights.

The CRC breaks clear of this logic by envisaging participation rights for children for the first time. Participation rights cannot be justified by *needs* but are based on the assumption that children have special *interests*, which they can point to and represent themselves. From a theoretical legal perspective, this discrepancy raises questions. Does it mean that participation rights stand alone, or do they also have an effect in dealing with the other rights groups? Stated differently, do the participation rights ultimately imply that children have a special sphere in life in which they act as subjects and can manage their affairs or do they suggest that the implementation of welfare rights must include the participation of children? The CRC does not provide clear answers to these questions. In the usual interpretations and in dealing with the CRC in practice, both rights groups are often dealt with separately. This is expressed by the fact that the participation of children, where it is thought of at all, is limited to 'children's affairs' and is seen as a sort of playground to practice and prepare for being an adult. However, I will demonstrate here why *all* rights groups are to be understood as agency rights of children or are to be seen and understood through the lens of children's agency.

If the so-called welfare rights are only understood as state obligations, they lose their meaning as special rights of children.[23] Welfare rights, if they are to be used in practice, always require interpretation and concretion. Their construction and the decision about their importance and implementation would be in the hands of adults only, and would be subject to their goodwill to act according to these rights. The fact that they are justified by the needs of children creates the impression that this is an objective criteria, which can be determined without any doubts, yet needs are changeable and in addition are not necessarily perceived or understood in the same way by adults and children. Therefore, over and above the needs, (differing) interests also have to be taken into account. These, again, can only be expressed and realized if children can participate in a meaningful way in the interpretation, concretion and implementation of protection and provision rights. We elaborate this here with the example of protection rights.

Generally, we assume that protecting children is mainly an adult task, as they are more far-sighted and have more means, power and influence to protect children against dangers than children themselves. However, the protection of children can lead to a limitation of their freedom and space for decision-making. This can go as far as increasing children's helplessness and need for protection despite all good intentions, as they are asked to settle into dependence and to rely on adults. Even if this limitation can be justified, adults can use it to implement *their* interests in making use of their power advantage over children or to even extend their scope of power.[24] This can be seen, for instance, in the efforts to observe children around the clock – even by using new surveillance technologies or by using special 'security services' – so that nothing happens to them or that they don't 'get out of hand'.

In order to prevent a one-sided instrumentalization of protection measures by adults, it is vital that children are not only objects of these measures, but that they can decide in which way they should be protected or whether in certain situations they might not need protection at all. Such participation ought to be practised also because all protection becomes all the more effective the more it is accepted and supported by the children who are being protected. Children can contribute actively to their protection, for instance by informing themselves, or by being sensitized, by learning certain rules or techniques of prudence, getting together with other children, to defend themselves better, to know/be aware of possible dangers. Apart from the question of efficiency, specific interests of the children would be taken into account also.

The CRC clearly postulates that the premise when interpreting and implementing children's rights must be the 'best interests of the child'. Since this concept has been introduced there are controversial debates over how to identify best interests and who can detect them in the most appropriate way (see, for example, Zermatten, 2007). Because interests are not timeless, the context and the points of view of the interests' holders have to be taken into account, in this case those of the children. In the CRC this is expressed as the child's right to be heard in all decision-making concerning him/her. Such decisions are not limited to select ambits or rights but include all areas, which affect children's lives now and in the future and by this also all rights belonging to children. Consequentially, children must have the opportunity to claim all their rights without exceptions. This implies that the bare minimum is that they can participate in a significant way in their construction, interpretation and implementation.

Arguing along this line, the separation of welfare rights from agency rights is meaningless in (legal) theory but not necessarily in (legal) practice. One reason is that the so-called protection and provision rights continue to be seen in a paternalistic and individualizing way, as if they were a selfless performance by (adult) society for children, and as if they had equal value for everybody and would be good for all children equally. A second reason is that in the existing political systems, in which political decision-making is a privilege of adults, children are inhibited from participating in the conceptualization and if required (re-)design of the protection and provision rights according to their interests and thereby connect them to their experiences and perspectives on life.

The debate on children's rights is mainly limited to the question of how children can come by and enjoy *legal rights*, meaning how they can use them. The codification of rights in the CRC or in national law is regarded as the highest attainable 'endpoint of the dialogue' (Roose and Bouverne-de Bie, 2007: 434). Seen as such, only one question remains to be discussed and that is how the codified rights can be 'implemented'. The way of solving specific problems seems to be based more on formal regulations than on a dialogue between involved persons. Yet if all focus is put on implementation, there is a tendency to ignore or even hide social contexts and inherent unequal power structures. There is a danger to lose sight of the possible and widespread instrumentalization of rights as well as their paradoxes. This can only be avoided if the debate on children's rights is contextualized and understood as part of political practice.

Like citizenship, participation is to be seen neither as a status that needs to be attained nor as a goal to be reached, but rather as a continuous learning process. This process always takes place in a certain context and has to be understood as *contextual practice*. This does not imply that participation and citizenship are only learning processes in an educational sense. Rather, we need to emphasize that in both cases the process is never-ending. Their meaning will be measured by the practical goals achieved by their means and by how they are reached. In the case of participation and citizenship of children, the issue at stake is whether they actually contribute to granting social recognition and human dignity to children. Therefore, it is most important that children are accepted as equal co-actors in the dialogue about their 'best interests' (see Roose and Bouverne-de Bie, 2007).

Frequently, children whose human rights are violated in the most aggressive ways are seemingly indifferent to them and seldom claim them. In order to achieve that children embrace their rights and make use of them for themselves, they have to be conceptualized in a context-specific way and have to give answers to the children's life experiences. The task cannot be to 'implement' formally existing children's rights, they must rather be reflected according to their cultural, political and structural coherence and weighed against the possible consequences for the children's lives. In doing this, the vast differences between living situations of children across the globe have to be considered and can lead to different meanings of the same rights. If need be, the rights have to be specified and extended with children participating in a significant way. The children are to be respected as persons who (co-)construct their rights and participate in and design the handling of their rights.

Conclusion

If law is not to be a weapon in the hands of the powerful but a 'power in the hands of the powerless' (Federle, 1994: 345) the discourse of children's rights as it has been led so far must be urgently revised. Rights are important because they signal to those who have them that they should not feel as mere petitioners or objects of some benevolent or beneficent act, but as holders of those rights. But 'rights without remedies are of symbolic importance, no more' (Freeman, 2007: 8). In the same way, we agree with Katherine Hunt Federle with regard to her experience in the United States almost three decades ago:

> Having the right means having the power to command respect, to make claims and to have them heard. But if having a right is contingent upon some characteristic, like capacity, then holding the rights becomes exclusive and exclusionary; thus, only claims made by a particular group of (competent) being will be recognized. ... Children, however, have been unable to redefine themselves as competent beings; thus, powerful elites decide which, if any, of the claims made by children they will recognize. (Federle, 1994: 343–344)

Children's rights become rights of the children and can be understood and practised as such by them only when they themselves reach the necessary power and means to set their own priorities and to use the rights according to their own discretion. The children's rights movements described in the first sections of this chapter show that these considerations are not unrealistic fantasies.

3

Children's rights studies in search of its own profile

With Rebecca Budde

Introduction

For about two decades now, research on children's rights or children's rights studies have been developing that claim to be a particular branch of research. Similar to social childhood studies and human rights studies, which have a longer history, they consider themselves as a scientific field with specific cognitive interests and questions that differ significantly from those of other fields of research. Although children's rights have been considered for more than a hundred years, we believe that it makes sense to understand studies on children's rights in the strictest sense of the term as research that systematically reflects on these rights. On the one hand, it should examine their social and ideational origins and, on the other, their meanings and impacts in particular contexts. This can be done in a theoretical and an empirical way. Also, it can be related to history and to the present. Logically, it is to be expected that these studies will also contribute to sharpening the contours of children's rights theory just as they are oriented towards certain theoretical approaches (see Cordero Arce, 2015a; Freeman, 2020; Hanson and Peleg, 2020). In this chapter, we only deal with the question of the meanings and effects of children's rights.[1]

So far, the debate on the profile of children's rights studies has been conducted mainly in English. Some similarities can be identified in this debate, but the question also arises as to how the profile of these studies can be refined, expanded and, in some points, reconceptualized. When discussing some of these questions in this chapter and considering the future prospects for children's rights studies, we will also draw on some contributions in Spanish.

There is general agreement that children's rights studies should not be limited to one of the usual academic disciplines, but should be interdisciplinary or even transdisciplinary (Moody and Darbellay, 2019; Vandenhole, 2020). This is a claim that can only be fulfilled in an approximate way. However, it can make us aware of the fact that children's rights, like any other right, are not just a normative legal construct, but a complex social factual situation in which different social interests manifest themselves and which can influence children's lives in very different ways. In this chapter, we will identify some of the aspects and contexts that seem to us to be most important. This necessarily results in close links to New Social Childhood Studies, where some of the children's rights researchers come from or are anchored.[2] However, the search for a profile of their own not only has professional political reasons for marking a distinctive location in the academic landscape. It also serves to specify the knowledge goals and methodology of research on children's rights and thus to increase its practical value for children and a policy which is committed to their interests and rights.

In this chapter, we identify some of the aspects of such a profile that we consider most important. In particular, we discuss the legal understanding and political implications of children's rights studies and ask to what extent the concept of *living rights* can serve as a guideline for research. We then turn to the question of the Eurocentric bias of the discourse and practice of children's rights, the necessity of their decolonization and the tense relationship between universalism and cultural relativism in understanding and dealing with children's rights. Finally, we address the question, which has been increasingly discussed recently, of whether children's rights studies should see themselves more as a form of 'enlightenment' or as a contribution to 'political intervention'. In a first step we summarize the present controversial discussion on the aims of children's rights studies.

Conflicting aims of children's rights studies

In the programmatic debate on the aims of children's rights studies, a difference can be seen above all in how the relationship to children's rights action is determined. This action is identified partly as 'advocacy' and partly as 'children's rights movement'. Didier Reynaert et al (2015) claim the starting point of children's rights studies as 'the dissatisfaction with dogmatic children's rights activism and the desire to move beyond the intellectual poverty of children's rights research that focused exclusively on the implementation gap as the one and only challenge for children's rights' (Reynaert et al, 2015: 11). In this sense, children's rights studies are sometimes called *critical*. Children's rights studies as new research field is based primarily on the intention to question the norms, values and logics of children's rights practice. Daniella Bendo (2020: 174) emphasizes as a special characteristic of children's rights studies that they are 'politically committed to exploring, analytically, how to understand children's situations in context in order to inform policy and advocacy more fully'. According to Ellen Desmet et al (2015: 425), children's rights studies comprise three 'key dimensions'. The authors refer to:

- the '*diagnostic* dimension', that is the identification of social problems and possible solutions to which children's rights can contribute;
- the '*deliberative* dimension', that is the continuous reflection, interactive forming of opinions and different interpretations of children's rights practice; and
- the '*emancipatory* dimension', that is the contribution to a transformative perspective of children's rights practice that goes beyond the mere application of existing rights.

Some authors emphasize that children's rights studies must follow a 'bottom-up approach', start from 'local settings' and examine the rights of children 'in their daily lives' (Vandenhole, 2012; Harcourt and Hägglund, 2013; Quennerstedt, 2013). This accentuation is also crystallized in terms such as 'children's rights from below' (Liebel, 2012a) and 'living rights' (Hanson and Nieuwenhuys, 2013; 2020) or in the explicit question of 'who is (to be) the subject of children's rights' (Cordero Arce, 2018). It is also linked to the question of the ethical foundations of empirical research (Beazley et al, 2009; Ennew, 2009; Bessell et al, 2017; Markowska-Manista, 2018; Alderson and Morrow, 2020). Some authors explicitly call for the use of participatory research methods in which children act as co-researchers (Lundy and McEvoy, 2011) or even as researchers on their own behalf under the assistance of adult researchers (for example, Alderson, 2008; Kellett, 2010; Liebel, 2012a: 215–223; Desmet et al, 2015; Kim, 2016; 2017). It is not postulated that children do research specifically on their rights, but rather that empirical research is guided by children's rights and that children must therefore be given a proper place in the research process.

Partly in contradiction to the emphasis on the bottom-up approach and participatory methods, the demarcation from the so-called children's rights movement occupies a broad space in the debate. The focus of this demarcation is the practical impetus, which crystallizes in the term 'advocacy' (Quennerstedt, 2013). This is usually understood to mean a 'paternalistic' or 'saviour' focused practice of adults in favour of or on behalf of children and their rights. In our opinion, this understanding of practice does not go far enough, since advocacy can also take place in an emancipatory way and can even be a practice of children themselves (*child-led advocacy*). The children's rights movement also represents far more than a movement for the protection of children (*protectionism*). Although Karl Hanson (2012) had already pointed out various 'schools of thought' on children's rights years ago,[3] a distinction is still rarely made between the protectionist and emancipatory lines of this movement (see, however, Adams et al, 1971; Gross and Gross, 1977; Veerman, 1992; Renaut, 2002; Liebel, 2012a: 29–42). The Global South is rarely taken into consideration.

With regard to the 'protectionist' or 'paternalistic' variant of the children's rights movement, Karl Hanson, under the critical motto 'killed by charity', demanded in a much acclaimed editorial in the journal *Childhood*, that children's rights studies should 'emancipate' themselves from the children's rights movement (Hanson, 2014; for discussion see Bendo, 2020). In a later text, Hanson and his co-author Olga Nieuwenhuys extend their call for a demarcation to any form of political activism, which, in our opinion, is problematically summarized under the technocratic term 'social engineering'. Instead of aiming for social transformation, their primary task is 'enlightenment' (Nieuwenhuys and Hanson, 2020). In contrast, Reynaert et al (2015: 11) emphasize that children's rights research itself has 'an emancipatory objective: it considers children's rights as a framework for social action and a lever to change societal conditions towards greater respect for the human dignity of children'.[4] This, in our view, fundamental contradiction raises the question of how future children's rights studies will be understood and located. We will therefore devote special attention to it.

On the legal understanding of children's rights studies

Children's rights studies cannot avoid making sure what they understand by children's rights. As do other children's rights researchers (see, for example, the contributions in Invernizzi and Williams, 2016), we understand children's rights as human rights that belong to both children and adults. Although children's rights are subject to special requirements arising from the specific characteristics of the stage in life and social status of children, they should not be understood as lower-ranking human rights ('small human rights'). As human rights, they are also ambivalent. Resulting from the liberal historical origin of these rights in the European Enlightenment, that is, an image of men (male, White, adult, civilized) predominates, emphasizing individual self-responsibility. Moreover, they revert to the circumstance that they can be instrumentalized by certain groups of people or groups of power in their own interest and have been used in this sense again and again. Franz Hinkelammert (1999) speaks of 'the ideological inversion of human rights'. As such, their universal claim is also related to particular interests in specific contexts where they are brought into play and are applied.

Against this background, for instance, Immanuel Wallerstein distinguishes, with a view to human rights, a 'European universalism' and a 'universal universalism'. He tries to show 'that the universalism of the powerful has been a partial and distorted universalism' (Wallerstein, 2006: xiv). He calls it a European universalism 'because it has been put forward by pan-European leaders and intellectuals in their quest to pursue the interests of the dominant strata of the modern world system' (Wallerstein, 2006: xiv). According to him, the struggle between European and universal universalism is 'the central ideological struggle of the contemporary world' (Wallerstein, 2006: xiv). He describes European universalism as a 'morally ambiguous doctrine', as justifying 'simultaneously the defence of the human rights of so-called innocent and the material exploitation engaged in by the strong' (Wallerstein, 2006: 28). It attacks the crimes of some and disregards, closes its eyes to, the crimes of others. Wallerstein does not deny that global universal values exist and must exist, but they only gain meaning for all if they cannot be monopolized by the fittest. This requires a worldwide 'structure that is far more egalitarian than any we have constructed up to now' (Wallerstein, 2006: 28).[5]

In the case of children's rights, the concept of childhood on which they are based and the way in which the biographical development of capacities is conceived are of particular importance. According to Western bourgeois understanding, on which the Convention on the Rights of the Child (CRC) is based, childhood is a stage of immaturity that is characterized by having fewer capabilities than adults. In our opinion, children's rights studies cannot limit themselves to measuring these capacities against the supposedly superior capacities of adults. Nor can they merely be considered as a preliminary stage of these capacities. Instead, children's rights studies are faced with the task of acknowledging the special characteristics of children's capacities. This must be done in a non-hierarchical way and in consideration of always being influenced by the children's living conditions. Their specific meaning can only be grasped by taking these conditions into account. This applies in particular to what is understood by rationality. The way in which rationality and emotionality relate to each other and the importance that is attached in particular to the mimetic and artistic capacities of children is key. Some Latin American authors (for example, Fals Borda, 2009; Escobar, 2014; Restrepo, 2016) speak of 'sentipensar' or 'sentipensamientos', however without referring to childhood. In other words, it must take into account the subjectivity of children in all its forms of expression, including non-linguistic ones.

The question of capacities is important because children's rights, like human rights in general, cannot to be understood as objective rights only but also as *subjective* rights. They are not only rights that oblige adults or state institutions to act in favour of and in the interests of children, but can also be claimed and exercised by children themselves. Hence the need to explore the conditions that enable children to exercise their rights is the first step. This is occasionally expressed with reference to the *Capability Approach*. Having said this, not only the development of *capacities* but also of *capabilities* must be considered (Liebel, 2014b). An important component is that children are informed about their rights, but they must also have a real possibility to translate this information into their own actions. Since the effectiveness of rights is always subject to interpretation, children's views of their rights must carry at least the same weight as adults' views.

This leads to the question what law actually is and what it is based on. A distinction is usually made between legal rights (that is, codified in state laws or interstate conventions) and moral rights. Legal rights have a greater weight in social life because they are backed by the power of state institutions. Nonetheless, legal rights are based on moral understanding and ethical considerations. Human dignity is an example. Moreover, legal rights can only claim legitimacy if they meet certain ethical standards. If we also bear in mind that legal rights are the result of social disputes or movements and the legal concepts that arise from them (Stammers, 2009), it becomes clear that moral rights are just as important and legitimate. With regard to children, this means that moral rights conceived by children themselves can also claim to be recognized and transformed into legal rights. This is especially true when children produce and articulate such rights collectively. Since children have only limited political rights, they can neither set rights nor legally administer justice. For children's rights studies, this implies determining possibilities for children to formulate and articulate their own rights and achieve their (legal) recognition. This also concerns the question how to counteract so-called legal paternalism, according to which rights-oriented action takes place top-down and essentially via the state.

An inherent problem of legal rights is that they are linked to the existence and actions of state institutions. Legal law is always state law or law recognized and enforced by the state. For children's rights as subjective rights, this is a limitation, since children can only claim their rights if the rights are cast in a general legal form and state institutions base their actions on it. That said, we see an important task of children's rights studies in exploring ways in which children's rights can arise and gain weight beyond state intervention. This consideration is on one hand based on a lifeworld understanding of rights that goes beyond a legalistic construction of children's rights. On the other, it challenges the 'normative fetishism of the legal system' (Salamanca Serrano, 2018: 134)[6] that is fixed on the state and understands children only as beneficiaries of legal norms. An example of this is the legal understanding of the Polish Jewish paediatrician and educationalist Janusz Korczak (2007; 2009).

In Korczak's idea, articulated more than a hundred years ago, children should have their own rights, by which several intentions crystallize. He hoped that children could thus most easily escape the arbitrariness of adults and become independent. Korczak sees this arbitrariness not only in the violence practised against children, their 'despotism', but also in the at first sight positive signs of favour which present themselves as 'love' for the child. He hoped to be able to replace the favour granted to children with a relationship of (mutual) recognition and respect. Although he had in mind primarily the inequality in the educational relationship, rights should generally place the relationship between adults and children in society on a new viable basis, which would guarantee children equal protection from the power of the stronger and freedom in the sense of a self-determined life. Korczak understood the rights of the children less in the formal legal sense as laws enacted by the state, than as based in the lifeworld as a mutually agreed regulation of social relations. They cannot be decreed or enforced, but require the voluntary recognition in the respective community and in everyday life. As such, they are also understood as a binding self-commitment and are fixed by rules that provide a reliable basis for a daily living together and, if necessary, for the settlement of conflicts (on Korczak's understanding of rights see Liebel, 2018a).

The understanding of children's rights presented here is characterized by the fact that it is not fixed on the state and legal rights. Rather, it brings back the creation and implementation of rights into society and to the acting subjects. This does not mean keeping the state out of everything and declaring the 'private subjects' according to a (neo-)liberal pattern to be the creators of their own happiness (and unhappiness) regardless of their economic and social position. State obligations are indispensable and must be insisted upon as long as states in the traditional sense exist. Nevertheless, they must be recognized in their conditionality and limitations, and must be expanded by an understanding and practice of human rights in which children themselves act as legal and social subjects and can influence decisions as well as make them themselves. This concerns not only decisions that directly affect children living today, but all decisions that are essential for a dignified life for all people in the present and future, including the lives of future generations. Children's rights studies could contribute to concretizing such perspectives and designing corresponding strategies for action.

Political implications of children's rights

In our opinion, the way children's rights (as well as human rights in general) have been dealt with so far is characterized by two problems. First, fundamental structural problems are approached as individual problems and challenges. Second, the assumed equality of rights ('everyone has the same rights') does not actually mean that everyone can benefit from and claim these rights in equally.

The assumption contained in the discourse on human rights and children's rights that rights can be claimed individually by autonomous persons and used in their own interest can have paradoxical or unintended consequences. It can exacerbate marginalization, especially for people who are in a weak and already marginalized social position. The assumption that a person has rights and only has to make use of them can lead to persons being held responsible for his/her situation in general. In the case of children, for example, the assumption that they can play a decisive role in decisions about their lives on the basis of their granted participation rights can lead them to being held responsible for actions that are beyond their reach. Actual (continuing) dependencies as well as structural reasons for their marginal status or their social or generational disadvantage are thus easily ignored or underestimated. Children's rights studies can contribute to making this problem visible and counteracting it.

The frequent linking of participation rights with provision or development rights can also have a depoliticizing effect. This occurs when the impression is created that social problems can be avoided or eliminated simply by claiming the rights you have. In this process, the right to participation is effectively cut off from its political roots and stylized into an arbitrary personal matter.[7] In this context, children's rights studies face the task of conveying a differentiated and relational understanding of participation. After all, participation is not a social norm that has to be fulfilled, but a prerequisite for achieving. Although all people participate in social life, the question arises to what extent and in what way this happens. This includes the idea that participation can also have negative or marginalizing effects.

> Participation does not automatically lead to emancipation, but emancipation is defined as the antidote of marginalisation. The mission of participatory work is then to breach marginalisation. Participation remains a key concept in this approach, but not as a goal or method. Participation, in this view, is defined as an essential condition in the definition of social problems. (Vandenhole et al, 2008: 13)

In this sense, the participatory approach can be used to make the dominant policy the object of analysis and press for its change. The main aim is to safeguard human dignity. Accordingly, children's rights studies are faced with the task of questioning various approaches and forms of participation as to whether and to what extent they contribute to guaranteeing or achieving human dignity. This also applies to many other topics to which children's rights studies can refer, such as the question of children's citizenship, the conception and handling of protective rights, the question of individual and collective rights, the relationship between law and justice, or the understanding and constitution of children's interests and their relationship to children's rights.

Children's rights studies do not take place in a space freed of power. They cannot escape the fact that children's rights themselves are not per se critical of power, but that they can be instrumentalized to maintain power structures, like the law as a whole. This applies as much to the conception of children's rights as to their application. With regard to the CRC, it is customary to highlight three groups of rights: the right to participation; the right to protection (including prevention); and the right to provision. In practice, however, protection and prevention are at the centre of political and legal action, while participation and provision occupy a distant second place. Even more distant are such rights as, for instance, freedom of conscience for children, which are even explicitly rejected by many States Parties to the CRC. This should not come as a surprise, because the 'primary forces behind the CRC are not disenfranchised groups that are seeking to gain full participatory rights in society, but rather enfranchised adults who seek to spread a protective mantle over the world's children' (Rosen, 2015: 157). They strive for 'nothing less than the global restructuring of age categories along with the rights and duties of children and adults' (Rosen, 2015: 157). This restructuring is based on a childhood pattern that emerged in Western societies and now serves as a benchmark for the production and evaluation of a 'good childhood'. According to this pattern, childhood is fixed as a social status separate from the adult world, characterized primarily by vulnerability and by excluding forms of childhood in which children are co-responsible social subjects.

Groups of people whose human rights are most severely violated frequently appear to be indifferent to their rights and rarely claim them. This also applies to children. In order for children to make rights their own and to see them as useful, they must be conceived in a context-specific way and respond to the life experiences of children. They must be reflected in their cultural, political and structural contexts and weighed up in terms of their potential impact on children's lives. In doing so, children's rights studies will have to pay attention to the fact that the life situations and thus also the interests of children vary and that even the same rights can take on different meanings. By investigating such connections, children's rights studies can contribute to the specification and expansion of children's rights with the significant participation of children. Children are to be respected as persons who help construct their rights and who participate in determining and shaping the way in which their rights are handled.

'Living rights' as a guideline for children's rights studies?

I see a central task of children's rights studies in exploring what meanings rights have or can acquire in the lives of children. This question is central to the concept of *living rights* (Hanson and Nieuwenhuys, 2013; 2020; Van Daalen et al, 2016). The concept challenges an 'essentialist' understanding of children's rights, according to which children's rights speak for themselves and always have the same meaning regardless of the specific circumstances in children's lives. Instead, the concept invites us to look at how children's rights are understood and expressed in children's actions: 'The concept of living rights contends that the meaning, interpretation, and practice of children's rights constitute a living, dynamic process. The concept of translations challenges the one-way idea of implementation to analyse what happens with children's rights in the complex encounters of children's and other actors' perspectives' (Hanson and Nieuwenhuys, 2020: 101).

Children's rights are therefore not only considered as legal rights, but also in their interaction with the ideas children have about their rights in local contexts. It is assumed that complex 'translations' take place in both directions, in which different interests meet, especially those between adults and children or between institutions that manage children's rights and have power, and groups of children who act or are willing to act. According to the concept of living rights, children's rights studies are not only faced with the task of reconstructing these processes, but they should also contribute to making children's ideas and voices visible in a 'child-centred' manner and to help them find their own way. 'There should be, at least conceptually, sufficient space for including children's situated knowledge and understanding of their rights' (Hanson and Nieuwenhuys, 2020: 113). The following questions, among others, shall find an answer:

> What are children's conceptualizations of their rights? How can we have access to children's positions? How do children's interpretations of their rights interact with other, concurring, competing or alternative views on children's rights? How do the notions of living rights and translations interact, and how can they help apprehend, question, and interpret children's rights law? (Hanson and Nieuwenhuys, 2020: 114)

As argued before, in order to recognize the 'situated knowledges'[8] or the knowledges that arise from children's experiences of life, there is a need for an open concept of children's rights inclusive of legal, moral and ethical rights. Consequently, in empirical studies, children would not only be questioned about codified rights they know and how important they are to them. In addition, children's actions and, possibly, also their verbal expressions would be interpreted in light of the rights the children claim for themselves and how they want to see them enforced. In situated knowledge and under certain circumstances, completely different ideas of rights and their relevance to one's own life can be expressed than those suggested by the universalistic children's rights discourse in an abstract way. This is illustrated in the following example from the Indian metropolis of Calcutta (with reference to Balagopalan, 2013).

As in all markets in countries of the Global South, many children in Calcutta are busy picking up leftover vegetables or fruit. Sometimes they also steal something from the stalls. Most of the time they move in groups and divide work among each other. While some of them collect or steal, others drag the prey away in small bags to divide it up among themselves or sell it at other places in the market. One morning, some children brought a small boy to the meeting place of an aid organization and said that he had been caught by a trader and beaten on the spot by a policeman. The boy was bleeding in several body parts and looked badly beaten. When the boy was reasonably recovered, he was told that the policeman had done wrong and would have to be brought to justice. After the boy had listened calmly, he said:

> Aunty, it would have been much worse if he had arrested me. They would have put me in the lock-up until I got bail and in the lock-up worse things would have happened. He was doing his job and helping me by beating me at the market itself. I know him because during the times that I have fought with someone at the shelter and decide to sleep on the station platform he often asks me to run small errands for him and gives me a blanket to cover myself at night. (Quoted in Balagopalan, 2013: 142)

Obviously, the boy saw little point in being made aware of his rights. He could not imagine to what extent the invocation of these rights could contribute to improving his situation. However, it would be short-sighted to argue a lack of understanding of children's rights. The problem is evidently, on one hand, the way in which the boy was to be taught and made aware of his rights. On the other hand, the problem lies in the political and social constellation in which he found himself, making it almost impossible for him to feel as a subject of his own rights. The boy's refusal to insist on his rights vis-à-vis the policeman who had maltreated him shows that generalized written rights can take on quite different meanings depending on the concrete situation and experience. The boy had not only had more complex experiences with the policeman than his carers could have imagined, but he also had far more in mind besides the abuse he had just suffered. Since he still had to reckon with the policeman in his daily (and nightly) life, it was quite obvious for him to weigh up the pros and cons of a legal appeal. Far from an attitude of submissiveness, he showed a remarkable sense of the real existing dependencies and power hierarchies and knew how to handle them in his own way.

The conclusion drawn from this is that children's rights must not only be 'applied', but culturally 'translated' and communicated through local traditions of thought and action as well as legal concepts and practices. This includes understanding children's rights not only in terms of individual claims, but also in terms of mutual references and obligations, including between members of different generations. This also includes, irrespective of cultural or regional characteristics, ensuring that rights do not become effective simply because they are attributed to people as 'natural' or are enshrined in laws and rules. To refer to them makes sense only if they are not undermined by actual inequalities in power and possession. In view of their often marginalized status, this is especially true for children living under conditions of extreme poverty and oppression. In order to turn rights into living rights for them, not only must they know their rights, circumstances must also change.[9] This raises the question whether children's rights studies can be content to interpret children's living situations or whether they must also contribute to changing them (see Cordero Arce, 2015b: 305–314).

Eurocentrism and decolonization

A problem that is rarely mentioned in the programmatic contributions to children's rights studies is the Eurocentric bias of large parts of today's children's rights practice. Contributions that do point to this problem nonetheless mostly remain biased in their analysis. The contributions are limited to the developmental discourse and reduced to the question why children's rights are not understood there. Only few authors advocate and pursue research approaches that discuss the entanglement of children's rights practice in the postcolonial asymmetry of power, also called 'coloniality of power' (Quijano, 2000; 2008), and connect it with a decolonial perspective.[10]

In this section, we will outline some specific tasks that we believe arise in this respect for children's rights studies. The focus here is on children whom we refer to as children of the Global South. By this, we mean children who are particularly affected by the aftermath of historical colonialism and the current forms of postcolonialism or 'informal colonialism' (Goldsmith, 2002). These are, for one, children in the former colonial areas who live in precarious conditions and are affected by the persistence of structural racism. Examples include Indigenous children and children of other minorities, children living in extreme poverty, working children and children living on the streets, children affected by and involved in wars, in short, children of classes and population groups that continue to be oppressed, exploited and discriminated against. In our understanding, this also includes children who live under precarious conditions in the former colonizing countries. These are especially those who had to migrate or flee from Southern regions of the world for different reasons, those belonging to discriminated minorities and all those children who are directly or indirectly affected by (relative) poverty and who are exposed to structural and personal forms of violence.

With regard to these children, children's rights studies face particular challenges. We argue that children's rights studies must go beyond uncovering particularly serious rights violations and researching their causes. Equally, they must include research on the meaning and significance of these rights for children themselves. The research aims to gather knowledge on the preconditions for children to consider their rights as true rights, which they can claim. This requires more than just promoting children's rights and working for the implementation of the CRC. Rights only become important for children when they experience that they are related to their lives and have a real chance of making these rights a reality. With regard to the CRC, it must also be borne in mind that the underlying childhood pattern is far removed from the actual experiences of the vast majority of children in the world and usually has little in common with the childhood patterns that exist in their social and cultural environment. Developmental policies and international aid programmes often devalue local convictions concerning childhood as backward and to be fought against as they are seen as contrary to children's rights. In the Global South, such lack of cultural sensitivity is often perceived as a presumptuous new edition of the colonial civilization mission. Children's rights studies cannot avoid analysing these practices and making visible alternative ways of children's rights practice that are understood as part of decolonization efforts. This includes to fathom children's 'situated knowledge' of their rights and thus to prepare the way for research that takes up and appreciates non–Western ways of knowledge and cognition. In the following section we will present some children's rights studies that pursue such a decolonial perspective.

As a first example, we refer to a study by Argentinean anthropologists (Szulc et al, 2016) analysing a UNICEF campaign for the rights of the child. In this campaign, UNICEF had accused the violation of the rights of Indigenous children in Argentina (UNICEF, 2009). Although the campaign explicitly spoke of Indigenous children, their precarious living situation was not placed in the context of their colonial and postcolonial history of oppression, but was measured solely against the assumed universal norms of the CRC. The specific rights of Indigenous peoples – as codified in the UN Declaration on the Rights of Indigenous Peoples (UN, 2007) and the ILO Indigenous and Tribal Peoples Convention (C 169) (ILO, 1989) – were not addressed either. As a consequence of this limited understanding of childhood and children's rights, the campaign focused mainly on poverty and insufficient education. The structural racism, however, that still prevails in Argentinian society and the associated practices of exclusion towards Indigenous children were not mentioned anywhere. Szulc and her colleagues also point out that the campaign was not created with the participation of the Indigenous population, who have been fighting for their rights for decades. The only form of 'participation' was that some of the children were chosen to present the campaign's messages at its public presentation, according to a scenario set out in advance by UNICEF.

As a second example, we refer to three studies presented in an anthology on humanitarian interventions (Cheney and Sinervo, 2019). These studies focus on the processes and problems of 'affective commodification' and 'objectification' associated with humanitarian aid for children. These terms mean that living beings (here: children) are degraded to a kind of commodity and object, and involve the mobilization of emotions in those who provide humanitarian aid. In one of the studies, Kristen Cheney and Stephen Ucembe (2019) trace how the widespread desire in the Global North to help 'orphans' has created a multimillion-dollar orphan care industry involving a variety of actors, from religious organizations to private travel companies. The authors argue that the 'manufacture' of orphans associated with commercialization can have serious consequences for the children, families and communities concerned. Another study in the volume examines how children in certain contexts are transformed into emotionally charged objects that lead to misinterpretation of their plight and needs. Miriam Thangaraj (2019) uses the example of India to discuss how activists in a campaign against child labour and for the right to education contribute to the stigmatization of working children. She sees the construction of the children's plight and needs influenced by the colonial-paternalistic ideology that aid can only be provided 'from outside' and 'from above' by particularly enlightened and civilized people. In a concrete case, it led to ignoring the reasons and motives that children associate with their work and further disadvantaged the children. Sara Lahti (2019), for her part, describes how adult actors who want to provide humanitarian aid to *talibés* (Koran students) in Senegal tell various stories about the suffering of children. Children begging on the streets is sometimes attributed to child trafficking and forced labour, sometimes to religious traditions. In the fixation on one of these alleged causes, the aid organizations lose sight of the experiences and perspectives of the children, and they are not able to search for solutions to their plight together with the children. The bottom line of these three studies is that humanitarian interventions frequently fail to take into account the local context and the realities of the experiences, ambitions and aspirations of local children and young people. Sometimes, they create even more difficulties for the children whose rights are supposed to be at stake, for example, by undermining their survival strategies.

As a third example, we look at studies included in an anthology on the 'international child protection regime' edited by Neil Howard and Samuel Okyere (2021). They focus on the prevailing way in which states, UNICEF, the International Labour Organization and many internationally active children's aid organizations headquartered in Europe and North America deal with the risks children of the Global South are exposed to. Some of the studies collected in this anthology deal with specific groups of children identified as 'risk groups' in international campaigns and programmes, such as 'child labourers', 'child prostitutes', 'child soldiers' or 'children on the move' (often portrayed as victims of child trafficking or new forms of slavery). The studies address the labelling and scandalizing rhetoric common in the child protection regime. Some contributions are based on regional studies, some of which have been conducted over many years. Others, with reference to research in various countries, deconstruct the ideological constructions, illusions and unintended but accepted 'side effects' associated with child protection, which are also referred to as 'collateral damage'.

A central point of criticism of the studies is that the risks for children are measured by standards from outside, without taking into account the local living conditions and cultural contexts in which children's actions arise and acquire specific significance. This includes measuring the endangerment of children against an idealized Western childhood pattern that has nothing to do with the actual life context of the children and is projected onto the children in an abstract way. In doing so, the children are usually not portrayed as acting subjects, but as victims who are to be 'saved' (called 'saviourism' by the authors; see also Mutua, 2002; Liebel, 2020: 130–131). In the authors' opinions, this also results from the fact that the capacity of children to judge and act is measured solely by their age. The assumption is that below 18 years, according to the CRC, children do not have the ability or only insufficient ability to judge and act. With the schematic orientation towards the age of life, they see ideas of childhood, which contradict the globalized bourgeois ideas of 'age-appropriate behaviour', delegitimized and stigmatized by the international aid organizations.

In many humanitarian and child protection practices, a childhood pattern is embedded in the formula 'childhood = school + play'. This is particularly problematic when dealing with communities where there is no clear-cut division between adults and children. Here, responsibilities are shared and it is common for children to take on various vital tasks outside the family and sometimes away from it. Since the aid programmes discussed here disregard such ways of life, they do not help to address the structural determinants of children's suffering. Such an approach also corresponds, intentionally or unintentionally, to imperial patterns of action. Due to the power imbalance, actors in the South see themselves forced to comply with the proposed measures even if they disagree with them or consider them unfeasible.

Legal scholar Wouter Vandenhole (2012; 2020), who is one of the founders of critical children's rights studies, draws the conclusion that children's rights studies need to pay more attention to local contexts and cultures. He understands this not as need to preserve traditions, but rather in the sense of 'balancing between hybridisation and replication' (Vandenhole, 2020: 187). The mere emphasis on the universality of human rights and the belief that they can be easily applied to any situation makes them misleading in practice. Conversely, mixing the rights with local traditions may lead to a dilution of normative universality. As such, there is a need to rethink and go beyond 'sterile cultural relativism'. This also applies to the rights of children. However, more is required in order to achieve, as Vandenhole postulates, a 'decolonization' of the human and children's rights discourse and its practice. The continuing 'coloniality of power' (Quijano, 2008) must be questioned in theory and practice. This is the only possible way to bring to bear 'situated knowledge', counter-hegemonic ideas and claims of human and children's rights, which are due to and partly articulated by children in Southern regions of the world. This would be equivalent to what Boaventura de Sousa Santos (2014: 200) calls 'emancipatory interculturality', or Catherine Walsh (2018: 57) 'critical interculturality'. We will pursue this question in the following section.

Children's rights between universalism and cultural relativism

Shortly after the adoption of the CRC some childhood researchers (for example, Boyden, [1990] 1997; Burman, 1994) pointed out already that it is based on the dominating Western concept of childhood. The main characteristic of this concept is an understanding of childhood 'as a time of innocence and vulnerability' (Cregan and Cuthbert, 2014: 32) in which children are dependent on protection and care by adults, the state or child aid organizations. The implicit presumption is a society that harms children if they are not protected against it. This is supplemented by the idea that as a first premise, children must be supplied with all they need. Children's relationship with adults or the state is not presented as interdependent but as dependent.

It is true that this concept has been modified in comparison with the Declaration on the Rights of the Child of the League of Nations of 1924 and the UN Children's Rights Declaration of 1959. Children are now recognized as legal entities capable of action and participation, although the basic paternalistic pattern is preserved (see Cordero Arce, 2012; 2015a). According to the CRC, the participation of children is limited to the promise that adults and adult-led institutions fulfil their obligations to listen to them and take their views into account in their decision-making. A further limitation is the supposition that children must reach a certain maturity to be worth listening to and making decisions. The implicit point of reference here is the adult, who is presented as perfect or at least superior, not least by including the rationality embodied by him or her. Such assumptions confuse a paternalistic or adultist order of power with personal properties of children.

While other authors assume that the CRC and the concept of human rights are open to different cultures, they also take a critical look at the ways in which human rights and, in particular, children's rights are interpreted. Among other things, they criticize the fact that the discourse of human rights and children's rights is instrumentalized by certain power groups and that these act as 'moral watch dogs' in order to 'modernize' and 'civilize' backward cultures and ways of life (Pupavac, 1998; Valentine and Meinert, 2009; Montgomery, 2017). A 'colonialist paternalism' would be encouraged 'where Northern "child experts" offer their help and knowledge to the "infantilized-South"' (Cockburn, 2006: 84).

The objections to this way of dealing with human and children's rights are not necessarily guided by cultural relativist considerations. They expressly distinguish 'real culture' and the 'culture presented to outsiders by governments and intellectuals' (Freeman, 2002: 30; also Harris-Short, 2003). Their objections are, above all, that human rights and children's rights are ordained from above by state orders and by power elites. They argue for a 'localization' of the understanding of the law and 'dialogical' procedures (for example, Vandenhole, 2012; Cheney, 2014: 27–28). This requires not to depreciate lifestyles and cultures as fundamentally backward, but recognize and promote diversity and their particular meaning. This suggests that the concept of childhood on which the CRC is based is not understood as the historically most advanced stage of childhood ('childhood of modernity') nor as the absolute norm for supposedly left-behind societies and cultures.

The CRC is based on a quite simple formal definition of the child by naming an age range within which young people are considered to be children (up to the age of 18). Such a definition may be difficult to avoid in a legal document, but it does not necessarily correspond to what is understood in a specific society or culture as a 'child' or 'childhood'. The age range is very broad and is possible to grasp only in a considerably abstract manner, according to the specific interests and self-understanding of young people in this age group. The subjective interests of a 16-year-old have little in common with the subjective interests of a toddler; a child who lives in absolute poverty will set other priorities than a child living in prosperity. Likewise, the children's and young people's agency competences differ and demand for specific concepts and arrangements for protection and participation. Children who take responsibility for others at an early age often feel 'infantilized' by being called a child. The sharp distinction between childhood and adulthood, marked by chronological age, easily leads to misunderstandings, inappropriate classifications or discrimination (see Sloth-Nielsen and Klep, 2020).

With these critical remarks we do not want to disesteem the advances made by the CRC, for the first time, children are granted the status of legal subjects under international law. We do however want to raise awareness of its limitations and (contrary to human rights principles) its conditionality. We also do not deny that the CRC contains wording that includes recognition of other cultures and of the childhoods practised there. The preamble states that the state agreements enshrined in the CRC and all corresponding measures are to be understood as 'taking due account of the importance of the traditions and cultural values of each people for the protection and harmonious development of the child'. Nevertheless, the CRC leaves little scope for imagining other childhoods and child rights concepts that do not correspond to the structural pattern of 'modern' Western childhood. Such childhoods and children's rights are indeed practised in some cultures, and are possibly brought forth by children themselves.

With regard to the debate between universalism and cultural relativism, we would like to address some of the problems that arise in the application of the legal principle of the best interests of the child, which is a fundamental principle of the CRC (Vandenhole and Erdem Türkelli, 2020). Like international human rights law, this legal principle is legitimized by its claim to universality, but must be adaptable to different cultures and local circumstances. For example, rules of life or child-rearing practices that are considered negligible or inappropriate from a Western perspective may be well thought-out and justified rules in community life for some people.

The recognition that certain aspects of child-rearing may vary between different social groups should not lead to blind acceptance of all practices or viewpoints that are described as 'part of the culture'.[11] Anthropologist Marie-Bénédicte Dembour (2001: 56), for example, warns of the dangers of pushing either universalism or cultural relativism too far. She characterizes 'universalism as arrogance and relativism as indifference' and stresses that while universalism can disregard the experiences of minorities, excessive relativism can also be used to excuse and justify any violent action. Without reflection and nuance, cultural relativism can be as harmful to minorities as Eurocentric universalism, because it treats minorities as clearly defined, homogeneous groups and ignores the internal dynamics and diversity of opinions within these communities.

The prevailing discourse is based on an essentialist concept of culture, according to which culture is a quasi-biological property that a group of people 'has', rather than understanding cultures as a diverse and varying combination of practices and beliefs which are developed and used to adapt to different circumstances. The danger of this approach is that minority cultures, in particular, are treated as fixed and immobile, so change is inevitably viewed negatively and homogeneity is assumed within the group. While Western or mainstream culture is assumed to be able to develop and is even expected to do so, some children's rights activists never tire of praising the 'preservation' of Indigenous and minority cultures. They are expected to stagnate in order to be considered worthy of preservation. This desire for preservation and supposed authenticity of Indigenous and minority cultures ignores the reality of today's interconnected world and limits the possibilities of these communities by painting 'traditional cultures' as general opposition to international human rights, trade and communication technologies, which are themselves seen as purely 'Western' by dogmatic cultural relativists.

Cultural relativist criticism of the international human rights regime often sees it as an instrument of neo-colonialism, for example by using women's rights rhetoric to legitimize military interventions. While this criticism is justified and necessary, it tends to ignore the fact that the idea of universal human rights has also been taken up and applied by minorities and colonized peoples, often against Western powers. It is striking, for example, that the main supporters of cultural relativism in the 1950s were not from Africa or Asia. It was the imperialist powers that used cultural relativist arguments to justify the disrespect for human rights in their colonies. At that time, 'rights were an anticolonial threat, not a neo-colonial weapon' (Burke, 2010: 114). The colonial powers even made considerable efforts to portray human rights as only suitable for 'civilized societies' and in contradiction to traditional cultures.

Cultural relativism that is not questioned but unconditionally applied can also endanger the rights of persons belonging to minorities. In discussions about practices such as Female Genital Cutting, for example, the fact that this practice does not have the unanimous support within the community can be easily ignored by relativists. Insisting on certain cultural practices on behalf of an entire community often only serves the interests of those who have special power in that community. The voices of those who are excluded from power remain silenced. These are usually children and women. That communities consist of different individuals, each with their own identity, is easily overlooked. If individuals are assigned to certain groups or if assumptions about their needs and preferences are made solely on the basis of their membership in that group, it becomes more difficult for them to express their own ideas.

No matter how valid it is to criticize the Eurocentric tendencies in discourse on human rights, care is required not to overemphasize cultural-relativist arguments. As social subjects whose views are usually valued the least, children are particularly vulnerable when universalism or cultural relativism is understood and practised in a dogmatic way. This applies in particular to children who belong to a population group defined as an 'ethnic' minority or who deviate from the dominant standards of normality (for example, due to extreme poverty or their sexual orientation). They run the risk of being marginalized and discriminated against, on the one hand by the absolute Eurocentric childhood pattern, and on the other hand by denying their individual beliefs.[12]

In view of the claim to universality of the CRC, children's rights studies face the task of understanding children's rights in an open, dynamic, processual, culturally sensitive and context-related manner (see Freeman, 2020: 272–276; 339–340). This includes dealing with the rights codified in the CRC in a critical and reflective manner and recognizing that they are not the final stage of a development but can and even need to be changed. Special attention must be paid to the views and demands of children, namely those of the Global South, especially when they themselves express them as their rights and legal entitlements. Only then is it possible to speak of a decolonization of children's rights in theoretical and practical terms.

Research and activism – a contradiction?

In a recent contribution, Olga Nieuwenhuys and Karl Hanson, the scholars who introduced the concept of living rights, have argued that children's rights studies are challenged by a field of tension between activism and enlightenment. As children's rights researchers, they see their task not in 'influencing the social world', but 'to better understand it' and on this basis 'to enlighten' (Nieuwenhuys and Hanson, 2020: 130). In our view, this opposition is based on problematic premises for two main reasons. First, the question arises whether researchers can at all 'understand' what moves children with regard to their rights if they only look at their situation from the outside or from above, instead of entering into a dialogical relationship with children in research and acting together with them. On the other hand, there is the question of what use it is to children to understand their situation and be enlightened about it if it does not make it possible for them to claim their rights. In both cases, researchers are in a distanced position, which can only be understood as indifference or even arrogance by the children whose rights are at stake.[13]

The relationship between research and (political) activism is undoubtedly complex and full of contradictions that can never be fully resolved. In our view, it is important to become aware of these contradictions and to deal with them in a way that benefits children and their rights.[14] We believe it is necessary to seek and, wherever possible, create an epistemological environment that allows researchers to get close to children and to understand their views, concerns and hopes in terms of their rights.

Children's rights studies take place at different sites and in different contexts. The universities are a privileged site. Despite neoliberal restructuration attempts aiming to turn them into mere production sites for human capital, research and reflection can still be carried out largely independently. There is still space for critical thinking that should not be underestimated, especially in educating students, if the aim is not to convey and acquire only practically applicable but also reflective knowledge. Nevertheless, research conducted at universities also has a flip side. The people involved are usually far removed from the reality of children and are exposed to the risk that their research serves their own scientific reputation rather than the children whose rights are at stake. Younger researchers in particular are urged to 'publish' and achieve a 'ranking' in the academic world, where the benefits of research for children are often overlooked and ultimately fall by the wayside. With a view to the children of the Global South, it should also be borne in mind that the universities usually claim a monopoly on knowledge. This is based on academic standards that largely exclude the ways of thinking and knowledge in non-Western cultures or have an instrumental ('extractivist') relationship to them (see the contributions in Cupples and Grosfoguel, 2019; Cornejo and Rufer, 2020).

Mexican sociologist José Manuel Valenzuela Arce sees the danger of the social sciences becoming heteronomous in the 'niches of comfort' from which academic researchers 'exercise their knowledge-power' and therefore affirm the violence of the powerful in social life:

> Social science heteronomies refer to research methods and processes, in which the others, the savages, the researched, the objects of study, the natives, the informants, the sample population, the pilot groups, the focus groups or the target populations, become involved in rules, norms, doxas, world views and knowledge imposed by academia. This all means little to nothing to their own interests, knowledge and worldviews. These subordinate forms of participation are subject to the rules of the game of researchers whose interests and objectives have little in common with the individual or community investigated. Furthermore, studies are carried out from monological positions loaded with symbolic violence that (re)produce heteronomy. (Valenzuela Arce, 2020: 14)

Children's rights studies conducted in the context of non-governmental organizations, which advocate children's rights, are often closer to children, as they are fed by the practical needs of children and are intended to contribute to improving their situation. Often, children's rights studies conducted here arise as a kind of accompanying research from practice and are led by actors who are familiar with the situation of children from daily experiences. But here, too, children's rights studies have another side. They are seldom independent, are frequently not planned thoroughly, and are bound to the specific interests of the organizations on whose behalf they are conducted. It is also by no means guaranteed that the knowledge resulting from social and educational practice, for example, corresponds to the children's views. These contradictions and problems are addressed in the concept of living rights and the question of 'translating rights' explained earlier.[15]

Research that seeks to explore the meaning of children's rights in children's lives cannot be done from a bird's eye view. Its actors must participate in the lives of children and be 'touched' by them. This applies especially to children whose lives are very different and far removed from the life experiences of the researchers. Therefore, researchers cannot, in our opinion, simply involve children only as informants or try to 'give them a voice'. Rather, they must share children's concerns and understand their own research as part of the children's (possible) actions. In these circumstances, researchers learn from children, just as they can help to facilitate children's reflections and actions with the knowledge gained. At its best, research can be 'a pedagogical tool for social transformation that enables children and young people to produce their own knowledge, to use it for the purposes of their organisation and to generate a context for the construction of new political subjectivities in both adults and children who participate' (Nichel Valenzuela, 2018: 18).

In such forms of research, children are not to be seen as mere participants in a research project designed and controlled by professional adult researchers. They must have the opportunity to plan and decide on the process of gaining knowledge themselves. So-called *participatory action research*, in which children are involved in the whole research process, from developing and deciding on research questions and the choice of methods to the formulation, presentation and use of results, is an important step towards this (although still very rare in reality). But we think it is also necessary to encourage children to act as researchers and to accompany them in solidarity. Only children's rights studies conducted in this participatory and supportive manner will create the necessary *epistemological environment* to make the situated knowledge and expectations visible which children associate with their rights (recent examples of this type of study are: Morales, 2020; Morales and Shabel, 2020).

We are convinced that it is equally important and necessary to take seriously ways and forms of knowledge that can in a specific way only be found in children (for example, in their sense of justice). Since children however hardly ever express themselves in an elaborate and purpose-oriented way, they are easily misunderstood or dismissed as 'kids' stuff' or even 'children's noise'. This is particularly striking for children of the Global South who live under precarious conditions and/or are rooted in cultures that differ from so-called Western civilization. Corresponding considerations are expressed in concepts of an 'epistemology of the South' (De Sousa Santos, 2014), 'Indigenous methodologies' (for example, Tuhiwai Smith, 2005; 2012; Kovach, 2010; Chilisa, 2020; Kleibl et al, 2020: 161–257) or 'horizontal methodologies' (Briones, 2020) without referring to children and their rights directly. They also challenge children's rights studies to reconsider the truth criteria and immanent logics of the sciences that dominate at universities, to strive for a (self-)critical intercultural perspective, and to renounce any claims to academic monopoly. Keeping this in mind and acting accordingly could ultimately contribute to a decolonization of children's rights discourses and practices.

One result of such research can be legal concepts the children develop by reflecting on their own experiences, articulating them together and implementing them partially or completely themselves. One example of this is the '12 Rights', which the African Movement of Working Children and Youth first formulated in 1994. The grassroots groups united in the movement work to implement these rights and every two years they meet to review how far they have come. These processes often arise out of necessity, for example, when HIV/AIDS or war orphans join siblings and other affected children in so-called child-headed households; or when children who oppose their exploitation at work establish their own cooperatives where they organize their work together, manage processes according to their own ideas and practice approaches of a solidarity-based economy. These are by no means always emergency solutions to guarantee mere survival. Frequently, they contain elements of a society in which children are no longer subject to the decision-making and the monopoly of knowledge production of adults, but rather shape their lives themselves. The existing legal systems do not yet take this into account and are more of an obstacle than a support for children. The CRC does not provide any solutions for this either, as, despite the promise of participation, it places the rights of children exclusively in the responsibility of states, parents and other adults.

Conclusion

Research on children's rights should not lose sight of the fact that these rights serve a practical purpose and should contribute to the emancipation of children and strengthen their social position in a societal power relation constructed to their disadvantage. This requires reflecting on (and investigating) the deeper reasons for the violation of children's rights or conceiving and contextualizing children's rights in a way that children can relate to them. In referring to the political implications of children's rights studies, we do not mean that researchers should leave their independent and critical thinking at the coat rack, following the motto 'serving the people'. On the contrary, they are invited to reflect on their epistemological environment, the risks and opportunities involved, and the ethical responsibility of their research. In this context, orientation towards a concept of living rights can be helpful, that is, in the sense of 'insurgent cosmopolitan law' (De Sousa Santos, 2014: 51), committed to social justice and the perspectives of children as a subaltern population group all over the world.

Ethical challenges of research with children of the Global South

With Urszula Markowska-Manista

Introduction

No one will doubt that ethical standards are at least as important and necessary in research with children as in any research about or with humans (and animals). And it is to be welcomed that interest in ethical aspects of research has increased in the last two decades and has even led to agreements that cross national borders and are understood as a worldwide professional commitment. The International Charter on Ethical Research Involving Children (ERIC), which was drafted under the umbrella of UNICEF's Innocenti Research Centre,[1] for example, emphasizes that:

- children, their views and their cultures must be respected;
- all children must be treated equally and obstacles to their participation based on discrimination must be challenged;
- the benefits for individual children or children as a social group must be maximized;
- the results of research must benefit children;
- possible harm resulting from children's participation must be prevented;
- children must agree to their participation, as must their guardians;[2] and
- the researchers must constantly reflect on the impact of their own assumptions, values, beliefs and practices on children (summarized according to Graham et al, 2013).

But as meritorious and plausible as these general principles may be, they are not beyond doubt and cannot eliminate all the problems, ambivalences and contradictions that arise in research practice even with the best will of the researchers. Their apparent plausibility may even contribute to concealing such problems and contradictions. In our opinion, this is especially true in the case of problems that arise from different life situations, interests and unequal power positions of the persons and institutions involved in the research. Furthermore, it is important to distinguish whether ethical principles are applied in legally regulated testing procedures ('procedural ethics') or whether they relate to practice in the research field and the use of research results ('practical ethics' or 'participatory ethics') (see Abebe and Bessell, 2014). In the first case, they contribute little or can even make it more difficult for ethical sensitivity to develop among researchers.

In this chapter, we would like to draw attention to selected problems that arise in research with diverse groups of children from the Global South, insofar as it is conducted by adults residing in countries of the North especially in the European Union countries. We identify some reasons for these problems and ask to what extent ethical principles can be of help in dealing with and overcoming these problems. We first present the inequalities in the globalized postcolonial world as a political and ethical problem and ask about the possibilities of adopting ethical symmetry[3] in childhood studies. Then we discuss the attempts to give a voice to children of the Global South, and finally we show why childhood studies need to free themselves from Eurocentric premises and decolonize themselves as well as in what way this can be achieved.

Global inequalities as a political and ethical problem

For the past three decades or so, children of the Global South have become a research topic for childhood studies departments based at European and North American universities.[4] To this day, however, their research is often still based on categories that do not do justice to the realities of life for children in other continents or for children of Indigenous minorities in their own continents, and sometimes even favours discrimination against them (see, for instance, Hunner-Kreisel et al, 2022). On the other hand, this basic attitude, which is occasionally described as Eurocentric, is also increasingly being problematized. Ethical principles are being formulated and research approaches and dialogical collaborations are being sought that are culturally sensitive and open to perspectives and experiences beyond the European understanding of culture and science. In this context, since the 1970s there have also been calls to decolonize the sciences themselves (see Stavenhagen, 1971; Kovach, 2010; Tuhiwai Smith, 2012; Strega and Brown, 2015; Chilisa, 2020).

We see one of the greatest challenges of childhood studies today as understanding the connections and contradictions between the global and local dimensions of childhood and children's lifestyles, at the level of the objective-material as well as at the level of subjectivity, thinking, feeling and acting. Children are just as influenced (though not in absolutely the same way) as young people and adults by what is happening in other parts of the world, because closed-off niches no longer exist. Nevertheless, the way they are influenced also depends on which parts of the world they live in and under what conditions. The globalization of childhoods is neither a unilinear nor an absolutely inevitable process, but implies many interdependencies. It does not produce a single uniform 'global childhood', but many, quite different 'global childhoods' (Cregan and Cuthbert, 2014).

It should not be overlooked that the interdependencies in the formation of global childhoods are embedded in an extremely unequal global power structure. How unequal these global interdependencies can be is most evident in the widening gap between wealthy regions and those regions of the world where absolute poverty prevails and children have much fewer opportunities in life. The growing social inequalities worldwide reflect the unequal distribution of power between the Global North and the Global South that emerged in the colonial era and persists today in hidden institutional forms. It is no longer openly expressed in colonial expansion, conquest and domination, but in the less visible dependence of seemingly independent nation-states in the South, which in turn internally reproduce social and political inequalities (see World Inequality Lab, 2018; UNDP, 2019; Piketty, 2020). This is not only a fundamental political problem, but also a challenge for the scope of ethical principles, which are based on the idea of (individual) self-determination as well as on the idea of human dignity and globally understood social justice.

Ethical symmetry as a precarious challenge

The ERIC Charter calls for respect for children, their views and cultures, as well as the requirement to treat all children equally and to prevent discrimination. This is intended to counteract the power asymmetries that have developed over centuries in the relationship between adults and children and are associated with an undervaluation of children and their abilities. This is sometimes called adultism today and results in numerous discriminations (see Liebel, 2014a; Chapter 5, this volume), of which we as adults are rarely aware, even when we act as researchers. In order to avoid age-specific discrimination, it is necessary not to degrade children to research objects, but to respect them as subjects with their own rights and competences (see, for instance, Thomas and O'Kane, 1998; Thomas, 2015). With the development of studies on children and childhood that are oriented towards children's rights, subjectivity and agency, the conviction has grown that only research *with* children is suitable for understanding the situation of children. It is also considered crucial for bringing children's voices to the fore.

Participation in research is considered particularly important, but is also particularly difficult to implement in the case of children who are socially disadvantaged and live in precarious circumstances. It is often limited to 'symbolic participation' such as periodic consultations or fragmentary interviews. Even when this is intended to enable children to be heard and seen, it rarely considers what this means in relation to the contexts and circumstances in which the children live. In such studies, children may be audible or visible (for example, in photographs or videos), but they usually have no real influence on what happens to their voices and images (see Markowska-Manista, 2020: 23). Under these conditions, research does not live up to the ethical claim of benefiting children.

This is especially true for research in which children's participation is limited to the role of informants or respondents, a common practice in survey research. In this case, the knowledge provided by the children is treated as a kind of raw material to be processed by adult experts as they see fit. Analogous to extractivist economies that ruthlessly exploit and destroy non-human nature, one could speak of an extractivist way of research here. This can only be countered if the children participate as co-researchers with their own rights and decision-making powers in all phases of the research process and can influence the research process right up to the use of the results (see, for example, Kirby, 1999; Clark, 2004; Alderson, 2008; Fiedler and Posch, 2009; Thomas, 2021; Nentwig-Gesemann, 2022; critically: Hammersley and Kim, 2021).

However, the inclusion of children as co-researchers has brought new ethical dilemmas and challenges in the case of children who are socially disadvantaged and marginalized (Markowska-Manista, 2018: 53). They arise from the fact that adult researchers, especially if they are only 'visiting', as it were, during their fieldwork, disappear again after the completion of the surveys. They find themselves in a social situation that is completely different from that of the children (see Lee-Treweek and Linkogle, 2000). Their perception of the world and the children's lives is shaped by their own experiences and preconceptions. This often means that only knowledge that is considered pleasant and valuable is taken up, while unpleasant knowledge is devalued as irrelevant and invalid and may even not be perceived at all. Knowledge that is unpleasant for the researchers is thus made invisible. We see an ethical challenge in this context in 'not only whose story it has the potential to tell, but also whose it will hide, why, for whom, and with what consequence' (Strega and Brown, 2015: 6).

The ERIC Charter, referring to a guideline from the children's rights organization Save the Children (2002), puts it this way: 'Harm can occur when children's voices are sought only when they match the interests of adult researchers, but are overlooked when they do not' (Graham et al, 2013: 32). Or the danger is pointed out that 'researchers from predominantly individualistic cultures interpret research findings within collective cultural contexts in ways that are consistent with their own views, beliefs and experiences, but inappropriate to the context in which the research takes place' (Graham et al, 2013: 37; see also Abebe and Bessell, 2014: 130).

While the professional researchers find themselves in a comfortable security, the children, even if they are included in the research process, remain subordinate and powerless; in the case of socially disadvantaged and marginalized children, their situation even remains precarious (see Markowska-Manista, 2017; Cronin-Furmann and Lake, 2018). The problem can arise that while the children's voices yield valuable insights for us researchers, they remain a trivial episode for the lives of the children themselves and may even have detrimental consequences. This also applies to the interpretation of the data obtained. It is often guided by beliefs or ideologies that we in academia consider normal, but which are not appropriate to the children's actions in their life contexts. For example, a British social researcher devalued the forms of action of girls working as domestic workers in a rural region of Tanzania as 'thin agency' (Klocker, 2007), because they did not correspond to the researcher's ideas of the autonomous, primarily individually acting person ('thick agency'), which emerged with the European Enlightenment (for criticism, see Esser 2016; Liebel, 2020: 23–30).

Afua Twum-Danso Imoh (2009), a social researcher from Ghana, also points out that participatory research with children in the countries of the South has become attractive not only because of the cognitive curiosity of the researchers. Its attractiveness stems not least from the fact that it is easier to obtain funding for studies conducted in 'developing countries'. According to Twum-Danso Imoh, however, there is no consensus on what participatory research with children in this field is and what practical consequences it entails in local settings. A recently published 'Global Ethics Code' (TRUST, 2018) articulates in general terms a self-critique by financially powerful institutions in the North of past funding practices for research projects in 'resource-poor settings'. It emphasizes the need 'to promote equitable research partnerships … using a new framework based on the values of fairness, respect, care and honesty'. The very name of the leading academic institution, which is based in the UK, expresses the guilty conscience and the hope that future funding will be trusted.

The ERIC Charter postulates that research should not only not harm children, but should also benefit them as much as possible, in other words, that their situation should improve through research. The latter basically requires researchers to take sides and characterizes research that is to be understood as committed to a practical purpose, in this case the improvement of children's situation. In our opinion, the postulate is very important, but also particularly difficult to implement. If we consider not only the possible harm but also the benefit for the children, we must ask ourselves, for example, which children we are referring to: to the children directly involved in the research process or to all children for whom the knowledge produced in the research is of relevance. In any case, we follow an ethics that not only demands responsibility for others (such as the feminist-inspired care ethics; see, for instance, Held, 2006; Barnes et al, 2015), but also respects them as social subjects with their own interests, rights and perspectives and has their emancipation or liberation in mind.

Such an ethic derives from the socially disadvantaged and politically oppressed people and population groups and their claim to human dignity. It can be found, for example, in the liberation philosophy of Enrique Dussel (1980). Also, it is a basis of the liberation pedagogy or *Educación Popular* associated with the Brazilian philosopher and educator Paulo Freire ([1968] 2000), or the pedagogy of tenderness elaborated by the Peruvian philosopher and educator Alejandro Cussiánovich (2007; 2022). Similar notions of ethics have also been present for at least three decades in the movements of Indigenous peoples and the descendants of slaves abducted from Africa, who recall colonial genocide and revolt against their degradation and enslavement during the last 500 years. They are expressed, for example, in a performative ethic of reciprocity focused on appreciative intercultural and intergenerational relationships (see Magnat, 2020; Romm, 2020).

Such ethical concepts also suggest encouraging children to act as researchers themselves and to accompany them in solidarity, taking into account the tangible and intangible aspects of their daily lifeworlds. Research conducted in this participatory and supportive way can create the epistemological environment necessary to make children's *situated knowledge* and potential for action visible and usable for themselves. The concept of situated knowledge refers to the fact that no knowledge is detached from its context or from the subjectivity of the person who expresses it. The social position of the person is taken into account, since viewpoints are never neutral in ethical terms. We will illustrate what situated knowledge means in the case of children with the question of speaking and silence, sometimes associated with double victimization of a particular group of children (Markowska-Manista, 2019).

Is it ethical to give children a voice?

In social science research on childhood, which has been developing since the 1980s, the question of children's voice and silence occupies a prominent place. The main issue is how to pay more attention to children's 'voice', but also what can be hidden behind children's silence. These questions are considered important because an essential task of childhood studies is agreed to be the deconstruction of the concept of childhood that dominates the modern Western world, which separates children from adults and places them at the bottom of the social power hierarchy. By making children's voices and views visible, that are possibly hidden behind silence, childhood studies aims to strengthen children's social status as a social group and contribute to their emancipation in relation to adults. This raises the fundamental ethical question of what it means for children to *give* them a voice.

For example, childhood researcher Sirkka Komulainen (2007: 23) points out that the 'voice' of children is consistently perceived selectively by researching adults and turned into an 'object' that 'can be possessed, recovered and verbalised'. Children's statements are subjected to a cognitive interpretive scheme that not only ignores the social conditionality and ambiguity of communication between children and adults, but also only 'hears' children's voices when they are put into words. Komulainen (2007: 25) expresses her criticism by playing with words: 'More listening may not inevitably mean more hearing' (see also Komulainen, 2020). Social work researcher Alison McLeod (2008: 21), referring to her own study, points out that adults and children often understand listening differently: while listening from the perspective of adults means that they pay attention to what children say, have an open attitude and respect their feelings, children expect listening to be followed by action.

Anthropologist Spyros Spyrou (2011; 2018) also emphasizes the need to reflect on the power imbalance and ideological contexts that influence children's voices in the research process. One answer to the question how children's voices, in their complexity and ambiguity, can be brought to bear and understood, might be for children to explore their reality themselves. Adults can certainly play a supportive role in this, but they must also reflect on their inevitable influence. This is usually missed in surveys conducted by children's rights organizations, which are well-intentioned to give children a voice. A recent example is a survey based on interviews and group discussions with more than 1,800 working children in 36 countries, mainly in the South (O'Kane et al, 2018).

Without a doubt, it is necessary to pay more attention to the contexts and conditionality of the children's voices captured, especially in participatory research approaches. Although these research approaches aim at overcoming the power imbalances between children and researching adults, this is not so easily achieved. Mary Kellett (2010: 91–92), a protagonist of this approach, draws attention to the fact that children are not unaffected by power differences found among different groups of children (for example, social background, gender, age, language skills, physical performance or popularity), which strongly influence the research endeavour. Adults, moreover, can never become 'natives' in children's worlds, not only because of their unequal physical size, but also because of the privileged status they always have, even as co-researchers. It is not enough to want to meet children 'at eye level', because this claim cannot override the continuing power inequality and can easily degenerate into a euphemism. Therefore, it is all the more important for researchers to be aware and accept that the children involved can resist the research goals and become 'counter-players' in the research process (Kämpfe et al, 2022; Storck-Odabasi and Heinzel, 2022).

The barriers to understanding the voices of children of the Global South are rarely reflected in childhood research. Although the Western bourgeois understanding of childhood is no longer used unquestioned as a yardstick for childhoods in such contexts, Eurocentric ways of thinking and forms of 'epistemic violence' (Spivak, 1988) influenced by them have not disappeared from childhood research or are rarely self-critically questioned (see Liebel and Budde, 2017). They can be seen, among other things, in the fact that little attention is paid to the forms of action and articulation of children in the South that are not individually verbalized as 'children's voices', or that they are hastily classified as not child-specific or externally controlled and thus made invisible. If the conclusion is that these children must first be given a voice or helped from outside to have more independence and participation, colonial patterns of relationships are reproduced – often unintentionally.

In the contributions from childhood research cited here, the social and discursive conditionality of children's voices is usually understood as a limitation or their authenticity is questioned. Very rarely is it asked to what extent the children's voices can also express interests that result from their situation in life, their social status or a particular situation. For example, children's voices may be guided and shaped by an interest in asserting themselves in a situation of unequal power – for instance, in relation to a teacher at school – and in tactically undermining or changing this relationship (Mandell, 1988; Atkinson, 2019). Such a voice can also express itself in deliberate silence or by going into exile and making itself known only to other children. In such a situation, it can also become a problem of participatory research or research aimed at empowerment to encourage children to speak. Contrary to its own emancipatory intentions, it contributes to depriving children of the secrets that are existentially important to them as persons subjected to power. When voices are interpreted as expressions of interests, it is also important to consider, in addition to individual expressions, correspondences and discrepancies between them and to relate them to the social or generational situation of the speaking or silent children. Consistencies can be found, for example, in collective expressions and actions of children who come together in groups or social movements to influence their environment.

We see an ethical challenge of childhood studies in becoming aware of the presuppositions and limitations of one's epistemologies and knowledge practices. The concepts we use as researchers – for example, agency, voice or participation – also emerged in a specific historical and geopolitical context and are associated with meanings and assumptions that cannot be transferred seamlessly to other contexts. They have to be questioned in the participatory process of research and reconceptualized together with the children involved in the research. This will only ever be possible in approximate terms and requires, especially in the North–South context, that the researchers, who stand in a Western academic tradition, reflect on their entanglement in (post-)colonial patterns of relationships.

Why childhood studies must be decolonized

The ERIC Charter calls for constant reflection on the impact of researchers' own assumptions, values, beliefs and practices on children. With regard to the children of the Global South, this means being aware of the fact that childhood sciences have colonial roots and have not freed themselves from this legacy until today. The Austrian educationalist Peter Gstettner had already pointed out 40 years ago that 'the scientific conquest of unknown territories precedes the conquest of the child's soul' (Gstettner, 1981: 15). He shows this in particular in the history of the emergence of developmental psychology, but also in the conceptualization of childhood (and youth) in the related sciences as a whole. Educationalists Gaile Cannella and Radhika Viruru (2004) have also shown that the dominant pattern of childhood in the West is the contemporaneous product of the same ideologies that served to justify colonial expansion and conquest. This is expressed in particular in the parallel application of the idea of development from lower to higher degrees of perfection. Childhood, like the non-European regions of the world and their inhabitants, is located at the lower end of the scale, which is also reflected in the fact that people subjected to colonization are equated with children who have yet to develop (see in detail Liebel, 2020: 43–49).

We conclude that childhood studies must decolonize itself to live up to its ethical maxims. By decolonization, we mean that it counteracts the 'coloniality of power' (Quijano, 2008) in both its material and discursive manifestations. This includes recognizing that there are no 'children without childhood' in the world, but a great diversity of childhoods. By ignoring this diversity or making it invisible through Eurocentric bias, many 'children out of place' are created, with multiple discriminatory consequences (see Invernizzi et al, 2017). In this sense, it is not enough to simply name the cultural diversity or plurality of childhoods. It is necessary to acknowledge and problematize that these childhoods are affected by postcolonial material and discursive inequality in different ways. For example, Indian social researcher Sarada Balagopalan (2019: 25) notes that 'mobilizing a "cultural" explanation around the differences that mark children's lives produces at best, a response in terms of "respect for their culture", a response that does little to destabilize the hegemony of a modern Western childhood'. Instead, she believes it is necessary to analyse children's lives in the context of larger global economic structures and changes:

This embedding of the culturally discrete lives of children within global economic processes not only offers us a more political handle with which to engage these lives but also allows us to discern shifts in everyday patterns that demonstrate how global realities affect local cultures and how these cultures adapt, adopt, resist, as well as desire these changes. (Balagopalan, 2019: 18)

Although childhoods of the Global South are more often the focus of attention in childhood and children's rights studies, they are still frequently studied and evaluated with theories and concepts that originated in and relate to Western bourgeois societies. This applies above all to a concept of childhood charged with universalistic pretensions, which originated in the European context and is now being used as a supposedly 'global child' as a yardstick for assessing the lives of children of the Global South (for a critique, see Sarmento et al, 2018; de Castro, 2020a; 2020b; 2021). It is true that in the meantime more sensitive concepts and research approaches have emerged in childhood and children's rights studies that are more open to the experiences and perspectives of children and differ from traditions of liberal-paternalist thinking. However, they are still rarely used in a way that contributes to a better understanding of the lifeworlds of children of the Global South and strengthens their social position.

A troubling legacy of colonization is also the fact that research on children continues to be dominated by researchers at Northern universities who absolutize the standards of academic excellence that apply here. These standards claim to be the only access to knowledge about reality and truth, and therefore exclude many other ways of thinking and knowing, especially those outside academia and in non-Western cultures.[5] The dissemination of research results also depends heavily on publishers and journals based in the North. They are usually only recognized internationally if they are published in one of the former colonial languages, particularly in English.

The increased interest in the lifeworlds and lifestyles of children of the Global South can contribute to their decolonization. However, it is also necessary that it opens up to ways of thinking and knowing from non-Western cultures and cooperates with researchers who are rooted in these cultures, and that these researchers are provided with scientific spaces in which their work and research methods are disseminated and taken seriously. This includes questioning the dominance and essentialization of one's own research paradigms and the accompanying 'epistemological privileges' (see Bhambra, 2014; Tlostanova, 2019; Pease, 2022: 62–71).

Compared to childhood studies, this process is already further advanced in feminist-oriented research (especially in Latin America and Africa). An example is the critical examination of the colonial implications of the category of the powerful and empowering (White and male) subject and by taking up so-called Indigenous or horizontal epistemologies and research methodologies. They are based on the idea that the separation between researcher and researched is abolished and new knowledge is produced jointly (see, for instance, Rivera Cusicanqui, 1987; 2010; Ball, 2005; Kovach, 2010; Corona and Kaltmeier, 2012; Segato, 2013; Tuhiwai Smith, 2005; 2012; De Sousa Santos, 2014; Rodríguez and da Costa, 2019; Chilisa, 2020; Cornejo and Rufer, 2020; Kleibl et al, 2020). This idea, which corresponds to the principle of ethical symmetry, is still largely uncharted territory in childhood studies. In order to decolonize knowledge and ways of knowing, the relations between knowledge and power must also be envisaged.

> There is a close connection between knowledge and power, which is shaped by the colonial deep structure. In this context, neither neutral knowledge nor pure research exists. ... Therefore, it is necessary to pursue an ethics and politics of research that does not start from the idea of an idealized academic field. Rather, political, economic and social aspects must be integrated and this must be done throughout the entire research process, starting with the definition of the topic, through the collection of data to the publication of the results, in order to advance the process of decolonizing knowledge. (Kaltmeier, 2012: 44)

Such critical self-reflections are also immensely important for childhood studies, as they can play an important role in the recognition of non-Western childhoods and the self-empowerment of children in the Global South. This is important not least because children experience violence, humiliation and discrimination in their various and interrelated forms directly.

Conclusion

The chapter is a plea to decolonize childhood studies via paradigm change, focusing in research on children's perspectives, participation and protection of children's rights. We wish to sensitize researchers to the asymmetries of methodological approaches, the failure to incorporate the specifics of local places, different, non-Western methodologies and children's rights. We draw attention to the failure to take responsibility for conducting this type of research and its consequences for children and their communities. Moreover, we advocate the need to adopt a non-Eurocentric approach, indicating that this research rarely incorporates non-Western epistemologies, decolonial approaches, local knowledge production and children's participation in childhood studies (which has to be also understood 'from below'). Further, we should consider the possibility of applying ethical symmetry in research about and with children, searching for the topography of ethics that is appropriate in this type of research.

The ethical dilemmas of participatory research with children of the Global South cannot be overcome by establishing ethical principles alone. They require researchers to critically self-reflect on the persisting inequality of power in the globalized postcolonial world and between adults and children. This requires that childhood studies not only expands knowledge about children, but also contributes to policy interventions that lead to greater equality and social justice. We see a fundamental condition for this in strengthening the social position of children and giving more attention and support to the ways of thinking, seeing and acting of children of the Global South.

Adultism, children's political participation and voting rights

With Philip Meade

Introduction

Since the UN Convention on the Rights of the Child (CRC) from 1989, children around the world have been regarded as persons with their own special rights.[1] These include rights that are intended to enable children to influence their environment and all matters that affect them. But how far these so-called participation rights go and whether they also include political rights is disputed. They oppose social structures that nail children down to a subordinate position, which today is subsumed under the term *adultism*. In this chapter, we will discuss the question of how far political rights, especially the right of children to vote, can contribute to counteracting adultism and thus contribute to overcoming the colonized status of children and childhoods. This question will be discussed not only in relation to children living today, but also in relation to future generations and intergenerational justice. First, we will outline what is meant by adultism and its conflict-laden relationship with children's rights.

Adultism and children's rights

What is called adultism refers to the belittling of children by adults because of their age. Adultism is based on the unequal power and power imbalance between adults and children and is usually understood as the 'abuse of power' of adults over children (LeFrançois, 2014; Bell, 2018; Bergman, 2022). It often arises in the context of superiority, privilege, convenience and blanket assumptions about being a child. It can also occur between young people of different ages, to the extent that they themselves have already internalized adultist behaviours. Adultism is a specific form of discrimination. It manifests itself in derogatory behaviour towards younger people, but can also become entrenched in social, legal, and institutional structures.

The term adultism as understood today goes back to the psychologist Jack Flasher (1978). It first became widespread in the United States and became a key word in the movements for equal rights for children and young people (see Bell, 1995; Fletcher, 2015). It was taken up in other world regions only after the turn of the millennium. It is mainly used to criticize educational methods and is associated with other forms of discrimination such as racism or sexism. While initially the relational aspects and psychological implications were emphasized, today systemic aspects and socio-cultural frameworks are also given more attention and there is talk of institutionalized or structural adultism, for example.

Adultism is widespread in all contemporary societies in the Global North as well as in the Global South. It permeates the daily lives of children and adolescents, it is found in family as well as in educational institutions, in public as well as in private life. Adultism is so common and considered so normal (for both children and adults) that it is rarely noticed or even considered a problem. Often, it even hides behind actions and measures that purport to serve child protection. It resonates when decisions are made *for* or *over* children at a family, school or political level.

Children experience adultism in many different ways: as disrespect, contempt, degradation, devaluation, imputation, attribution, stigmatization, appropriation, arrogance, heteronomy, subjugation, discrimination, marginalization, exclusion or punishment. It is sometimes experienced as direct or indirect violence by adults who have power over them. Adults, in turn, use this power consciously or unconsciously to achieve certain goals, to satisfy their own needs, to eschew fears, to give in to desires for dominance and control or to make their lives more comfortable. Sometimes simply because something 'is done that way' and supposedly has always been done that way.

Children deal with adultism in completely different ways. For some, adultism leads to insecurity, helplessness and self-loathing. For others, it leads to frustration, anger and resistance. Others give up, keep quiet or pass on the pain they experience to weaker people. Notwithstanding repressive conditions, many children do find ways to live comfortably and establish sustainable relationships with adults.

To counter adultism and gain more influence on political decisions, children's human rights can be an important lever. However, this requires understanding these rights in such a way that children themselves can claim them and use them to strengthen their social position. Since the adoption of the CRC in 1989, children's rights can be said to have become part of global reality, at least in the sense that every child in the world has a legally codified entitlement to them (if the national State Party has ratified the CRC, which has not yet happened in the case of the US). It is more than just an idea or the desirability of children's rights, as they have been formulated in writings and appeals since the late 19th century by committed children's thinkers such as Ellen Key, Janusz Korczak, Eglantine Jebb or Gabriela Mistral (see Chapter 2). But they are far from being a reality in the sense that children's living conditions and daily lives are based on them.

Having rights and actually being able to exercise them are two different things. In order to be able to exercise rights, social conditions must be in place that enable children to make use of them. And there must be the political will to fulfil the obligations towards children due to their rights. As far as their living conditions are concerned, there is only a modest political will that in turn is counteracted by a savage capitalist economy, which also harms the conditions for coming generations' growing up and endangers their lives and human dignity. Although some things have improved for children in most countries of the world, they have seldom been able to fully enjoy their rights. Moreover, the rights enshrined in the CRC are not in themselves incontestable. When the CRC was formulated, the idea that children could and should participate in the elaboration of their rights was very limited.

The CRC has stimulated numerous initiatives to address and combat the contempt, discrimination, violence and disadvantage that children suffer from the moment they are born. However, the positive impact of the CRC should not obscure the fact that it is a time-bound document based on diplomatic commitments, with weaknesses, gaps and shortcomings. Among these shortcomings is that the CRC has a protectionist tendency and that it challenges paternalism and adultism only half-heartedly. The basic paternalistic tendency is expressed in the concept of childhood, the disregard for adult-centric power relations, the absence and ambiguous formulation of some rights, and the understanding of participation. This basic tendency is reinforced by widespread conservative interpretations.

There are contradictions between what is promised to children in the form of children's rights and what makes it difficult or prevents them from exercising their rights. These in turn are part of existing legal constructs. To clarify this, we will look at two examples.

In the 1990s, some working children in Nicaragua (as in many other countries) wanted to unite to defend their rights and sought UNICEF's support for a larger gathering. The head of the local office was enthusiastic. But when the children asked for a grant for travel, rent and food, she referred them to an adult organization, since she could not enter into a contract with minors due to the country's laws and UNICEF's own statutes. In addition, the children, who contribute to their families' livelihoods through their work, had designed a poster for their meeting with the slogan: 'Yes to Work – No to Exploitation!'. The UNICEF representative shook her head apprehensively and said she could only support the meeting if the first half-sentence was removed. The children were grateful, but refused, as they felt this violated their right to freedom of expression and assembly and they did not want to be dependent on an adult organization.[2]

A second example is related to Germany. In a study on the meaning of children's work (Hungerland et al, 2007), the authors found that children, especially girls, often took on household chores that were not for educational purposes, but to relieve their parents. They kept the house in order, did the shopping or took care of younger siblings, sometimes also taking care of sick parents or other relatives. Particularly in immigrant families, the children helped their parents in their own shop or snack bar, or supported them with their often better German language skills in correspondence with the authorities. Other children, who had paid jobs in addition to school, contributed all or part of their income to the family budget. The authors had the impression that the feeling of supporting one's own family in a difficult situation filled the children with pride and contributed to their self-esteem, especially when they received social recognition for it. But this recognition was denied because of the widespread idea that all work is harmful to children (on concepts of harm in relation to children's work, see Maconachie et al, 2023). The right to work in dignity has not yet been granted to working children, not even in the CRC.

By granting children their own rights, which they can also claim for themselves as subjective rights, their moral status as human beings entitled to human dignity is underlined and affirmed. However, rights are still limited to the claim that adults take responsibility for children's welfare and give due consideration to their views, expressions and opinions. Political rights, in the sense of children being able to make vital decisions and participate in social and political life in a specific but equally important way are not yet provided. The principle of *the best interests of the child*, which is central to the CRC, is ambivalent, as it remains largely dependent on the interpretations of decision-makers and grants children their own judgement only to a limited extent. Participation in decisions that are supposed to serve the best interests of children are linked to maturity and rationality. Although the moral status of children as human beings entitled to human dignity is generally recognized, especially in the right to be protected from discrimination, violence and exploitation, the participatory rights as contained in the CRC now do not suffice to ensure a balance in intergenerational relations.

This raises the question how to expand children's spaces of participation and action. The dominant concept of family and childhood assumes that children are cared for by their parents and are therefore dependent on them, both in legal as well as financial terms. Although the breadwinner-wife-family model has long been questioned and an increasing number of women are moving away from biased gender-specific roles, not much thought has been given to the consequences for children until now. A basic child allowance, which is not only geared to the level of subsistence, but to the best possible development of the children's personality and capacity for action, and which would have to be available primarily to the children themselves, would be a possible way of enabling them to take more self-determined action, at least from a certain age onwards. However, the acquisition of the capacities required for this is not tied to a specific age, but depends on the specific experiences and developmental conditions in each case.

In our view, there are two reasons why an expansion and reformulation of children's rights codified in the CRC is necessary: first, certain facts were not yet known or there was no consciousness of them when the CRC was drafted and adopted. Second, a structural imbalance between children and adults is reproduced in it. The need for updating the CRC has already been highlighted on several occasions in relation to ecological rights that have not yet been explicitly codified. Likewise, digital media and their immense importance in the lives of young people are absent in the CRC.[3] The problematic of the CRC is also reflected in the fact that the understanding and need for children's political participation has expanded, especially in terms of how to go beyond the right to be heard. For this to happen, children would have to have political rights that allow them to directly influence decisions that affect their present and future lives. These changes would have to be made respecting children's views and demands raised individually or collectively.

This perspective challenges the existing power relations between adults and children. For this reason, some warn not to demand 'too much', as this could jeopardize what has been achieved so far, even if little. We, on the other hand, are of the opinion that children's rights can only achieve an emancipatory meaning and develop a corresponding effect if they are freed from their paternalistic eggshell.

Rights, however formulated, are initially little more than window-dressing. Even as subjects of rights, children depend on having them recognized and the conditions created to make them a reality. The basis for the underlying concept of the CRC is that parents and, subsidiarily, the state have the primary responsibility for the implementation of children's rights. It is incumbent upon them to orient themselves towards the 'best interests' of children and to 'guide' them in the exercise of their rights.

In the international discourse on children's rights, universally valid rights are said to be 'translated' into the local environment of the subjects, taking into account local specificities. In the case of child poverty, for example, this could mean that children invoke the right enshrined in the CRC to grow up in the best possible living conditions and to receive material assistance and support from the state 'particularly with regard to nutrition, clothing and housing' (Art. 27.3). Only through this contextualization can children's rights also become reality for the children, because they live in specific circumstances and have specific interests.

This raises the question of whether and how children themselves can dispose of their rights and help shape them. Legal or (according to legal terminology) positive rights cannot be thought of without a substructure of moral rights. This becomes especially clear in the concept of human dignity, since it cannot simply be derived from positive law. It is also the result of self-understanding and socio-cultural and ethical agreement on what is 'inherent' in human beings and constitutes their dignity (and is then legally codified as an indispensable guarantee, for example, in a constitution). The same is true of the 'best interests' principle, which is fundamental to children's rights.

If we are to understand children as subjects of their own rights and children's rights in the sense of the draft made here, children must have the possibility to constitute their own rights. Since, until now, they didn't have the possibility to participate in legislation or jurisdiction, their own ideas about what is rightfully theirs must at least be recognized as moral rights. And since children do not grow up and act in the free space of society, society or the 'world community' is obliged to support them in elaborating these ideas and formulating them as children's rights. They have a moral duty to open up social spaces in which children as a whole or as groups can become aware of their common interests, articulate them and collectively represent them themselves. However, this should not be confused with the frequently expressed postulate that children should be 'given a voice', as this is itself an expression of adult-centric power relations. The social space in which children formulate their interests and, where appropriate, their rights, should be as autonomous and child-shaped as possible.

This understanding of children's rights and their transformation into rights in the hands of children are termed 'rights from below' (Liebel, 2012a) or 'living rights' (Hanson and Nieuwenhuys, 2013; 2020). While power relations would have to be fundamentally transformed in favour of children, this would not happen by 'putting children in power', but by mutually recognizing adults and children in their equality and diversity, and communicating and interacting with each other in their own ways.[4] Given the foreseeable difficulties, this is certainly utopian, but it is not impossible.

Children's political participation and voting rights

We understand political participation as self-determined action that is directed towards and contributes to changing social conditions. It can be both actions that directly seek or bring about change and actions that try to achieve a transformation indirectly through representatives or by using existing political institutions. In the first case, these are social movements, self-help actions or temporary individual or collective initiatives aimed at improving living conditions. The second is characterized, for example, by participation in elections to political bodies or the assumption of political responsibilities in such bodies. Another indirect way of political participation is when people invoke their own rights before the courts. In reality, the different forms of political participation can go hand in hand and complement each other.

With the CRC, children gained participation rights in international law for the first time. These include the right to be heard in all judicial and administrative proceedings affecting the child (Art. 12), the right to information and freedom of expression (Art. 13) and the right to assemble peacefully and form their own associations (Art. 15), supported by the provision that the 'best interests of the child' must be 'a primary consideration' in decisions taken by state authorities (Art. 3). These rights granted to children limit political participation to being 'heard' by adults, thus not guaranteeing their active participation in political decision-making. Likewise, the right to participate in elections to political bodies or to take responsibility and make decisions in these bodies is also not provided. The interests of future generations and thus questions of intergenerational justice are also not explicitly addressed in the CRC. They are only indirectly addressed in the right to health care (Art. 24) and adequate living conditions (Art. 27).

However, political participation is not limited to the exercise of codified rights. It can also manifest itself in people 'taking the right' to the streets or to criticize grievances on social media and, in this way, generate political pressure for change. Forms of 'civil disobedience' are also part of this and can even be associated with deliberate violations of rules. In the case of children, these actions are often not taken seriously by state authorities (dismissed as 'childish things' for 'minors') or, if taken seriously, are not tolerated or are dismissed as manipulation by the adults concerned. Current examples are the 'school climate strikes' by the climate justice movement Fridays for Future or the calls for transport fare evasion as a protest against the increase in transport fares during the social outburst in Chile in October 2019, initiated by young people, who triggered the subsequent street protests. These examples demonstrate that these actions and movements can exert political influence, but are also sometimes associated with stigmatization, criminalization and considerable personal risks to life and limb.

According to children's rights researcher Laura Lundy (2007), children's participation should include four key elements:

- *Space*: Children must be given the opportunity to express a view.
- *Voice*: Children must be facilitated to express their views.
- *Audience*: The view must be listened to.
- *Influence*: The view must be acted upon, as appropriate.

For these elements to be fulfilled in reality, both children and adults must be able to prepare themselves fully and certain framework conditions must be guaranteed. If children's participation in public affairs is to take place outside formal institutions, there must be a safe environment for them. Such an environment offers children 'space' to raise their 'voice' and gain 'audience' by attracting attention in order to exert 'influence'. In this sense, social movements acting in public are a way for children to intervene effectively in public affairs.

Adultism in society is also revealed in the fact that children are not accepted as political actors despite the participatory rights granted to them in the CRC. Also, they are denied a hearing precisely because they make political demands and 'arrogate' powers that adults commonly attribute exclusively to themselves. We will show why this situation can only be overcome if children are no longer denied the right to vote. Universal suffrage is a basic element of any society or any political system that claims to be democratic. To deny it to children and young people is to deny them full citizenship. However, the right to vote is not a value in itself, it must be seen in the context of the respective form of state and society. Likewise, the children's right to vote must be seen in the context of other forms of political participation and structural changes in social power relations.

In 'representative' democracies that are based on a liberal (economic) state, the right to vote gives citizens only little influence on political decisions, as it is limited to periodic individual votes. Furthermore, politics is relatively isolated from their lives in the hands of professional politicians who usually belong to political parties. The latter are officially beholden not to their voters but to their conscience, but are often subject to the influence of powerful interest groups. One consequence is that disadvantaged population groups, in particular, have little trust in political institutions and participate less in elections. In societies with great social inequality, elections can even be used as a front that disguises unequal property and power relations by wrapping them in a largely inconsequential democratic cloak.

The right to vote is much more important in political systems where citizens have more frequent opportunities to vote on important issues and where members of parliament and state authorities are directly accountable to their constituents and can be voted out of office by them if necessary.[5] These systems are sometimes referred to as 'direct', 'participatory' or 'community-based' democracies. They often arise in social upheavals, where people are dissatisfied with the status quo and push for change. In postcolonial societies in the Global South, where there are several peoples with different cultures and ways of life, they sometimes take the form of plurinational democracies. These are decentralized and federal. Such forms of democracy sometimes oppose the idea of the unitary nation-state and have their strongest expression at the local or regional level. Here, too, the need for a central state power at the national level is often questioned. This is paradigmatically demonstrated today, for example, in the autonomous communities that emerged from the Zapatista uprising since 1994 for the dignity of Indigenous peoples in the Mexican state of Chiapas.

Whatever the form of government or political level, in all societies with democratic aspirations, universal suffrage is a fundamental civil right that belongs to all people. It is not the only means of ensuring that political decisions are made in the interests of all people living on the territory, but it is one of the fundamental ones. Denying this right to children and young people below a certain age is the opposite and a form of adultism.

Arguments in favour of children's right to vote are also found in some writings on the theory of democracy and justice. According to these, laws that create obligations can only claim legitimate validity for people who have directly or indirectly participated in their creation. Philosopher Jürgen Habermas (1996) says that the idea of self-legislation by citizens presupposes that those who are subject to the law as its addressees can also see themselves as the authors of that law. Political scientist Iris Marion Young (2001; 2002) argues that the legitimacy of a rule depends on the extent to which those affected by it have participated in the decision-making processes and have had the opportunity to influence the outcomes. The author warns that the problem lies in conceiving an egalitarian society without acknowledging cultural or group differences. This, in her view, causes theories of justice, for example, that of philosopher John Rawls (1999), to be more about injustice by fostering exploitation and domination, so that recognizing differences is an imperative of a just society. In this sense, social philosopher Nancy Fraser (2013) affirms that once the discussion of redistribution and recognition is overcome, we must arrive at guaranteeing the representation of disadvantaged groups. For Fraser, it is essential that these groups get the remedies that guarantee political representation so that they are in a position to defend their rights. These are, broadly speaking, the criteria that make up the principle of democratic legitimacy, the cornerstone of any democracy that claims to be just. To the extent that laws also bind young people and create obligations for them (for example, in criminal law), they must also be decided upon by young people.

There have been repeated objections to children's right to vote by arguing that children lack the information and skills necessary to participate in elections. Fears have also been expressed that they can be manipulated particularly easily by adults close to them (for a critical analysis of the objections, see Wall, 2021). These objections ignore the fact that such criteria are not a requirement for adults to participate in elections. Nor are all adults informed and competent and they can be influenced in their voting behaviour by other people or by the media as well. If children were given the right to vote, their interest in political information would presumably increase, as would their ability to make independent political judgements. Political parties and candidates seeking election would be obliged to make themselves and their programmes understandable to children. The information and political choices offered could be expected to be more responsive to children's interests and expectations. The numerous recent protest movements of young people in various parts of the world have shown that they are among the population groups particularly interested in political issues and that they are politically engaged. However, their engagement is hardly related to institutionalized politics. Many young people perceive these as distant and irrelevant to their own lives.

The question therefore arises whether children feel addressed by the framework of elections. However, two things should not be confused: on the one hand, the fact that political decisions, at least in today's parliamentary democracies, are only influenced to a limited extent by participation in elections; on the other hand, the fact that today elections are still only addressed to adults and therefore seem to children a boring and irrelevant event. If children had the right to vote, presumably, at least the form of addressing issues would change and more attention would be paid to their interests. This, in turn, could have the effect of shifting the priorities of the political agenda towards young people, as well as increasing their awareness of their own rights and confidence in their own abilities.

It should also be borne in mind that children's right to vote would have a power-balancing function, counteracting the structural degradation towards children in contemporary societies by reinforcing their social status and bargaining position. In this context, it is not enough to extend the right to vote alone. It is also necessary to create real conditions in children's lives for them to perceive this right as meaningful for their own lives. In this sense, it is also necessary to broaden the principle of capacity development to refer not only to children's subjective capacities, but at the same time to include the creation of the material conditions to be able to use these capacities. These, as well as the experiences of action themselves, influence the degree to which and the way in which subjective capacities are developed. The ability to recognize one's own interests and to exercise one's right to vote accordingly can only develop to the extent that children have practical experiences and become aware of their self-responsibility and co-responsibility towards others.

In recent decades, a number of options have been proposed on how to extend the right to vote to children.[6] They range from lowering the voting age to, for example, 14, to proposing that children should be able to participate in elections as soon as they express their willingness to do so. Another proposition is that parents should exercise the right to vote on behalf of their children until they reach a certain age or until they express the will to vote themselves. All these proposals are worthy of debate, as they could help to increase the political weight of the younger generations or to counterbalance the dominance of the older population (which is growing as life expectancy increases in many societies, especially the wealthier ones). However, we believe that the children's right to vote should not be exercised by adults close to them, but by the children themselves, as is considered normal for adults. To avoid distortions in voter turnout statistics (since babies will not yet want to vote), it could be regulated that all children who want to exercise their right to vote up to a certain age (for instance, 14 years old) should be registered on a voters' list and thus acquire the right to vote. At that age, they would automatically be registered as eligible to vote.[7]

As explained earlier, political participation is not limited to the right to vote. In many countries, children's and youth parliaments, children's and youth councils or similar forms of young people's participation have been established since the 1990s, inspired by the CRC. Or children have been offered special electoral procedures in which they can express their political preferences parallel to the 'real' elections. These forms of participation are often seen as a kind of 'citizenship in the making', intended to serve the political education of the younger generation and to awaken their interest in political issues. They rarely have a significant influence on political decisions, and this is usually not their aim either. Their scope is set by adults and they are often a kind of playground for young people who want to be active in some way. But here, too, their context has to be taken into account.

If children's councils or similar institutions of child participation serve as a substitute for 'real' voting rights, they divert attention from the issue of children's voting rights and postpone their possible introduction. They channel children's interests and energies in a way that is mostly predetermined by adults, and thus do not really contribute to counteracting adultism in society. However, if children's councils are part of a political process aimed at changing society, or even emerge as protest movements of young people themselves, they can help to give these processes and movements a more stable structure and thus increase their effectiveness. In general, it can be assumed that, even if children are given the right to vote, a greater impact can only be expected if it is accompanied by self-organized social movements.

Moreover, only in this way would it be possible to overcome an immanent limitation of the right to vote, which consists in limiting political issues to parliamentary institutions. For democracy to be taken seriously producing new rules and laws is unsatisfactory, instead, a change of the lived reality would be needed. In other words, society would have to be democratized in all areas, in the economy as well as in social and educational institutions. For young people this would mean, for example, gaining influence on the content of teaching and forms of learning at school, and to have legally binding possibilities to act against the violation of their own rights. With this extension of democracy into everyday life, it would go beyond the framework of a representative democratic form of government from the liberal model. Children's right to vote could contribute to making this perspective more visible.

One of the shortcomings of the debate on children's right to vote so far is that it largely revolves around the question from what age the right to vote is given, and whether it should be exercised by parental representation up to a certain age. But the question should not only be whether we, as adults, should give children the right to vote, or even at what age we should give them the right to vote, but what we can do to raise children's interest to participate in democratic politics and political decision-making. This comes down to the question what a just democracy for children and future generations should look like.

The issue of the right to vote is closely linked to questions of intergenerational justice. This does not only concern children living today, but also future generations yet to be born. Therefore, it also seems important to us to address the question how the interests of future generations can be safeguarded and what resources exist or should be created for this purpose.

Intergenerational justice

To counteract adultism, it is necessary not only to consider its immediate consequences for young people, but also its long-term consequences for their later life as adults and for the life of future generations. Many of the political decisions made today have serious impacts on later life and future generations, without those affected being able to influence them in the short and long term. With regard to children living today, the question of how their political participation can be expanded is important, for which, as we have shown, the right to vote is of particular importance. For future generations, however, additional solutions must be found that also allow for their political representation and to thus achieve intergenerational justice.

The issue of intergenerational justice has been addressed by some governments and the United Nations in recent decades. Almost 20 years ago, for example, the Austrian government included 'generation mainstreaming' in its action plan to counteract generational discrimination (Österreichische Bundesregierung, 2004). According to this plan, it is necessary to examine the effects of all political decisions on the different generations. As with 'gender mainstreaming', whereby the gender perspective is included in governmental action, the question of what a certain action means for children must always be asked. In addition to 'affirmative action' measures, which aim to accelerate de facto equality for certain disadvantaged groups – in particular children with disabilities and minorities – the Austrian Plan of Action calls for 'equal opportunities and equal rights for all children as a key policy objective and focus of awareness-raising measures'. This is to be achieved by reviewing the impact of all policies on the later lives of children and subsequent generations; taking account of generational discrimination in social reports on children; and promoting children's participation.

More generally, this issue is also addressed under the key term 'intergenerational justice' in the National Sustainability Strategy, *Perspectives for Germany*, which the German government adopted in 2002 and updated in 2017, referring to the global sustainability goals formulated in the UN

Agenda 2030 (Deutsche Bundesregierung, 2017). This strategy proclaims as a 'first rule of principle' for politics and society that: 'Each generation must solve its own tasks and must not burden future generations with them. At the same time, it must make provision for foreseeable future burdens.' However, it does not explain concretely how the interests of future generations can be taken into account in politics.

Legal scholar Edith Brown Weiss (1989; 1990; 1992) had already developed criteria for intergenerational equity in the 1980s. These are summarized in three principles:

- *Conservation of options*: Each generation should be required to conserve the diversity of the natural and cultural resource base, so that it does not unduly restrict the options available to future generations in solving their problems and satisfying their own values, and should also be entitled to diversity comparable to that enjoyed by previous generations.
- *Conservation of equality*: Each generation should be required to maintain the quality of the planet so that it is passed on in no worse condition than in which it was received, and should also be entitled to planetary quality comparable to that enjoyed by previous generations.
- *Conservation of access*: Each generation should provide its members with equitable rights of access to the legacy of past generations and should conserve this access for future generations (Brown Weiss, 1992: 26).

Since then, similar criteria have been included in several international environmental and human rights documents. As early as 1988, the United Nations General Assembly unanimously adopted a resolution on the protection of the global climate for present and future generations of mankind (UN, 1988). This resolution set in motion a process that led to other international climate agreements in the following years. For example, the Declaration of the United Nations Conference on Environment and Development, held in Rio de Janeiro in 1992 (UN, 1992), states as Principle 3 that: 'The right to development must be fulfilled so as to equitably meet developmental and environmental needs of present and future generations.' Although it is not further specified here what 'developmental and environmental needs' are to consist of and how they are to be 'met', some clarification can be found in subsequent international documents. For example, a UNESCO Declaration on the Responsibilities of the Present Generations towards Future Generations (UNESCO, 1997) states:

Article 5 – Protection of the environment
1. In order to ensure that future generations benefit from the richness of the Earth's ecosystems, the present generations should strive for

sustainable development and preserve living conditions, particularly the quality and integrity of the environment.

2. The present generations should ensure that future generations are not exposed to pollution which may endanger their health or their existence itself.

3. The present generations should preserve for future generations natural resources necessary for sustaining human life and for its development.

4. The present generations should take into account possible consequences for future generations of major projects before these are carried out.

Article 11 – Non-discrimination

The present generations should refrain from taking any action or measure which would have the effect of leading to or perpetuating any form of discrimination for future generations.

In 2015, two international agreements were reached within the framework of the United Nations that, while not explicitly referring to future generations, are of great importance to them. The first is the UN Agenda 2030, which incorporates the Sustainable Development Goals (UN, 2015a), while the second is the Paris Agreement, which establishes a global framework for avoiding dangerous climate change, keeping global warming below 2°C and continuing efforts to limit it to 1.5°C (UN, 2015b).[8] These agreements have been criticized, and rightly so, on the grounds that, for example, the development goals adhere to the dogma of economic growth or that the climate agreement does not go far enough. However, it should not be underestimated that both agreements reveal learning processes of the international community about the serious threat to the planet, which was not necessarily to be expected. However, practical results can only be expected if the pressure from below, especially from the young generation living today, continues and becomes even stronger.

From the point of view of the interests of future generations, there is a fundamental difference between the management of natural resources on the one hand, and economic and financial resources on the other. To clarify this difference, we refer to the reflections of a German educationist at the end of the last millennium:

As long as future generations cannot use any more fossil fuels that have been consumed, they are faced with the contributions they have to make for the repayment of the debts of the state obligations, which are in front of a well-ordered society with a supply of usable structures. While the excessive use of natural resources leads to an asymmetrical favouring of the present, the use of financial resources in the public sphere has a certain symmetry. (Brumlik, 1999: 1464)

The starting point is what the author calls 'a well-ordered society'. The author stresses that the available resources must really benefit all people equally and that they are taken care of in such a way that no social group or part of the world's population is privileged over others, neither in relation to the present nor in relation to the future. With regard to economic and financial resources, for example, care must be taken that the difficulties in financing state social benefits resulting from the changing age structure of a society are overcome in a spirit of solidarity, through measures such as broadening the base of the pension system or increasing taxes on high incomes, wealth and international capital transfers. However, the question how to deal with natural and cultural resources is at least as urgent. Brown Weiss (1989) rightly calls them not resources but livelihoods, since what is at stake is not their use (or even exploitation) but their preservation and further development. Here, for example, the debate is about how to secure:

- that natural and cultural diversity be maintained and nurtured;[9]
- that the natural and cultural bases of life are nurtured, protected from commercialization and made equally accessible to all people;
- that those responsible for the damage and destruction of these livelihoods be held accountable (states, multinational corporations);
- that all people, regardless of their origin and circumstances, receive an education that is not aimed at the economic utilization of knowledge, but serves the development of personal skills;
- that all people are able to provide for their livelihood in a humane manner;
- that all people can live a life free from fear and discrimination; and
- that a world order is established that does not oppress, harm or exclude anyone, and that is oriented towards understanding and peaceful coexistence.

A justly ordered society, in which the interests of children are also considered, would ultimately also require that power is no longer distributed unequally and that vital issues are not decided without those concerned, but that everyone – regardless of age – is given equal opportunities to participate in their solution. Since it can be assumed that children living today have a better feeling for the future than adults, such a society is more likely to take the interests of future generations into account.

The responsibility that children living today feel for future generations is most recently expressed, for example, in the Fridays for Future climate justice movement (https://fridaysforfuture.org), as well as in various legal complaints that children have filed against the governments of their own and other countries for violating their rights to a healthy environment (on Peru, see Instituto de Defensa Legal, 2019). In an international initiative, 16 children aged 13–17 from 12 countries have appealed to the UN Committee on the Rights of the Child demanding that states be held accountable for their inaction in the face of the climate crisis (UNICEF, 2019). In it, they accuse five states that are among the world's leading economic powers for their inaction in the climate crisis and hold them responsible for it (Children vs Climate Crisis, 2019). In its response, the Committee accepted the petition's argumentation, but forwarded its authors to the courts of their countries first, referring to the individual right of appeal enshrined in the Third Additional Protocol to the CRC. However, such a procedure would take years. The Committee has since begun work on a General Comment on the right to a healthy environment, with a particular focus on climate change, for which it is consulting young people for the first time alongside states and civil society organizations.

One of the problems of past systems of representative democracy is that they are oriented to the present and are thought of almost exclusively in terms of jurisdiction. This means that future and insidious problems, such as those arising from climate change or demographic development, lack public attention. To change this situation, for some years now proposals have been made in different parts of the world on how to take into account the interests of future generations in policies and legislation. These proposals include the institutionalization of independent 'ombudspersons for future generations' (analogous to ombudspersons for children's rights), specially elected and independent 'deputies responsible for the future' or special 'sustainability or future chambers' of parliaments with a veto right to postpone decisions. In Germany, a suggestion has been put forward that 'advisory councils on sustainability and future issues', which are currently appointed by the government and have little influence, should be replaced by 'future councils' at all political levels or complemented by a 'citizens' forum'. These should be chosen by lot from a representative sample of the population, including younger people. In the sense of a participatory understanding of democracy, the aim is to make underrepresented or insufficiently visible demands and needs permanently audible and visible, and to strengthen the responsiveness of political structures intergenerationally.

Some of these proposals, such as ombudspersons for future generations, have occasionally been taken up by governments and parliaments, but their implementation has been limited to very few countries and, often, they have been quickly abandoned or their functions limited (as in Hungary and Israel) when parliamentary majorities changed. Another problem is that the institutions for sustainable policy (as in the framework of the German government's sustainability strategy) are endowed with little or no power. Environmental and climate protection agreements are not legally binding and can therefore not be enforced. In addition, and in general terms, the proposals already show the shortcoming that children are not envisaged as possible representatives and members of such institutions. However, the institutions of the future can only be realized in a credible and sustainable way if they provide for children's right to vote. This right must also include the right to be elected as representatives and/or members of future institutions, and to participate in judicial decisions in these areas.

Nevertheless, in order to achieve intergenerational justice, it is not enough to create new forms of political representation for the hitherto ignored young and future generations. It is also necessary to counteract the destruction of the livelihoods, which is based on the globalized capitalist economic system and its immanent compulsion to growth. This requires a new non-capitalist economy that thinks and shapes 'economics from the standpoint of care' (Wissen and Brand, 2022: 278) and, we would like to add, does justice to the interests of young people and future generations. This is the case, for example, in some eco-socialist concepts (Williams, 2010; Löwy, 2015). Such concepts assume that it will not be possible to stop the destruction of nature either through a change in consciousness and collective humility or through new technological processes (renewable energies, recycling, and others). They also always question the extent to which natural relations, consumption models and lifestyles are intertwined with class and other relations of domination, including intergenerational ones.

Conclusion

Adultism dominates contemporary societies and not only harms the young people living today, but, along with other forms of unequal power, endangers the future of humanity. To counter this effectively, children's rights can play an important role. For this purpose, participatory conditions must be created so that children themselves can make use of them. Participation rights, and especially children's right to vote, are therefore of particular importance. Together with social movements and other forms of political participation, the right to vote can help to strengthen the social position of children and increase the likelihood that the interests of future generations will no longer fall behind. The efforts made so far by individual governments and the United Nations to achieve intergenerational justice are remarkable and offer starting points for a policy oriented towards the interests of today's young people and future generations. However, to go beyond general declarations of intent, it is essential that children and adolescents are recognized as political subjects and actors, and that their opportunities to influence political decisions are expanded to a far greater extent than before. This would also challenge the colonized status of children and childhoods.

PART II

Children in resistance

Children's rights and political subjectivities

Introduction

Among those who see children's rights as an important achievement and advocate for them, there is agreement that children must be respected and taken seriously as *subjects*. This is not only as subject in the legal sense, but also in the sociological and psychological sense. The recognition of children as subjects leads to the conclusion not to emphasize what children are not yet able to do, but to focus on their existing or emerging abilities to express opinions, judge and act (*agency*). It is therefore also important that children are able to express their views freely, gather with other children in their own interest and influence all decisions that concern them (*participation*). Since children and girls in particular are in a subordinate and marginalized social position, emphasis is placed on the need to strengthen them (*empowerment*). In view of the temporary or permanent difficulties that many children face in their lives, emphasis is also placed on their capacity to overcome adversities (*resilience*) and the need to promote it.

I consider all these concepts to be significant and the assumptions and intentions they contain to be relevant and necessary. Nevertheless, I also think it is important to draw attention to some blind spots and problems associated with them. These are not deduced from the concepts themselves, but from a more precise analysis of the social contexts and situations in which children find themselves, and in which the concepts have specific meanings. As the concepts of subject and subjectivity are central to this, I will focus on examining their various contexts, justifications and meanings in relation to children and their rights. Here, I put emphasis on childhoods of the Global South and engage in some reflections on its ambiguities and paradoxes as well as possible extensions and concretizations.[1]

Children as subjects of rights

In children's rights discourse, the concept of the subject has a central and consistently positive meaning. It serves to attribute to children their own legal and social status, which must be respected by society. By designating children as legal subjects or subjects with rights of their own, it emphasizes that they are not dependent on the goodwill of people who have more power than they do that is often exercised over them, but that these persons, just like the state, are legally and morally obliged to respect children as persons with their own dignity. Like human rights, children's rights are both objective and subjective rights. Reference to objective rights emphasizes the obligations of society or the state towards children; reference to subjective rights emphasizes that children themselves can claim and assert their rights. The assumption that children's rights should be understood not only as objective rights but also as subjective rights goes hand in hand with the assumption that children, as *social* subjects, also possess capacities that enable them to identify, claim and exercise their rights. Societies are obliged to recognize and promote these capacities.

I am of the opinion that it is necessary to understand children's rights in this sense not only as objective rights, but also as subjective rights. If this does not happen, the discourse of children's rights remains hollow, as this in fact leads to adults or state institutions reserving a monopoly on knowing better than children what is appropriate and good for them or what is in their 'best interests'. They then act in the name of children's rights, but the holders of those rights are excluded and have 'no say'. The often-raised objection that children must first develop the necessary skills before they can understand their rights and make use of them does not bear fruit. Very young children certainly do not yet have an explicit understanding of 'rights', but they acquire a sense of what is good for them and what is just at an early age. It is precisely by experiencing adults respecting them as subjects and giving them the opportunity to make use of their rights in their own individual and collective interest that children learn to manage and value their rights. Understanding the subjective nature of children's rights therefore implies that adults strive to understand children's views and opinions and to provide children with the necessary conditions that enable them to recognize the meaning of their own rights and, ultimately, to demand and claim them.

However, it should also be borne in mind that it is not sufficient, and may even have problematic consequences, to understand children exclusively as *legal* subjects. In contributions to the philosophy and sociology of law, it is repeatedly pointed out that some problems are connected with the historically developed figure of subjective rights. One of these problems is that the conception of human relations as legal relations may alienate people from each other, since they are dominated by individual interests claimed over others. In bourgeois–capitalist society, this is especially true of the right to property in the sense of *private* property that can be used, accumulated and bequeathed or inherited almost arbitrarily for one's own interests.

To understand a human being only as a legal subject means to reduce his or her qualities as a human being to legal aspects. Under these aspects, the human being is seen, on the one hand, as a person who is obliged or even subjected to certain laws and norms codified by the state (a rarely considered meaning of the category of the 'subject' in the sense of *being subjected*). On the other hand, as a person who has entitlements against other persons or institutions and can claim them. In either case, the relationship between the person and other persons or state institutions means a reduction of human life and coexistence to questions of obeying or demanding. It makes it difficult to imagine relationships of love, friendship or solidarity, and can thus contribute to an impoverishment of human relations. In the attempt to claim their own rights, those who are marginalized and whose rights are massively violated are forced to abstract from their concrete everyday experiences and to move into a terrain where they were already disadvantaged. This is especially true for children. Social philosopher Daniel Loick (2017) calls such legal thinking 'juridism'[2] and, like other critics of the 'scheme of subjective rights' (Fischer-Lescano, 2018: 378) that emerged with bourgeois society, argues for 'transforming' the rights ascribed to the individual into 'social and political counter-rights' (Menke, 2018) and arriving at a 'postjuridical law' (Loick, 2017: 22).[3] In order to attain emancipatory significance 'the atomizing and disciplinary moments of law' would have to be pushed back or neutralized (Loick, 2017: 181).

From a feminist perspective, social philosopher Wendy Brown points out that women's invocation of subjective rights or demands for 'equality' can lead to *paradoxes*:

> Rights secure our standing as individuals even as they obscure the treacherous ways that standing is achieved and regulated; they must be specific and concrete to reveal and redress women's subordination, yet potentially entrench our subordination through that specificity; they promise increased individual sovereignty at the price of intensifying the fiction of sovereign subjects; they emancipate us to pursue other political ends while subordinating those political ends to liberal discourse; they move in a transhistorical register while emerging from historically specific conditions; they promise to redress our suffering as women but only by fracturing that suffering – and us – into discrete components, a fracturing that further violates lives already violated by the imbrication of racial, class, sexual, and gendered power. (Brown, 2002: 432)

Therefore, in order to give greater importance to subjective rights, it is not enough to draw attention to the 'ambivalences of juridification' – as, for example, in the legal analyses by Habermas (1996) – it is necessary to move 'from a *state-centred* to a *lifeworld-centred* perspective' (Loick, 2017: 250; emphasis in original). From this perspective, such a change in perspective 'would also give a different version to the analysis of the ambivalent effects of juridification: instead of appearing as *dilemmas* arising from the implementation of state measures, they appear as *paradoxes* resulting from the fact that lifeworld-situated actors must both demand and reject rights at the same time' (Loick, 2017: 250–251; emphasis in original).

One reason for the paradoxes is that the freedom and power promised in the discourse on subjective rights meets non-egalitarian preconditions. 'The safeguarding of the factual non-egalitarian preconditions in the normativity of egalitarian law is the price for the legal safeguarding of liberal societies in the form of subjective rights. Subjective rights insofar designate the standards of justice, but also the limits of justice of liberal societies' (Hilgendorf and Zabel, 2021b: 3). Here it comes to bear that the function of subjective rights to enable politics has 'a formal and a material dimension. Subjective rights are formal because they can exist independently of the fact that the material preconditions for claiming them exist at all' (Schmidt, 2021: 150). That is, the juridical protection and equality promised by subjective rights 'do not include a claim to the material preconditions of the rights if these are not already given' (Schmidt, 2021: 150).

Similarly, in relation to children, legal scholar Matías Cordero Arce (2015a; 2018) draws attention to the fact that the conception and understanding of children's rights cannot be limited to an abstract understanding of the child as a legal subject, but must gain a 'dialectical' vision of children in their lived contexts. According to this author, the reality of children's lives is characterized by 'autonomous interdependence'. For example, the co-responsibility of children that is practised in many non-Western cultures should not be understood as a restriction, but rather as an extension of children's rights. In this way, children are both beneficiaries and actors of their rights, or in other words, 'subjects as citizens'.[4]

However, not all problems are solved at this stage. An approach that understands children as subjects and emphasizes their subjective rights is therefore not without risk. It risks trivializing objective or structural constraints that prevail behind children's backs and beyond their judgements and competencies.[5] It could also be used by interested circles or 'society' to divest themselves of their responsibility for children, and transfer them to children's own strengths and initiative. This happens, for example, when in the neoliberal state people are redefined from people in need of help into supposedly sovereign 'customers' or people who depend on the sale of their labour power into 'labour entrepreneurs'. In this way, rights as a claim to state guarantees for a dignified human life are perverted into an inconsequential conglomerate of 'post-rights' (Luciani, 2010) in analogy to the transformation of democratic forms of government into 'post-democracy' (Crouch, 2005).

Nevertheless, these risks cannot be avoided if children are seen solely as victims who must be fully protected and shielded from all risks. This would place children in an objectified position, amount to their incapacity and, above all, hinder the growing demand of young people everywhere to be able to act independently and to have a say in matters that concern them. A subject-oriented approach requires an awareness that all children are children of the society in which they live. Their views, judgements and desires do not develop in an empty space but are influenced by the ideologies and normative guidelines of this society. In all societies, the subject being is confronted with more or less pronounced structural, cultural and social constraints and is only formed in the face of them. Therefore, I see an indispensable component of subject-oriented interaction in dealing with these constraints. They include the fact that children are often unable to decide how and under what conditions they want to live, or that they often have to live in conditions that leave little or no room for their personal interests or needs to grow up. It is therefore important to ask how these constraints arise, for example, to what extent they can be attributed to extreme poverty, a particular mode of economy, dependence on power elites, age hierarchies, ideologies of children as an inferior group ('minors'), 'macho' mentalities and/or contempt for 'different' sexual orientations.

But also and especially in view of the given limitations of being a subject, the question of what role children themselves can play in addressing these conditions remains central. A theoretical analysis must also take into account children's (possible) judgements and (possible) actions. This is more than a question of research methodology. It is about who is most interested in overcoming the limitations of being a subject and how theoretical reflection and empirical research can contribute to achieving this.

Already three decades ago, educationalist Erhard Meueler, in a study on 'paths to the subject', drew attention to 'the fact that the desire to become the subject of one's own action develops in particular from the situation of the inferior, the dominated and the subjugated' (Meueler, 1993: 76). He sees this not as an almost automatic, linear process, but as a dialectical process. The stronger the power, the deeper he sees resignation, but also the more urgent the 'need for freedom' becomes. According to the author:

> The predetermined conditions, the unconscious, the uninfluenced and the still free form shape a contradictory unity, to which the individual must necessarily take a stand in his/her everyday practical actions. Influenced by his/her history, totally dependent on a multitude of conditions that sustain the present life, the individual is not completely absorbed in them. S/he is not autonomous, but in a self-confident, resistive and innovative action, s/he resists the oppressive world of the given. The freedom s/he takes in his/her actions is not absolute freedom. Making use of it is the result of his/her self-reflection and of the education that determines it. (Meueler, 1993: 81)

The self-reflection and education mentioned by Meueler is more likely to develop if children can communicate with others and find a listening ear. It is therefore essential that the training of the subjects respects their views and voices and emphasizes the legitimacy of their own opinions and judgements. It is no less important to highlight their competencies and strengths and to insist on their participation.

Nevertheless, children's *own voices* and *strengths* must be placed in the context of their de facto disadvantage and discrimination, and must be linked to a critique of the specific irresponsibility of the social and economic system towards children, particularly those in the popular sectors or being females. And children, with their voices and views, must not only function as an ornament to an adult-dominated society (called *adultcentrism* or *adultism*), but also have the opportunity to assert themselves in it. This includes enabling children to articulate themselves in a collective and organized way and to be formally and legally represented in decision-making institutions and organizations.

From a feminist perspective, some authors (e.g. Molyneux, 2007; Llobet and Milanich, 2018; Rosen, 2019; Llobet, 2021) also draw attention to the fact that the subjective rights of children codified in the CRC are primarily constructed through the family, which is made responsible for the well-being of children, especially in the figure of the mother. This relativizes not only the subjective rights of children, but also the rights of women, who are expected in a moralizing way to always care for and protect their children, especially by unpaid domestic and care work. Due to the abstract construction of rights, which are supposed to apply equally to all and are available to all, the material conditions of existence vanish, with the consequence that especially mothers from the lower classes end up in a situation where they are accused of not taking care of their children adequately. To the extent that children are only seen as dependent and to be supported, their subjective rights are also ultimately lost sight of.

Finally, subject orientation also means finding the 'objective' social trends that point beyond children's 'objectivity' and favour their subjectivity. These may consist of expanding children's capacity to make their own decisions and creating new possibilities and opportunities in which children have more space to act at their own discretion and responsibility. This goes hand in hand with the relativization of the strict and hierarchically structured relationship between adults and children, and can be facilitated by the spread of new communication technologies. Here it is important to identify the special 'innovative' strengths of children and the potentials for learning and participation that accompany them.

The forms of life and communication that are conducive to children's subjectivity are not naturally established and are not simply open to children. In the context of capitalist societies, they are often marked by exploitative interests and tend to instrumentalize children's subjectivity and 'innovative forces'. From a subject-oriented perspective, it is therefore indispensable to sensitize children to the subtle mechanisms of instrumentalization and to strengthen their self-confidence and their 'bargaining power' wherever they have to defend themselves against unacceptable living conditions. A widespread form of collective self-reflection and counter-power in several regions of the Global South is the networks and associations of children and adolescents, some of which have taken the form of social movements.

When referring to the subjective characteristics of children and their rights, it should also be borne in mind that the concepts of subject and subjectivity have different meanings and are used in different ways.

Ambivalences of subject and subjectivity

A look at the history of philosophy and the social sciences shows that the concept of the subject is conceived differently and associated with connotations that give rise to a cautious approach to it. It is marked by a history that culminated in the notion of an autonomous figure, conqueror of nature and ultimately conqueror of the world, largely identified with the White European male. Cultural researcher Andreas Reckwitz (2008) distinguishes three strands of this discourse of the classical subject. To summarize:

- Descartes' model of the self-confident self, which is expressed in the formula 'Cogito, ergo sum' (I think, therefore I am) and extends to the idealist philosophy of Kant, Fichte, Schelling and Hegel.
- The contract-theoretical individualism of liberal thinkers such as Hobbes and Locke, who model society as the product of selfish individuals.
- The 'romantic' conception of the subject as an expressive, predominantly aesthetic core of self-realization that is susceptible to alienation.

Despite all the differences, these strands of classical subject discourse are based on the same basic assumption of an autonomous subject. 'It appears as an irreducible instance of reflection, action and expression, which finds its basis not in contingent external conditions, but in itself. The classical subject of the "I" is a self-transparent, self-determined instance of recognition and action – moral, interest-driven or creative' (Reckwitz, 2008: 11). According to Descartes, man, through his reason, is confronted as a subject with possible objects to which he is superior in the autonomy of his thought. His conception of the subject has prepared the supremacy of a rationality superior to all other aspects of human existence. This also applies to the subsequent classical subject philosophy, in which the subject is understood as a being endowed with consciousness and rationality, thinking, recognizing, acting, and possessing a sovereign and autonomous 'I'. Kant opposes his concept of subjectivity as an idealistic utopia to the thoroughly regimented, censored and bureaucratized corporate society he experienced. At the centre of his utopia, as a 'categorical imperative', is the rational, self-conscious and autonomous individual who, in interaction with other 'free' individuals, produces a 'bourgeois society' that allows for the full – so-called 'moral' – development of the subjectivity of all human beings. At the same time, he has his eye on the bourgeoisie, which was gaining numbers and influence at the time.

Under the impression of the class antagonisms that arise in bourgeois society, Karl Marx and Friedrich Engels oppose the idealist conception of the subject of bourgeois Enlightenment philosophy with a materialist conception of the subject, at the centre of which is labour and the dispossessed proletariat dependent on the sale of its labour force. They argue that actors who see themselves as autonomous are in reality puppets of a system whose limits of action hardly differ from traditional dependencies. In contrast to the idealist conception of man, which revolves around the concepts of reason and freedom, they emphasize the historical, social and work character of the human being. In their essay *Die deutsche Ideologie* (The German Ideology), written in 1845/1846, but first published in 1932, Marx and Engels formulate the basic features of their materialist conception of the subject:

> The production of ideas, of conceptions, of consciousness, is at first directly interwoven with the material activity and the material intercourse of men, the language of real life. ... In direct contrast to German philosophy which descends from heaven to earth, here we ascend from earth to heaven. That is to say, we do not set out from what men say, imagine, conceive, nor from men as narrated, thought of, imagined, conceived, in order to arrive at men in the flesh. We set out from real, active men, and on the basis of their real life-process we demonstrate the development of the ideological reflexes and echoes of this life-process. ... Life is not determined by consciousness, but consciousness by life. In the first method of approach the starting-point is consciousness taken as the living individual; in the second method, which conforms to real life, it is the real living individuals themselves, and consciousness is considered solely as their consciousness. (Marx and Engels, [1844/1845] 1932: 9)

Marx and Engels understand human life and its history as the conscious activity of subjects, however stress that people can only shape their lives and their history under the given conditions. Relationships with nature and with other people must be established in order to survive. They claim these two types of relations as objective relations, as a result of the actions of previous generations. The subject, with her or his productive, intellectual and other forces and abilities, is subject to these conditions and has them at face at all times. She or he develops in practical social activity, making new areas of the world the object of his or her activity and knowledge.

Both conceptions of the subject, the idealist and the materialist, still constitute two essential fixed and frictional points in the debate on the 'opportunities of the subject'. Against the human-made backdrop of the catastrophes in the 20th century (two world wars, fascism, Stalinism, environmental destruction), the autonomous and free rational subject of Enlightenment was discredited. Likewise, the optimism of progress, embodied in the materialist subject, was being questioned.

Sigmund Freud, the founder of psychoanalysis, broadens the spectrum of the concept of the subject by the facet of unconscious psychic processes and judges the autonomous, free subject to be an illusion (Freud, [1915] 1963; [1923] 1957). Under the impression of Nazi regime, the German-Jewish philosophers and sociologists Max Horkheimer and Theodor W. Adorno[6] see the process of reasoning's self-destruction as inexorably progressing in an ominous 'Dialectic of Enlightenment'.[7] Their aim is to show 'how the subjugation of everything natural to the sovereign subject culminates in the domination of what is blindly objective and natural' (Horkheimer and Adorno, [1947] 2002: xviii). According to them, the self-gain, which characterizes the subject, is always paid with the self-loss:

> Humanity had to inflict terrible injuries on itself before the self – the identical, purpose-directed, masculine character of human beings – was created, and something of this process is repeated in every childhood. The effort to hold itself together attends the ego at all its stages, and the temptation to be rid of the ego has always gone hand-in-hand with the blind determination to preserve it. (Horkheimer and Adorno, [1947] 2002: 26)

A quarter of a century after the end of Nazi barbarism, Adorno posits a 'subject without a subject' (Adorno, 1970: 35), whose apparent individuality is presented only as a *mise-en-scène*. And almost at the same time, the French philosopher and historian Michel Foucault even proclaims the 'end of humanity' with the death of the subject: 'How can man *be* that life whose web, pulsations, and buried energy constantly exceed the experience that he is immediately given of them? How can he *be* that labour whose laws and demands are imposed upon him like some alien system?' (Foucault, [1966] 1970: 344; emphasis in original).

The critique is primarily concerned with the idealist conception of the subject mostly resonating with the materialist understanding of the subject. A different kind of critique of the subject is equally concerned with both positions. A critique that has emerged with feminism and popular and Indigenous movements, which are directed against the destruction of the life sources associated with capitalist globalization. The movements oppose separating the human subject from nature and making it its arbitrary object. A document from Peru, dedicated to the revival of Andean cultures, argues against the thematic thinking that has emerged in the European Enlightenment:

> This man who objectifies nature is the individual, a being without precedent in history, who asserts himself as such in his opposition to others, whom he considers objects. The individual is a solitary being who opposes other individuals because he considers them competitors in his own realization, he opposes nature which he considers a medium populated with resources to be exploited and he opposes God because he considers that He clouds his possibilities of rational explanation of the world. (Rengifo Vásquez, 1991: 33)

In contrast, Andean and other 'Indigenous' cultures do not conceive of 'a separation between something living and something inert' (Rengifo Vásquez, 1991: 34).

> The feeling of equality is experienced equally by humans, nature and *huacas* [protective goddesses], to such an extent that all are considered persons. ... In this personified world there is nothing outside nature. There is no supernatural. The *huacas* are patent, evident, and the dealings with them take place within the framework of a relationship of *ayni* [communal work] and not of worship, for all consider themselves incomplete, requiring each other for the healthy re-creation of life. Reciprocity manifests itself in the framework of this incompleteness, for one who feels complete does not need dialogue with others. (Rengifo Vásquez, 1991: 34–35)

Knowledge and education are not seen as the privilege of man who repairs it to be appropriate or submits himself to a non-human nature. Non-human nature is also considered living and 'educated' and allows human beings to learn from it, as long as they respect their environment and establish a dialogical communication and relationship with equal rights.[8]

What if the idea of the subject is necessarily accompanied by separation and subjugation from other people and nature? In my opinion, the subject can also be understood as mutual respect and social recognition, recognizing that all depend on each other as the indispensable foundation of human life. The idea of the subject turns against all forms of oppression and exclusion, without fighting for new constellations of oppression and exclusion. This social thinking is contained in both the idealist and the materialist conception of the subject. In the former, however, it is lost in the celebration of the selfish individual seeking his or her advantage; in the latter, it is lost in the fog of the abstract construction of a collective of those who have been ignored.

The idealist understanding of the subject, related to the rise and triumph of the bourgeoisie in Europe, arose from a situation of oppression. However, the concept is fixed on the bourgeois or educated individual and aims at his domination over other disadvantaged and non-human beings. Its modern ideal type is that of a technically skilled manager-entrepreneur who does not shy away from risk in order to win.

Although parts of the materialist understanding of the subject aim at domination as well, it sees the human being in his or her need and social references. Accordingly, the subject develops by working for self-preservation and creating the material bases that make life easier for everyone. And she or he evolves by establishing relationships with other people, in the differentiating division of work and cooperation and in the solidarity of the struggle for survival and a better life. In contrast to self-love and the dominant bourgeois subject, one could speak of a social subject and *intersubjective* relations. If I, in this context, also speak of subjectivities instead of subjects, I am dealing with an understanding of the human being that does not separate rationality from the body, but links rationality with bodily and psychic parts.[9] This is particularly important with regard to the recognition of children's capacities, which cannot be measured merely by the standards of a rationality that is directed solely towards the achievement of certain purposes that are determined in advance by those in power ('instrumental reason' in the sense of Horkheimer, 2013).[10]

The conceptual history of the subject also includes the fact that subjectivity was and is set in opposition to supposed objectivity and devalued as an arbitrary opinion. Thus, it follows the dogma that has long prevailed in the natural sciences and positivist social sciences: the subjective is opposed to the desired objectivity of knowledge and is a source of error.[11] There is hesitance to scientifically recognize that subjectivity and objectivity are not contradictory, but are mutually conditional in the process of cognition, and that objectivity cannot be had or endured without the recognition of its subjective parts. But the devaluation of subjectivity remains disturbing, for example, when children's 'subjective' interests are given less weight than their supposedly 'objective' interests. The devaluation of the subjective is still expressed in the traditional discourse on 'degenerate subjects' or 'suspect subjects' and similar word formations. It is directed against all those expressions of life which do not correspond to normality or to the given 'mediocrity' and which embody an immeasurable or controllable obstinacy. On the contrary, it seems to me important to recognize subjectivity as an indispensable component in maintaining or restoring self-confidence and the capacity to act. In this sense, subjectivity can also be understood as an expression of aliveness.

Optimizing the subject

In the most recent discussion on the subject, influenced above all by the thought of Foucault, the concept of subjectivation comes into play, as the concept of the subject is considered too rigid and, moreover, historically charged.[12] 'If one speaks of *subjectification*, then the focus is on the conditions that only produce the subject as subject: social practices, orders, norms and discourses. The question of subjectification is thus a question of the *conditions* under which individuals can be subjects in society' (Färber, 2019: 76; emphasis in original). With the concept of subjectivation, one also tries to avoid sticking to the figure of the autonomous subject that arose with bourgeois society and was emphasized by the philosophy of the idealist subject. In the concept of subjectivation, the subject is understood

> not as an *autonomous* subject in the face of circumstances, but as an ambivalent subject. The figure of the *ambivalent* subject must refer to the fact that the subject is constitutively related to the other, so that the subject can no longer be understood in the classical sense as identical to itself, as transparent to itself. (Färber, 2019: 77; emphasis in original)

The subject understood in this way is seen as both disempowered and empowered. This is also an attempt to go beyond the abstract opposition between power and freedom and to make their interdependence visible. The subject itself, understood as self and self-relation, is thus not a place free of power, but always conditioned and determined by power.

Following Foucault's discussion on subjectification, we should ask ourselves whether people today are 'subjectivized' in a new way. This refers to the tendencies of neoliberal policies and the 'activating welfare state' to make individuals responsible for themselves and to push them into 'self-optimization'. Striving for self-optimization corresponds well with the concept of neoliberal citizenship. People are called upon as actors to optimize their own opportunities through skilful self-management – Foucault speaks of 'technologies of the self' (Kelly, 2013). They are granted active participation and self-responsibility at the cost that, if things go wrong, they themselves are to blame and have to bear the consequences.

Some authors have tried to condense these new forms of subjectification into certain concepts. Sociologist Stephan Lessenich (2009: 130), for example, refers to the transition from state provision to self-care and speaks of the 'subjectification of the social'. According to him, the 'activation of the welfare state ... is not only the motor but also the driving force of general social mobilization' (Lessenich, 2009: 163). In the view of another author, domination now masquerades as 'self-empowerment and is based on the active participation of subjects' (Burghardt, 2019: 185), which is also known as 'entrepreneurial self' (Bröckling, 2015).[13] Bröckling considers the maxim 'managing the entrepreneurial' to be a categorical imperative of the present. According to him, entrepreneurship is not a given, but a constant striving towards a goal. Human beings become it, acting in all life situations in a creative, flexible, responsible, risk-conscious and 'customer' oriented way. At the same time, the mission statement is a frightening image. What everyone should become is also what threatens everyone. Competition subjects the entrepreneur to the dictates of continuous self-optimization, but no amount of effort can banish his fear of failure.

Such self-optimizing perspectives have also found their way into educational programmes for children. One example is a programme of the German Bertelsmann Foundation for school development that was carried out in cooperation with the state in one region of Germany between 1997 and 2002 under the name 'School & Co'. This project praised 'students' independent learning and work' as the 'ultimate reference point', and seemed to respect children as subjects and promote their liberation from dependencies (Bastian and Rolff, 2002). But a closer look reveals that the project followed the relentless 'logic of efficiency and utility' (Engler, 2005: 91). 'School & Co' is based on an understanding of 'economic education' and 'economic knowledge'. Until today, similar initiatives of business associations and some foundations are based on such an understanding in which the praised individual qualities, such as independence, open-mindedness, flexibility or self-management, serve mainly to practice thinking in market categories. And even social qualities, such as communication skills and team spirit, are downgraded to social skills and thus 'become a mere stock of topics, a reserve for the next customer talk' (Engler, 2005: 92) and self-marketing.

In many cases, this objective is also achieved through the creation of 'school mini-companies', sponsored by private companies and pending foundations. Sometimes they form part of 'educational agreements' between schools and companies. They give children the impression that they can do something for themselves. They feel attractive to many because the adults/companies allow them to be more proactive and experience doing something practical. However, they are often invested according to the model of private companies (as expressed in the legal forms of joint-stock companies or limited liability companies), where the main objective is to do business and make profit, to train market behaviour. Concrete experience with work or the reflection of working conditions, as well as manufacturing methods and characteristics of products and services, are rarely addressed (see European Commission, 2005; Liebel, 2007b). An exception are the few mini-companies that are set up as cooperatives or projections of a solidary economy.

In Latin America, these trends are expressed, for example, in 'Clubes de Emprendedores', in which children as young as seven years old are taught by 'financial education' to set up micro-enterprises and to understand themselves as 'entrepreneurial children'.

> Fortunately, more and more educational institutions at all levels, civil organizations and some government agencies are working to generate an entrepreneurial culture. Because of their importance, special mention should be made of institutions that focus on cultivating this entrepreneurial vision in children and adolescents, such as the Howard Gardner School in Mexico, where children from preschool to high school live the entrepreneurial culture in their classrooms. Or the Club de Emprendedores in Colombia, which through the Emprender para aprender method contributes to the formation of the entrepreneurial spirit and entrepreneurial thinking from an early age. (Aguilar Morales and Ocampo Carapia, 2018: 16, see also Cárcamo Solís et al, 2017)[14]

As in the European examples, children are taught to optimize themselves to cope with life's increasing difficulties. Although children are encouraged to work, the focus is not on the work itself, but on the financial management associated with it. Therefore, children should not see themselves as working children, but as young entrepreneurs (of their labour).[15] Magically, by creating a 'success mentality', the hitherto demonized 'child labour' is reinterpreted as a career stepping stone to social advancement. It seems as if the problem of child labour disappears into thin air, while children who continue to work continue to be discriminated against as a kind of failure.

There is also a tendency towards self-optimization in ideas and practices aimed at creating the 'perfect dream child'. Using new reproductive and genetic technologies, parents are encouraged to give birth only to those children who possess the qualities they consider optimal.[16]

The resistant subject and political subjectivity

The references to the perversion of the subject through 'subjectification' resemble Adorno's earlier diagnosis that individuality has degenerated into 'mise-en-scène'. This analytical vision is paramount to falling back into the trap of constructing a subject, which praises the absolute freedom and autonomy of the individual and places it above the relation to others. But, for its part, it runs the danger of throwing the child out with the bathwater and inducing people to be instrumentalized or manipulated as it pleases. It is precisely the vision of people in precarious situations, or – like children – seemingly powerless that can show that they resist a 'subjectification' that attempts to extinguish their subjectivity.

They cannot give up, or they sink. They unite traits that can be described as the 'small ego' and the 'big ego' (Löwenthal, 1989). German-Jewish philosopher Leo Löwenthal uses the term 'small ego' to describe the desire directed towards the 'next', with which the individual seeks to assert himself in a society that is not conceived as supportive and to seek self-affirmation herself. The 'big ego', on the other hand, recognizes that isolated individuals deny the reality shared with others, by which Löwenthal means 'turning away from the reality of the suffering of the human and non-human creature' (see Jay, 1987, on the biography of Löwenthal). The before-mentioned educationalist Meueler observes that the two egos only seem mutually exclusive, but that in fact the 'small ego' can gradually pass into the 'big ego':

> The small ego uses all available power for its own self-preservation, no matter what the cost. If I only have myself in mind, I only perceive what is important for my own survival and well-being. Only that makes sense to me. Pure self-preservation is realized through difference to the point of aggressiveness towards the suffering and destinies of others. ... The autonomy for which one strives only becomes a human value when one takes into account his/her counterpart, which applies to the other and the other to me. (Meueler, 1993: 90–91)

With reference to the 'small ego', Meueler also speaks of a 'quite functional subjectivity ... which is in the service of self-preservation' (1993: 92) and which makes everyday life possible. Since people would have to search again and again for previously unknown answers and paths, mere functional self-preservation would be transcended by the subjects. Again and again

> an excess of spontaneity, contradiction, stubbornness, and the ability to cope with conflict, productive disruptive material in the concept of functionality. These surpluses are not only found among those who are materially well positioned, heal in less alienated occupations and can look back on satisfying and stimulating educational careers. They can also be discovered in another way in those who have to live in degrading conditions, completely insecure, below the subsistence minimum. (Meueler, 1993: 93)

It is precisely the vision of the everyday life of the oppressed that makes us doubt that the subject is really dead. It only seems to be lost from sight when we measure it against the pathetic cubit of philosophical systems. It is also remarkable that the more vividly the subject is asked again, the more human societies threaten to sink into catastrophe and even the end of history is conjured up. Perhaps there is something in Meueler's assumption that subjectivity 'only becomes visible in loss' (Meueler, 1993: 95).

This includes the recognition that subjectivity arises from a sense of vulnerability (Butler, 1997; 2015: 123–153). However, this cannot simply be attributed to natural characteristics, but is always driven by social conditions. It can even arise when children and other supposedly more vulnerable people are protected from assumed risks and dangers as best they can. If this is achieved by protecting these people by keeping them sealed off, an underlying new powerlessness arises, as individuals cannot learn to cope with these risks and dangers. Having said this, it is important not to construct an abstract opposition between strength and weakness or strong and weak. Possible resistance, also from the vulnerable groups, must be considered, even anticipated, and, wherever possible, sought out and encouraged. Resistance from the supposedly weak people counteracts the tendency to stylize them as mere victims and thus deny them any subjective capacity to act. Subjectivity would in this case be reduced to the capacity to suffer and the possible support and help to act out of compassion. In this way, those who are shown this compassion degrade themselves to objects or are 'de-subjectivized'.

The question how resistance emerges among people in precarious living situations is often discussed as *political subjectivity*. The corresponding discourse has many facets and theoretical references which cannot be discussed in detail here. 'Its perimeters range from a traditional search for the substantial subject of politics in entities such as the state, civic movements, or individuals, all the way to the total dissolution of the subject of politics in radical posthumanist philosophies' (Häkli and Kallio, 2018: 58).[17] Here is an example with regard to the Global South. A few years ago, the journal *African Diaspora* dedicated an issue to the political subjectivity of African people who are forced to leave their traditional places of life and are particularly threatened by uprooting and social exclusion. The editors explain why and how they use the term:

> The focus on political subjectivity ... allows us to pay closer attention to the relational dynamics through which power comes into being. ... The heuristic tool of political subjectivity enables us to consider the dimension of emotional attachment in formalized relationships with the state and other institutionalized forms of authority. ... In our understanding political subjectivity is a helpful notion to describe how people relate to governance and authorities. It denotes how a single person or a group of actors is brought into a position to stake claims, to have a voice, and to be recognizable by authorities. At the same time the term points to the political and power-ridden dimension within politics of identity and belonging, by encompassing the imaginary and emotional, as well as the judicial-political dimension of claims to belonging and citizenship, including moments of exclusion and non-incorporation. (Krause and Schramm, 2011: 128 and 130–131)

In one of the rare contributions addressing political subjectivity with regard to children (Häkli and Kallio, 2018), the authors emphasize that the political should be conceptualized in a processual and everyday sense in order to understand the emergence of political agency in unequal power relations throughout the life course. Their case analysis of an 11-year-old girl's life story in Finland shows how political subjectivity

> can be studied by assessing experiences of situations and events that make the subjects attentive to power relations vested in the subject positions that are offered to them in their everyday life. As experientially grounded in the flux of everyday life, political acts can concern anything that human subjects become attentive to, with the potential of maintaining, challenging, and transforming the conditions from which they spring. (Häkli and Kallio, 2018: 70–71)

Unlike the common discourse on the subject rooted in the European Enlightenment that emphasizes rationality, the Latin American discourse on political subjectivity aims to underline that affectivity and the whole body also play an important role. 'The experiences of encounter and misencounter that occur in communal life are always charged with emotions, passions and feelings' (Duque Monsalve et al, 2016: 136). Some approaches even recognize that political subjectivations are mainly based on desire and affection, rather than on processes of reasoning. In this sense, it can be said that political subjectivity is also 'incorporated' (Díaz Gómez and Alvarado Salgado, 2012). The body embodies what is sometimes not possible to narrate (Alvarado, 2014), but also what is symbolized by political discourses. 'The political subject is necessarily a subject with a body, since this is the first territory of power, which can house both practices of domination and liberation' (Duque Monsalve et al, 2016: 137). Feelings, not only cognitions, become catalysts for the decision to take a position on the realities experienced and to take political action (Arias Vargas et al, 2009). The latter feelings are associated with the pleasure of forming the desired community with others. Humour and laughter, for example, are associated with political action in the 'carnivalization of life' (García Rodríguez, 2013) and they generate meanings that disrupt the dominant contexts and values.

With regard to children from popular sectors, Peruvian educationalist Alejandro Cussiánovich (2010: 15) speaks of the 'challenge of reworking installed feelings and meanings'. In confronting hostile conditions for their existence and their search for belonging and recognition, he sees the emergence of 'a new social subjectivity' that cannot be limited to the isolated and segregated field of a privatized childhood.

It is a matter of decolonizing the world of subjectivities of societies which historically concealed perceptions, feelings, empathies, sympathies and antipathies that inhibited the development of children's status as social subjects throughout history, of feeling and conceptualizing children as a matter of state, as a political link with the rest of society and the state. In other words, to shake off the historical relagration to the domestic and private sphere to which children were confined. (Cussiánovich, 2010: 15)

Andrea Bonvillani (2012), in a study with adolescents and young people between 14 and 25 years of age in the Argentinean city of Córdoba, points out that political subjectivity arises when subjects, in their desire for emancipation, enter into conflict with the established and ordered structures and relationships and question their apparent 'naturalness'. According to her, the political activism of young people is emotionally intertwined with feelings of pain and fear associated with lack of recognition. On the other hand they are also filled with the joy and self-confirming emotionality that the subject feels when he or she discovers his or her creative power in political life. Consequentially, a relationship with politics is established, which also has an emotional impact on the formation of identity. Uruguayan writer Raúl Zibechi (2007; 2017), for his part, gives the important indication that it is the affections that generate cohesion in neighbourhoods, popular and Indigenous communities. Above all he points to the common and joint experience of pain and its important role. Political subjectivity in the sense of resistance arises from the fear, pain and indignation experienced by the subjects, but also connects with courage, passion and hope. In this way, '"societies in movement" or, as they name themselves, "peoples" or "nations" fighting for their sovereignty and self-determination' (Zibechi, 2017: 17) are created at different levels, both in the rural areas and in the cities, collectively.

To trigger such processes, especially in children from popular and Indigenous backgrounds, the experience of exclusion and oppression needs to be complemented with experiences of hope for change, through their own actions. These can be spontaneous groups of children with different backgrounds, all with the experiences of discrimination, sometimes on double or triple grounds. Intersectional discriminated children, such as girls or same-sex groups, get together in mutual solidarity and build relationships and attachments. There is frequent space for experiences of self-efficacy in using their competencies. To act with these competencies, an environment in which children experience recognition and, if necessary, support from people who have some influence in the community. The basis for this recognition is that children are understood to be as important to the community as any other living being, not just as the embodiment of a better future. They are actors who largely contribute to family life and to the community. The framework for such processes of recognition and encouragement is often a result of 'projects', 'networks' or 'movements' of committed adults or youth groups who feel connected to children and are interested in a dialogue with equal rights. The awareness of having their own rights and of being heard due to these rights can provide an additional stimulus for children.

With reference to the then emerging social movements of working children, Alejandro Cussiánovich pointed out in the early 1990s that a 'subjectivity of subordination', which results from the painful daily experience of being wounded in their dignity, gives rise to a new protagonist political subjectivity in children from the popular sectors:

> Consciousness and a feeling of dignity are built up, of which opposition, antagonism, the vocation for protagonism and self-determination are components and expressions. In other words, a new subjectivity no longer in subordination but in struggle for its social and political protagonism. This is an important level in the gestation and consolidation of subjective power and the beginning for many of a feeling of belonging to a broader popular and even national entity with the same characteristics of self-determination, self-identity and protagonism. (Cussiánovich, 1990: 373)

In the following years, a lively debate emerged in Latin America on the concept of children's protagonism, focusing initially on working children and now, in a broader sense, on children of the Global South (see Chapter 8).

Conclusion

If we consider children as subjects with own rights, and if we want them to be able to act and be recognized as social subjects, we have to consider the subjectivity or subjectification that is involved in this process. In any case, reference to subject status is not enough for this purpose. In order not to let children fall into the trap of the 'entrepreneurial self' and the permanent need for self-optimization, contrary to the intentions of the emancipatory and subversive discourse of children's rights, another understanding of subjectivity is needed. Such an understanding gives children the confidence and enables them to defend themselves against their degradation and the instrumentalization of their own initiative and agency. In exchange for an economic subjectivation that is based on permanent self-optimization, perspectives of political subjectivation should be developed that enable more or less subjugated subjects to object to their orientation towards 'human capital'. I see an important element in the fact that the desired liberation from constraints is linked to the struggle for dignity, equality and social justice (see Balibar, 2014).

Flexible adaptation or resistance? Paradoxes and pitfalls of discourses on resilience in children

Introduction

In the 1980s, I came into contact with children in Nicaragua who lived in great poverty in the midst of a cruel war during which they had witnessed a massacre or lost relatives. I was amazed at how these children mastered their complicated daily lives. They did what needed to be done, they built their own toys, and they brought life to the rural cooperative where I stayed for a few weeks. To my great surprise, they were generally in good spirits. A few years later, when I started working with children in a city in the same country whose parents had disappeared, who lived on the streets and kept themselves afloat with odd jobs or petty theft, I had similar experiences. I kept asking myself where the strength of these children came from, not to lose courage even in seemingly hopeless situations.

This and subsequent similar experiences have led me to explore theoretical concepts that can help to understand and support coping with extremely stressful life situations. One such concept is called *resilience*. It has witnessed a boom in recent decades and has advanced to become a key concept to explain such behaviour in view of the extreme difficulties experienced. 'The idea of resilience seems to be associated with an almost magical quality that is now almost indispensable in any field of practice' (Gebauer, 2017: 15). It has been repeatedly pointed out that the concept cannot only be understood in different ways, but is also often used arbitrarily. The emancipatory intentions originally associated with it have increasingly been reversed and begs an answer to the concept of resilience's suitability for emancipatory action. This also applies to social and educational work with children.

First, after an outline of the development of the concept of resilience, I will examine some of its applications and critical objections. I will then discuss some immanent limitations and contradictions of the resilience discourse and ask whether it is possible to conceive of other concepts within its framework. Finally, I will formulate some reflections on the extremely stressful conditions children live in and how they can defend themselves and address the causes of their suffering. I will focus on what needs to be considered here. To this end, I will take up reflections and concepts that are discussed and lived under the term resistance in the social movements of Indigenous and popular class people, especially in Latin America. They revolve around the question how oppression and exploitation can be resisted and how a dignified life can be possible.

How the concept of resilience came about and how it is changing

Originally, the term resilience was introduced in connection with the physics of materials. It refers to the property of an elastic material to return to its original state after having been exposed to a heavy load. In the human sciences, it was first used in medicine to characterize the recovery of patients after physical trauma, such as surgery or accidents. Almost simultaneously, the term was also introduced in clinical psychology, in particular in developmental psychopathology, to diagnose 'developmental disorders' and to find out how to treat them. According to this understanding, research on resilience offers 'indications on the genesis of psychological abnormalities and disorders, as well as on how to cope with stress and crisis situations' (Petermann, 2000: 14).

In addition to people-related approaches, systems-related approaches have emerged and are now mainly used in security policy, disaster control, developmental policy and management theory. They date back to the concept of 'ecological resilience' developed by Crawford Holling (1973) and have since received a number of new features. This concept is based on the assumption of a fundamental elasticity and regenerative capacity of ecosystems that develops in response to external shocks and disturbances. According to Holling (2001), the principle of 'non-linear complexity' contained therein applies not only to ecological systems but also to socio-ecological systems and thus also to social developments (Folke et al, 2010). Recently, resilience has also been discussed as a sociologically relevant concept (Blum et al, 2016; Endreß and Maurer, 2016).

Resilience research focusing on children first examined the coping patterns of children who had lost their mothers or whose mothers were mentally ill. The concept of resilience was also used to study the psychical processes of the terminally ill. Until now, most research on resilience has been concerned with individual and micro-social factors, while community or macro-level influences are hardly addressed. Only since the turn of the millennium has the idea of resilience been taken up in the social sciences and concepts have been developed to understand and promote the ability to actively cope with particularly stressful living conditions, for instance, extreme poverty or wars. In addition to individual dispositions, increasing attention has been paid to social, environmental and cultural aspects. This applies in particular to the so-called socio-ecological approach, which was introduced by the social psychologist Michael Ungar (2005; 2013; Ungar et al, 2007; for an overview, see also Masten, 2014).

Despite its roots in clinical psychology, the study of resilience paved the way for a paradigm shift, which in part 'turned the mind-set of the discipline upside down' (Zander, 2008: 28) and shifted the focus away from 'developmental disorders' and 'maladjustments' towards resilient forces in humans. The possibilities and conditions of a 'positive development', which can result from the confrontation with risks and burdens, were increasingly in demand. Thus, the view shifted from a deficit-oriented view to a resource-oriented or subject-oriented view. The impetus for this reorientation came from long-term studies with children since the 1950s (Rutter, 1979; Garmezy, 1981; Werner and Smith, 1982; 1992), which revealed that most of the children who participated in the study proved to be able to survive and withstand adverse living conditions and constant psychical stress.

The focus on the phenomenon of 'mental resilience' has sparked a new interest for knowledge in research and practice. The two central questions are the following: 'What factors can contribute to children (or adults) demonstrating resilience despite adverse living conditions, stress and risks? How can children's (and adults') resilience be promoted and strengthened?' (Zander, 2008: 29). This implies an interdependent interplay of 'risk factors' and 'protective factors'.

The following are commonly identified as risk factors: 'family factors' such as depression, alcohol and drug abuse of adult family members; 'family processes' such as divorce and separation, loss of one or both parents, family violence; and 'extra-systemic and socio-demographic risks' such as poverty, low income, urban violence (Luthar, 2003). Margherita Zander (2008: 33) considers it necessary to 'broaden the concept of risk by taking into account the social conditions of growth and socially generated problems, such as discrimination against minorities and disadvantaged groups'.

Protective factors are generally identified as personality traits of the child and distinguish between resources in the family and community or personal resources of the child and social resources within the family, in educational institutions and in the wider social environment. This often results in a conglomeration of fixed qualities, such as temperament, intelligence, first-born status; of acquired or acquirable qualities and capacities, such as problem-solving ability, self-efficacy beliefs, self-regulation ability, high social competence or creativity. Social resources, such as the presence of at least one stable reference person, family cohesion, appreciative educational climate, positive peer contacts or the presence of pro-social role models in the neighbourhood also pertain to these.

Occasionally, attempts are made to weigh protective factors in their importance for different ages. Emmy Werner, who participated in one of the first long-term studies on children's resilience, the so-called Kauai study in Hawaii, emphasizes that:

> Constitutional dispositions – health status and temperament – have their greatest influence in infancy and early childhood. Communication and problem-solving skills, as well as the presence of 'surrogate parents' and responsible and competent teachers, play a central role as protective factors in school life. In adolescence, internal control beliefs and goal setting are important protective factors. (Werner, 2007: 26)

Social researchers Jo Boyden and Gillian Mann (2005) emphasize the importance of informal peer groups for the development of resilience in childhood and adolescence, especially because children and adolescents experience each other as valuable and learn to relate to each other in a supportive way. Regardless of their particular importance in the life course, protective factors are no longer conceived of as temporary, stable, life-long characteristics, but 'primarily as a temporary characteristic that can change in the course of life' (Opp and Fingerle, 2007: 15).

The listed protective factors refer only to developmental conditions that are generally considered positive. Therefore, it has to be kept in mind that 'resilience is only demonstrated in coping with a risk and that the general protective factors listed may have more specific effects in a risk context' (Zander, 2008: 41). However, a fundamental problem becomes apparent, which Stefanie Graefe (2019: 23) describes as the assumption of a 'productive force of misfortune'. Boris Cyrulnik (2011), one of the most influential representatives of the concept of resilience, explicitly emphasizes affirmatively that the emergence of resilience presupposes the experience of misfortune and suffering.

To speak of protective factors is an indication that this does not necessarily mean the resistance of acting subjects or that 'resilience' is understood as 'flexible adaptation'. Brad Evans and Julian Reid (2014: 6), for example, speak of an 'effective blending of the terms resilience and resistance'. Or, Ulrich Bröckling (2017: 120) concludes: 'Instead of looking for resilient individuals, constellations of resilience are identified.' According to him, resilience programmes are aimed at 'adapting people to risks. Instead of reducing burdens, adaptive capacity is increased' (Bröckling, 2017: 122). In other words, 'the "power of the resilient", which is supposed to constitute resilience and strengthen the promotion of resilience, does not resist but survives' (Bröckling, 2017: 136–137).

Different approaches to resilience research also differ in what should be understood as 'normal' or 'healthy', that is a successful reaction to adverse circumstances. In this context, the culture and class goodness of some of the assumptions of normality are critically discussed. Differences can also be seen in how the dimensions and potentials of resilience are conceived. Generally, a distinction is made between coping capacities, adaptive capacities and transformative capacities. Even if the focus is on human individuals, they are understood as part of systems or social units.

> The dimension of *coping potential* refers to the short-term handling of disruptive events, whereby an assumed status quo ante should be maintained or *adaptation potentials*, on the other hand, refer to a medium- and long-term perspective and describe the capacity to adapt to new contextual conditions within a certain framework and thus to secure the existence of the resilient unit. *Transformation potentials*, finally, address the capacity of resilient units to undergo long-term and comprehensive change (also beyond paths taken so far) in order to not only secure their existence but also to generate new potentials. (Blum et al, 2016: 170; emphasis in original)

Other authors in the resilience discourse (Voss, 2008; Lorenz, 2013) emphasize participatory capacities in addition to coping and adaptive capacities. By this, they mean whether people in a given social unit have the opportunity to participate in systemically relevant and vital decisions or to make them themselves. It addresses questions of power inequality, social inequality and justice, both within certain societies, communities, and between powers in different regions of the world. A minimum of equality and social justice in society and throughout the world is seen as a prerequisite for the respective social systems to be able to cope with and emerge strengthened from disruptive developments. However, serious differences in the understanding of the concept of resilience must be considered. Daniel Lorenz (2013) sees participatory capacities as the necessary condition for maintaining the flexibility of the system and being able to react successfully to surprising risks and catastrophes. Martin Voss (2008), on the other hand, focuses on people who are ultimately unable to make themselves heard due to large power differentials and social inequality, thus becoming vulnerable and losing any potential for participation. They are at the mercy of the powerful. However, in both conceptions the focus of interest is not on people's subjective wellbeing, for example, their life satisfaction, but on the functionality and durability of the system.

Political instrumentalizations of the concept of resilience

Resilience, like any subject-oriented concept of action, is a thought construct that is both promising and ambivalent. It can contribute to recognizing, respecting and trusting people's capacity to act. This is especially important in the case of children, as they are often accused of 'not yet' being able to think and act independently or their statements in life are not taken seriously. Nevertheless, also subject-oriented or subjectivizing concepts of action such as resilience can be abused. This often happens nowadays with the resilience discourse, if, for example, under the motto 'Don't worry, be happy!' the impression is given that people can easily come to terms with difficult life situations, if they find an optimistic attitude to life. Training courses and corresponding guides have been flourishing in business today, seeing resilience as 'big business' (Evans and Reid, 2014: 98). The guidance literature 'mainly suggests ideal processes and standard sizes regardless of context-specific conditions' (Wink, 2016: 5). Focusing on successfully coping with crisis situations 'may lead to increasing pressure to adapt and change for those (individuals, groups, regions) who are not (yet) able to cope successfully with such situations' (Wink, 2016: 5).

By emphasizing the 'strengths' or 'resources' of individuals, the resilience discourse and resilience-oriented concepts of action tend to divert attention from the structural causes of difficult life situations and to burden those affected with the responsibility of coping with them. These practices are particularly fatal if they are accompanied by political intentions that only have reactive crisis management in mind and thus justify precisely the circumstances that cause such crises in the first place. In this context, Thomas Gebauer (2015) speaks of the 'resilience paradox' or Vanessa Pupavac (2001b) of 'therapeutic governance'. Ulrich Bröckling (2017: 137) sees a 'discursive strategy of depoliticization' at work in resilience programmes. Gebauer criticizes that in the case of the resilience approach

> it is no longer about social ideals, but about the question of how people and systems can protect themselves from disturbances, that is from a world that has gone off the rails. Its corset is no longer the effort to correct destructive behaviour, but adaptation to the progressive process of destruction. (Gebauer, 2017: 16)

It is also rightly pointed out that resilience can be understood as a conceptual response to the 'creed of flexibility, speed and activation' (Dörre, 2009: 64), which is characteristic of today's capitalism and, at the same time, no longer unquestionably credible. Stefanie Graefe (2019: 18–19) sees this as a response 'that does not break with this creed, but stabilizes it even more under changed normative signs'. She emphasizes this especially in view of burn-out and other crisis phenomena interpreted as psychosomatic illnesses, which are spreading everywhere in today's deregulated and flexibilized capitalist societies. If the concept of resilience becomes the basis for political action, the necessary fight against the structural causes of human suffering is prone to be replaced by psychological modelling and permanent adaptation of the affected people.

Some governments, the European Union (European Union, 2016; European Commission, 2013; 2016), the World Bank (World Bank, 2013), the World Trade Organization (WTO, 2021), the International Red Cross (IFRC, 2018) and other international organizations, which aim to involve local people in crisis management, now advocate this idea. The German government, for example, has declared resilience to be a key concept in its security strategy. The 2016 White Paper of the Ministry of Defence states:

> Strengthening our country's resilience and robustness against current and future threats is of particular importance for the provision of national security services. This implies intensified cooperation between state agencies, citizens and private operators of critical infrastructure, as well as media and network operators. It goes without saying that we must all work together to ensure common security. (Bundesministerium der Verteidigung, 2016: 48)

In this regard, the German government's Federal Academy for Security Policy has chosen resilience as one of its main themes. Under the motto 'Forward Resilience! – Suggestions for Advancing Resilience in Germany', Michael Hanisch, personal advisor to the academy's president, has suggested a 'National Action Plan for Strengthening Resilience' to the federal government. The aim is to strengthen one's own resilience in the face of crises: 'Effective circumvention, adaptation and coping with unavoidable shocks, such as environmental disasters, terrorist attacks or related propaganda is a basic element of comprehensive security measures at the national level' (Hanisch, 2017: 1).

In terms of resilience concepts, the US Army has been putting its units through a 'Comprehensive Soldier Fitness' programme for several years now. The training, which was developed by psychologists around positive psychology guru Martin Seligman, focuses on preparing for traumatic events. Soldiers should learn to regard extreme experiences as a challenge to personal maturation processes. Related experiences should give them self-confidence and strength. The goal is 'an invincible army' (Reivich et al, 2011; for critique, see Brown, 2015). A rather whimsical, but no less serious, use of the term resilience can be found in the *Military Child of the Years® Award* programme, in which children of members of the US military are honoured annually for being especially resilient (Operation Homefront, 2019). 'The resilience work performed by children of military families contributes to making invisible and otherwise managing the meaning of significant social costs of contemporary militarism' (Beier, 2020: 229).

The resilience discourse has also found its way into international economic and trade policy. Numerous International Monetary Fund publications mention that the global financial system must be resilient. National and regional economies are expected to develop resilience, and 'sustainable adjustment' is seen as a means to develop this resilience (for example, International Monetary Fund, 2019; Simison, 2019). The World Economic Forum speaks of 'systemic financial resilience' (World Economic Forum, 2011–2012). In the preface to a report on global risks, Klaus Schwab, founder and chairman of the World Economic Forum, writes:

> The more complex the system, the greater the risk of systemic breakdown, but also the greater the potential for opportunity. Together, we have the foresight and collaborative spirit to shape our global future and particularly the survival instinct to move from pure urgency-driven risk management to more collaborative efforts aimed at strengthening risk resilience to the benefit of global society. (World Economic Forum, 2012: 8)

In its recent World Trade Report (WTO, 2021), the World Trade Organization praises 'economic resilience' as a means of countering the increasingly frequent disruptions and threatening collapses of global trade. In the 208 pages of the report, the word resilience is used no less than 738 times. Instead of strengthening local economies, for instance, by relocating production and increasing self-sufficiency, the World Trade Organization's reference to resilience serves to dispel emerging doubts about the sense of unrestrained free trade.

In several publications, the World Bank recommends 'social resilience' as a means to combat poverty (for instance, World Bank, 2017). Together with the United Nations, the World Bank even came up with the remarkable idea a few years ago to 'increase the wealth of the poor' by means of resilience (World Resources Institute, 2008). The British social researcher Marc Neocleous comments: 'The beauty of the idea that resilience is what the world's poor need is that it turns out to be something that the world's poor already possess; all they require is a little training in how to realise it' (Neocleous, 2013: 4–5).

The promotion of resilience is now also accorded a central function in the foreign and development policy of the European Union. The European Commission has developed a special *Action Plan for Resilience in Crisis-prone Countries 2013–2020* (European Commission, 2013). In a summary, the 'key message' of this and other resilience programmes is expressed in this way:

> The costs of humanitarian crises are rising and become increasingly unaffordable, as climate change generates more severe weather-related events and as the world faces new pressures such as population growth, urbanisation, land and eco-systems' degradation, scarcity of natural resources, fragility of states and complex conflicts. There is an urgent

need to help people and communities to withstand and recover from increasing shocks and stresses. In other words, help them build their resilience. (European Commission, 2016)

By shifting the perspective from weaknesses and vulnerability to strengths and resilience, local coping skills are now perceived, but at the same time, the antecedents of catastrophes and crises are lost sight of. 'The focus is on the affected people and communities, who must change and adapt, not on the catastrophic state of the world' (Merk, 2017: 137). With the concept of resilience, the European Union and international organizations aim to involve people on the ground in crisis management and to make them responsible for this. This is expressed above all in the expanding discourses of 'resilient communities', 'resilient cities' or 'resilient societies'. They assume that the most frequent disasters and crises require not only individual, but also collective and, above all, 'systemic' responses. Although catastrophes and crises are understood as human-made, they are seen as inevitable. It is no longer a question of preventing them, but of finding ways to cushion them and limit their negative consequences. The '100 Resilient Cities' network launched by the Rockefeller Foundation in 2013, for example, defines resilience as:

[T]he capacity of individuals, communities, institutions, businesses, and systems within a city to survive, adapt, and grow, no matter what kinds of chronic stresses and acute shocks they experience. Shocks are typically considered single event disasters, such as fires, earthquakes, and floods. Stresses are factors that pressure a city on a daily or reoccurring basis, such as chronic food and water shortages, an overtaxed transportation system, endemic violence or high unemployment. City resilience is about making a city better, in both good times and bad, for the benefit of all its citizens, particularly the poor and vulnerable. (100 Resilient Cities, 2018)

The network explicitly claims to go beyond 'disaster risk reduction' and to make cities 'better' in the short and long term through proactive 'transformative measures'. However, it also points out that the resilience concept 'can accomplish many goals with one project, saving time, money, and effort' (100 Resilient Cities, 2018), and sees it as 'a perfect tool for an age of austerity' (100 Resilient Cities, 2018). In this context, the president of the Rockefeller Foundation, Judith Rodin (2014), explicitly speaks of a 'resilience dividend', in plain language: a worthwhile investment. It is worth mentioning that the cities that have so far belonged to the network are mostly 'global cities' that have long since reached the limits of their functionality.[1] Since 2017, the World Bank has also been developing a Resilient Cities

Programme under the motto 'Bigger and Better Investments for a Resilient Future'.[2]

The discourse on resilient societies is similar, but pursues disparate objectives and uses different elements of control. Benedikter and Fathi (2017) distinguish four schools of thought. One returns to the security discourse and strives for systemic harm reduction in addition to precautions and emergency response. Accordingly, special attention is given to improving the durability of large cities' smart, technologically functioning infrastructure to cope with catastrophes, the starting point being terrorist attacks and natural disasters. The concept includes earthquake-proof architecture, fail-safe power supply, resilient telecommunications networks and heat supply. The second, more innovation-oriented concept focuses less on risk minimization and disaster management than on risk adaptation and 'disaster transformation'. The analysis of factors influencing social and technological change has priority here in order to harmonize and make society more flexible in a rapidly changing environment. Having said this, risks must be absorbed by a flexible network rather than concentrated at a vulnerable point of contact. The third approach aims to provide the tools to transform social resilience, understood as 'natural', into practical criteria for formulating recommendations for action. The main objective is to protect societies from social conflict, with a focus on preventing social protests and unrest. The fourth school of thought seeks to make society's network more capillary and thus more flexible through 'participatory technological innovation'. Especially in digital technologies for decentralized use, in order to be able to react more quickly and effectively to disruptions of all kinds. Resilience serves here

> as an overall figure for coping with risks, hazards and incalculable events of disruptive change, the aim of which is not so much to prevent their occurrence as to enable people to adapt to them and cope with their effects. ... In short, it is not the crisis and catastrophe events themselves that are prevented, but their destabilizing and destructive effects. (Bröckling, 2017: 114, 116)

In view of the catastrophic consequences of climate change that can be observed worldwide, it cannot be denied that, just as preventive measures are needed to combat the causes of the climate crisis, adaptation strategies are also needed to protect people from these consequences. However, these have so far been dominated by technical measures that do not take into account the fact that the consequences of the climate crisis are already affecting disadvantaged regions of the world and population groups particularly. For example, the Intergovernmental Panel on Climate Change points out that adaption policies which do not consider that 'opportunities for climate resilient development are not equitably distributed around the world' could 'exacerbate vulnerability and social and economic inequities' (IPCC, 2022: 29). An adaptation policy that is based on solidarity must therefore understand adaptation in a proactive way as an entry point for fundamental societal changes towards more social justice. 'It combines protection against the no longer avoidable impacts of the climate crisis and a focus on those most affected with the question of how we want to and can live in a manner that is actually sustainable' (Brand et al, 2022: 39).

Concepts of *resilient communities* are mostly different depending on where they emanate from, whether from globally active institutions or from local communities themselves. An example of the first concept is the European Union's comprehensive strategy for foreign and security policy (European Union, 2016; similar to European Commission, 2013). In it, the term resilience conveys the message that the responsibility for dealing with crises must be transferred to local communities, as they cannot be prevented and can only be intercepted to a certain extent by states (see Wagner and Anholt, 2016). In the International Red Cross operational concept for Preventive Crisis Management (IFRC, 2018), the community is declared a social actor precisely because it is particularly affected by diseases, natural disasters and political and economic crises. The people in the communities have similar habits and cultural resources that can be used to cope with them. Community resilience has also become a key concept in the field of international development cooperation. In view of the dramatic increase in humanitarian challenges, it is seen as an appropriate method to stimulate the self-help power of local populations and thus to banish criticisms of the postcolonial paternalism of wealthy 'donor countries' and 'donor organizations'. In the same vein, community resilience is conceived as a 'technocratic crisis and risk management strategy' (Merk, 2017: 217), which allows for cost reduction through the targeted identification of vulnerable people in endangered areas. The question arises whether collective resilience concepts developed by local communities, that is 'from below', can represent an alternative. I will address this later when I ask whether more far-reaching resilience concepts can be devised or whether alternative concepts are required.

Impending limitations and contradictions of the resilience discourse

Some authors who operate within the resilience paradigm (for instance, Ungar, 2005; 2013; Boyden and Mann, 2005; Ungar et al, 2007) also point out that the resilience discourse and the construction of the various factors and assumptions about their interaction are based on assumptions of normality that are class, gender and/or culture specific and therefore not easily generalizable. The assumption, for example, of what should be considered as 'successful' or 'healthy' development depends on certain ideas about what characteristics the 'developed' or 'healthy' individual should have and how he or she should live, act and relate to others. Furthermore, assumptions about competencies and capacities, which are seen as the basis of resilience, are often normative and culturally specific, without this always being taken into account in research.

Risk and protective factors are often conceived in such a way that they act on the individual from the outside, thinking of the individual as a separate entity from society. It overlooks the fact that in many non-Western cultures people are closely involved in social communities and experience themselves as an inseparable part of these communities. In these societies, social relations are seen as key factors for individual wellbeing. Nevertheless, for Western culture, too, the question can be raised whether the notion of the 'separate individual' corresponds to real life. In this sense, Michael Ungar finds it problematic to say that the 'I' is resilient:

> The *I* of which we speak is a cultural artefact, a perspective that is social and historical, relational and constructed. Instead, we might better say, 'There is resilience in this child and his or her community, family and culture'. Resilience is simultaneously a quality of the individual and individual's environment. To the extent that a child accesses communal health resources and finds opportunities to express individual resources, so too will resilience be experienced. (Ungar, 2005: xxiv; emphasis in original)

Consequentially, resilience must be more than a combination of individual characteristics. A culturally reflexive and context-related understanding of resilience would correspond to considering individuals' belonging and participation in communities as a possible resource for the emergence of resilience. In this sense, one could speak of a socio-ecological concept of resilience (Ungar et al, 2007; Ungar, 2013). This would also include taking into account the specific life situation by identifying resilience in certain behaviours and ways of feeling and thinking. Accordingly, resilience is not an absolute personality trait, but is demonstrated as such only in relation to and in confrontation with the burdens in this specific situation.

Different socio-political perspectives can also be manifest in ideas of resilience. In some concepts of resilience, for example, the criterion for success is that the individual must be able to adapt flexibly to different situations. In other concepts this criterion is seen in the ability to show resistance and to have a changing effect on one's environment. This difference is also expressed in the fact that resilience is seen, on the one hand, as a more or less *passive* consequence of protective factors, while other concepts see resilience arising in *active* action.

These differences can have serious consequences, especially in studies related to children. They often follow a certain pattern of childhood, which perceives children more as beings to be protected than as subjects with agency, determining their development and influencing their environment. Jo Boyden and Gillian Mann (2005) see in this a predominance of Western thinking, in which a family-oriented, middle-class understanding of childhood prevails, and the dominance of an adult perspective, as research is generally conceived and conducted by adults rather than together with children.

> Most of the studies on children's vulnerability and resilience draw on researchers' preconceived ideas about what constitutes adversity or risk for children. Often, adults (parents, teachers, and others who are also close to children) are used as respondents. The result is that, in many cases, we do not have accurate information on children's own perceptions. This is problematic given that there is emerging evidence that children do not share the same understanding of risk and adversity as do adults. The privileging of adult perceptions over children's experiences has sometimes meant that, in practice, resilience is conceived of more as the absence of pathology rather than the presence of personal agency in children. (Boyden and Mann, 2005: 11)

Furthermore, the vast majority of resilience concepts are exclusively adapted to the normative guidelines and expectations of the dominant society. This means that researchers often fail to reflect on and self-critically question their own *ideological* assumptions.

> A major limitation of the concept of resilience is that it is tied to the normative judgements relating to particular outcomes. If the outcomes were not desirable, then the ability to reach the outcomes in the face of putative risk factors would not be considered resilience. Yet it is possible that the socially defined desirable outcome may be subjectively defined as undesirable, while the socially defined undesirable outcome may be subjectively defined as desirable. From the subjective point of view, the individual may be manifesting resilience, while from the social point of view may be manifesting vulnerability. (Kaplan, 1999: 31–32)

Take, for example, the behaviour of pupils who 'skip' classes in school. From the point of view of teachers and school authorities, this is misbehaviour and a sign of a lack of ability to successfully complete school and learn what is important for their lives. However, pupils may be absent because they consider the knowledge they learn to be useless or because they do not agree with the way teachers treat them. What appears to be a risk factor from the point of view of teachers and school authorities may be an expression of stubbornness and resistance from the pupils' perspective.

Another example can be the walking behaviour of children who depend on the street as a place to live. In a study with Colombian children who gather in street cliques, the so-called *galladas*, this action is interpreted in a non-pathologizing way, for example:

> Although the galladas' involvement in crime and violence must be recognized and combated, it must first be recognized that these children do not join together to wage war and steal from others; rather, they join together to meet the most important physical and emotional needs that are not met anywhere else. (Felsman, 1989: 66)

A normative component is almost always introduced into studies on resilience, which does not do justice to children in precarious living situations. Canadian social researcher Sheila Martineau is therefore critical of the fact that '[o]bscured behind the well-meant intention of teaching resilience is a call for disadvantaged children and youth to conform to the behavioural norms of the dominant society (associated with social and school success) by overcoming or being invulnerable to the systemic distresses and adversities of their everyday lives' (Martineau, 1999: 3). Martineau's critique is based on an understanding of resilience that sees it as active resistance to liberation from oppressive or marginalized social conditions. This understanding differs greatly from the psychological discourse that dominates resilience research. 'Thus, the resilience discourse imposes prescribed norms of school success or social success upon underprivileged identified as at risk. The effect is that non-conforming individuals may be pathologized as *non-resilient*. Emphasis remains wholly on the individual and, thus, *individualism* is a dominant ideology embedded in the mainstream resilience discourse' (Martineau, 1999: 11–12; emphasis in original).[3]

It is therefore important to understand the meaning of children's actions from their own perspective and their importance in coping with their life situation. How children react to stressful circumstances cannot be adequately interpreted 'without reference to the social, cultural, economic, and moral meanings given to such experiences have in the contexts they inhabit' (Boyden and Mann, 2005: 15). This is especially true for children from socially disadvantaged or marginalized groups. To understand, for example, how children cope with growing up in poverty or with experiencing economic deprivation and what empowers them, it is not only different regional and historical contexts that must be taken into account. Rather, it must be borne in mind that certain personality or behavioural traits, often interpreted in psychological research as 'mental illness' or 'dysfunction', are necessary for children in socially disadvantaged living conditions and must be understood as appropriate coping strategies.

This requires research approaches that do not approach the children from the outside or from above and with prefabricated categories of analysis, but are planned and carried out together with them and can be a supportive experience for the children.

In the previous explanations, I examined and critically discussed the shimmering relationship between flexible adaptation and resistance in resilience research, which has so far taken place primarily in the Global North. In the following part, I will ask, with a view to research approaches in the Global South, whether there are more far-reaching resilience concepts and which research approaches can be found here that could possibly overcome the limitations of the resilience paradigm that dominates in the Global North. To this end, I take up thoughts and concepts that are discussed and lived under the term *resistance* in the social movements of Indigenous and marginalized population groups, primarily in Latin America. I give examples of how children resist the impositions they experience on a daily basis and ask about the possible reasons for and scope of such a resistant practice. Finally, I outline the methodological baselines of a research practice that can contribute to making children's resistance practice visible, to understand it better and to support it.

Are other concepts of resilience possible?

In Latin America, an approach to resilience has emerged around the turn of the millennium that is explicitly distinguished from individualistic and pathologizing concepts of resilience and is seen as community-oriented.[4] The Argentinean health scientist Elbio Néstor Suárez Ojeda (2001) locates its background in the need to deal with extreme emergencies and catastrophes of various kinds that affect many people at the same time and can only be dealt with together. As an additional source, he refers to pre-colonial Indigenous traditions, whose basic existence includes social solidarity and joint efforts to cope with emergency situations. The key elements are not seen in characteristics of the individuals, but in the social conditions, group relations, cultural peculiarities and values of the respective community or society.

According to Suárez Ojeda, the basic 'pillars' of resilience are collective self-esteem, cultural identity, 'social humour' and state honesty with its officials. Collective self-esteem, for example, is expressed in a sense of pride in the living place, whatever its constitution. Cultural identity is understood in the sense of a cultural diversity that asserts itself against the uniformizing pressure of globalization and gives people the feeling that they are not being outdone. Social humour manifests itself in the capacity of groups and communities to 'find comedy in their own tragedy'. Suárez Ojeda (2001: 74) sees in it 'the capacity to express in words, gestures or bodily activities the comic, incongruous or hilarious elements of a given situation, achieving a calming and pleasurable effect'. The integrity of the state consists in the decent, responsible and transparent management of public affairs, including the group consciousness of resisting contrary practices. Other elements that Suárez Ojeda identifies as contributing to resilience include 'the capacity to generate authentic and participatory leadership, the exercise of effective democracy in day-to-day decision-making and the "inclusiveness" of a society in which there is no discrimination' (Suárez Ojeda, 2001: 76).

'Malinchismo',[5] fatalism, authoritarianism and corruption are mentioned as opposing forces that hinder the emergence of resilience. By weighing the factors that promote and hinder resilience, Suárez Ojeda (2001: 80) argues that it is possible to estimate the actual group resilience, either to make a prognosis or to design interventions with greater precision leading to the reinforcement of resilience.

In two more recent papers, some authors from Mexico (Díaz Barriga and Reséndiz, 2017; López Bracamonto and Limón Aguirre, 2017) see community resilience as an approach that differs from the mere analysis of individual responses to stress which are typical for resilience research in the Global North. According to López Bracamonte and Limón Aguirre:

> Research on community resilience in countries such as Chile, Colombia and Mexico has confirmed the existence of a relationship between the quality of the interactions and interrelationships of group members and the possibility of a resilient process. Populations in these countries that faced environmental or socio-political crises proved to have a better possibility of overcoming and rebuilding themselves than other groups. They maintained an organized participation around community networks, with established institutions and with the natural and constructed environment of community interaction. Specifically, populations that had suffered environmental disasters such as in the commune of San Pedro de La Paz in Chile, and in the state of Veracruz in Mexico were able to overcome the experience of disaster. Political violence such as in the municipalities of Marinilla, Peñol and San Luis in Colombia, were also overcome by acting in collaboration, cohesion and equity, as these practices facilitated more expeditious access to available resources and their adequate distribution and management (see González-Muzzio, 2013; López Jaramillo, 2007; Maldonado and González Gaudiano, 2013). (López Bracamonte and Limón Aguirre, 2017: 3)

Díaz Barriga and Reséndiz (2017: 152) use the example of the 1985 earthquake in Mexico City. According to the authors, 'community capacities, which include solidarity and mutual aid are effective when mobilized in the face of disasters and are sometimes more effective than the external resources that could be received or the actions of the authority itself' (see also Uriarte, 2013). However, López Bracamonte and Limón Aguirre (2017: 4) emphasize that resilient practices and processes require 'a clear recognition of the components involved in social interaction and the life history of collectives, families, groups and peoples'. Consequently, as an indispensable part of this, they consider

> that community practices associated with the resilient process are based on collective cognitive components such as *cultural knowledge* and *social capacities*, formulated throughout their life history, which allow them to exercise desirable actions and even formulate *organizational strategies* based on unity and hope in the face of conditions of vulnerability, risk, threats and adversity. (López Bracamonte and Limón Aguirre, 2017: 4; emphasis in original)

As mentioned earlier with reference to concepts of community resilience, this understanding of resilience is just as problematic and can be abused if responsibility for disasters and grievances suffered and their resolution is put into the hands of local people. The problem is that both material and discursive power are distributed extremely unevenly between local and global actors and can severely restrict the possibilities of asserting own ideas and interests.[6] On the other hand, if the members of the respective community become aware of the real causes and responsibilities for their suffering and do not take responsibility for themselves, they can secure their own possibilities for action, free themselves from power-based dependencies and practically question the unequal power relations that underlie them.

This can be seen, for example, in the social movements of Indigenous peoples, Afro-descendants and the popular sectors in general in the Global South, who are defending themselves against the aftermath and new forms of colonial domination. The people involved are strengthened by an awareness of common interests and mutual solidarity. They create autonomous ways of securing their existence and shaping their lives, which often relate to and revive pre-colonial ways of life. It is of importance to them not to see themselves as disadvantaged minorities dependent on state support and promotion, but that they rely on their own power of self-organization, including also an education of the next generations aimed at emancipation and liberation (so-called *Popular Education*). It is striking that in such movements that they do not resort to the category of resilience, but describe their actions as a collective *resistance* that attacks the causes of their misery from below (see Zibechi, 2017).

Resilience or resistance?

Is the concept of resilience (still) adequate to understand the processes that make people not give up and resist despite extremely stressful living conditions? Not only is the concept poisoned by its inflationary and increasingly instrumental use, it is also understood in a purely defensive way and fundamentally oriented towards the restoration of a supposedly original condition, ensuring that people or systems function, or it is oriented to mere survival. It can impede thinking about and understanding actions aimed at changing social power structures and unequal living conditions. Therefore, I will only resort to the term resilience if I refer to studies that continue to work with this term, otherwise I will speak of resistance or resistant action.

Even talking of resistance also has its problems, because, like resilience, it can mean different things and can be used in different ways. The term resistance alone does not indicate what the action is directed to/against and what its aim is. With the European Enlightenment and the bourgeois revolutions, the concept of resistance found its way into the political and moral-philosophical debate on human rights. This was and still is about the legitimacy or illegitimacy of state authority expressed in laws and normative obligations (see Douzinas, 2019: 153–167). In politics, the term resistance was used to describe the struggle against Nazi and other totalitarian dictatorships. Today, the term is also instrumentalized by right-wing populist groups and parties as they wish. Nevertheless, the concept of resistance, like the concept of emancipation and other concepts aimed at liberation from oppression and imposed hardship, remains an indispensable resource for the preservation and restoration of humane living conditions. This equally applies to research oriented to such maxims (see, for instance, Mignolo, 2009; De Sousa Santos, 2014). In the Latin American discussion, to which I refer next, the term resistance – similar to the anti-fascist French 'Résistance' – has an emancipatory and decolonial meaning and aims at a society in which social equality, justice and human dignity are guiding principles. First, I will refer to the sociological discussion.

There is broad agreement that resistance is an intentional action that is directed against someone or something, not just an opinion or intention (Hollander and Einwohner, 2004: 539). Pierre-Alexandre Cardinal (2016: 46) defines resistance as 'the performance of a collective will that does not recognise itself in a set of social circumstances and rules given effect by the existent legal order'. In general, a distinction is made between everyday resistance and organized forms of political mobilization. Both can merge and stimulate each other (Lilja et al, 2017). Resistance is always about power, as Michel Foucault expressed in the phrase: 'Where there is power, there is resistance' (Foucault, 1978: 95). Resistance is directed against a power and tries to change the balance of power, so it also depends on power itself.

> Everyday resistance is ... historically entangled with (everyday) power (not separated, dichotomous or independent). Everyday resistance needs to be understood as intersectional as the powers it engages with (not one single power relation). And, as a consequence, it is heterogenic and contingent due to changing contexts and situations (not a universal strategy or coherent action form). Thus, the heterogenic and contingent practice of everyday resistance is – due to its entanglement with and intersectional relation to power – discursively articulated by actors, targets and observers, sometimes as 'resistance', and sometimes not. (Vinthagen and Johansson, 2013: 39)

In the current philosophical and ethical discussion, the concept of resistance is expanded beyond demonstrative forms of resistance such as large-scale revolutionary events, mass uprisings or protest movements, and also takes into account 'the shallow, scattered, low-threshold, and failed forms of resistance' (Därmann, 2021: 55). This look at the 'microphysics of resistance' was inspired by Foucault, according to whom there are 'resistances that are possible, necessary, improbable; others that are spontaneous, savage, solitary, concerted, ram pant, or violent; still others that are quick to compromise, interested, or sacrificial' (Foucault, 1978: 96). Both the sociological and the philosophical debate on resistance remain unclear about the sought concrete changes and how far they go. In addition, both have not asked under which conditions experiences of violence and suffering turn into resistance. Moreover, the concept of resistance has very rarely been examined with regard to children (see Holmberg and Alvinius, 2019).

To understand children's practices of resistance the microphysical perspective is particularly important. For these practices to succeed, however, it is also important, especially with children, to 'orient the political sense of direction of resistances to the self-understanding of those who practice them' (Därmann, 2021: 54). With this in mind, I will now reflect on children's resistant actions and illustrate them with concrete examples. My aim is to find out how extremely overwhelmed children do not give up and do not put up with everything, and how they can be supported and encouraged to do so. In this way, the deeper causes of the misery experienced can be addressed and the need for more far-reaching policy solutions becomes apparent.

Under certain stressful living conditions risks can become a provocation to act, and people can learn from their experiences of risks and acquire the necessary skills to master their lives and, if necessary, to change their environment. This is not to be confused with the assumption that resistive action arises only from supposedly inevitable suffering. It can also be seen and understood as inquiry into the necessity of suffering even in the awareness of one's own vulnerability (see Butler, 2016). In this way, it creates what we call resistance and evokes questions similar to the prominent concept of agency in social childhood studies, which is understood to mean both the capacity and the possibility of action.

The concept of agency is often attributed to children without taking into account the intentions, scope and social preconditions of the respective action in which their agency is used. If it is considered, as is increasingly demanded today (see Esser et al, 2016; Abebe, 2019), children's agency is mostly constrained by living conditions and is identified as 'weak agency' (Klocker, 2007) if used in dire situations without any appreciable potential for change. What is left out of sight is that oppressive life experiences can also trigger far-reaching impulses for action. However, this in turn presupposes specific conditions in the children's living environment that enable them to find confidence in their capacities and to imagine not only individual but also collective options for action. This occurs in Latin America, for example, in social movements led by children and adolescents from popular sectors and often crystallizes in the concept of *protagonismo infantil*. 'Protagonism affirms the subject as a social actor in a permanent struggle to transform the established order, when this involves the denial of the other and the submission of imposed roles' (Nuñez Patiño et al, 2017: 13; see Chapter 8). I will use a few examples to show how children manage to resist oppressive living conditions and sometimes even attack their causes.

Children's resistance practices

I will begin with the observations of the Chilean historian Gabriel Salazar. He observed some neighbourhoods of the city Rancagua and combined them with reflections upon the role of children in the 'neoliberal crisis'. Rancagua is located in Chile's central valley south of the capital Santiago. In the poverty-stricken areas of the city, Salazar accompanied the lives of children in the 1990s. Pinochet's military dictatorship had come to an end and parliamentary democracy had been restored, nonetheless the Chilean state continued to pursue neoliberal policies. We will reproduce some of the historian's observations, which give a concrete expression to the way in which children cope with the adverse circumstances of their lives. Salazar lets some of the neighbours, teachers and representatives of the local people speak. Street vendor Norma Carrasco reports:

> What strikes me most is the loyalty that these children have among themselves. In other words, if one of them makes a mess, none of

them accuses the other, even if you are pressuring them to say so. It's an incredible loyalty, because in other sectors the children will always accuse the other one of doing something. But not in this sector [of the city]. There is no way the child will betray you or tell on you. Even so, if you bring a loaf of bread, you share it with all your companions; they have an incredible sense of sharing. (Quoted in Salazar, 2012: 107)

Policewoman Veronica Bravo agrees:

They are very supportive of each other; the children look after each other. Especially with the younger ones. We have one child who is six years old and they all look after him a lot. Suddenly they can't stand each other and they fight, there are even fights and things like that. But most of the time the problems are solved, because this is a house and they are like a family, so they are brothers and sisters. (Quoted in Salazar, 2012: 107)

Salazar comments:

With their parents far away and the system threatening, the children open up to the only ones who can understand them: themselves. Where there is little filial love and protection, only fraternity, comradeship and solidarity can grow and develop. Thus, even when children grow up with serious affective deficiencies, they also grow up with a growing experience of 'fraternity'. Which is undoubtedly the mother cell of society and humanity. (Salazar, 2012: 108)

He compares the 'compensatory fraternity' of the children to a 'synergetic honeycomb' that attracts many young people and adults from the neighbourhoods. The children's groups represent 'a human molecule' of social regrouping and neighbourhood fraternity and contribute to the regeneration of resistance forces.

The atmosphere of fraternity that the children create among themselves and see growing around them gradually shapes a human and supportive experience that transforms, within them, into an attitude similar to that expressed by Don Carlos Pinto [another neighbour]: 'if we can give, let's give'. In this way, in the midst of the outbursts and splinters, children's gestures appear that are as much or even more supportive than those they receive from the young people and some adults in 'their' territory. A re-humanizing reciprocity that contrasts with the harrowing experiences that come down from the neo-liberal system. (Salazar, 2012: 111)

Salazar also points out that the bond between the children has not only an emotional but also a material dimension: the children contribute to the livelihood through their work. He quotes Maria Teresa, a teacher:

There are children who work, and there are a large number of children who, in the opposite day to their studies, go to the supermarkets to pack, carry bags, do cleaning, and so on. And they also work in the agricultural sector, especially in the summer season. They come from all grades. I even have kids from first grade who help their parents as street vendors, selling calendars, herbs, different things. When they are little they are in the street trade. (Quoted in Salazar, 2012: 111–112)

Salazar is ambivalent about children's work. He sees the danger of working within the capitalist system, allowing it to reduce the cost of labour and generate ever more profit. In his view, by showing solidarity with adults and supporting their families, children are also putting their own future at risk. 'The glowing ember of humanity with which they come into the world is soon spent in this kind of solidarity with adults, and their fire, by the same token, is slowly extinguished. Sometimes forever' (Salazar, 2012: 113). Just as important is to also recognize that the children

are stimulating, by their own action and mere presence, the solidarity response of the people against the underhand and dehumanizing attack of the neo-liberal crisis. And this response – which is essentially social and cultural – contains in a notorious and relevant way, as has been said, the fundamental components of the re-humanizing condition: fraternity and rebellion. ... They do not subjectivize the crisis in order to hide it – as the system does – but, on the contrary, they socialize the responses to it precisely in order to make visible what a different world can be. A better society. (Salazar, 2012: 124–125)

Salazar describes the children's actions and their sibling relationship as a kind of natural rebellion. He relates them to neoliberal impositions and sees them as a promise of a better and more humane society. Having doubts whether the children understand their actions in this political sense is legitimate, but they certainly show that they do not behave in the merely 'functional' way expected of them. Their functioning may help to keep the system going, but it also contradicts the official ideology of childhood. Instead of being led by an uncertain yet supposedly prosperous future and by fulfilling the expectation of being prepared for it in school, they take the present into their own hands, so to speak. Some studies on working children show that their own work often makes children aware of their 'worth' and involves them in 'adult affairs'.[7]

This was evident, for example, in studies with working children in which they themselves were given the opportunity to speak out about their experiences. According to these studies, despite the burdens and constraints they face, their work gives them a sense of pride for doing something important for others and contributing to the family's livelihood. Children sometimes gain a strong sense of independence and self-confidence, even in cases of work that some child labour experts consider to be obviously subordinate, exploitative and even dangerous. This is especially the case when children's work in their environment is seen as a legitimate activity and when it goes hand in hand with social recognition. In an environment where 'child labour' is generally classified as being negative, children find it much more difficult to cope with the pressures and feel excluded and degraded (see Liebel, 2004; Ennew et al, 2005; Woodhead et al, 2007; Bourdillon et al, 2010).

The goals that children want to achieve through their actions depend on the occasion and the situation in which they find themselves. In the case of working children, they are often related to their work and aim to achieve better working conditions. Nevertheless, frequently, they also include demands related to their education and health. For example, when working children demand the right to work in dignity, they take into account all their living conditions and insist that they can live in dignified conditions, with free access to education and health care.

In recent years, environmental issues have played an increasingly important role.[8] Today, children are often committed to doing more in their neighbourhoods in removing rubbish from streets and wild dumps, promoting public rubbish collection and sewage systems, and ensuring clean water supplies. In some districts of the Peruvian capital, Lima, for example, children have begun to plant their own trees and gardens, some of which serve for family self-support (they call them 'chacras de ternura', that is, gardens of tenderness). In a settlement in northern Chile inhabited by migrants from Colombia, Bolivia and Peru, children have worked to ensure that places are kept clean and can be used by them for play and sports activities. They themselves ensure that the other inhabitants of the settlement no longer dump their rubbish in these places, and have demonstratively planted flowers and shrubs on the edges of the site, which they themselves maintain and guard. In the Peruvian Amazon region, children have come up with suggestions on how villagers can better protect themselves from flooding, which has increased dramatically as a result of climate change.

A very frequent reason for children's direct action is the discrimination and violence they experience on a daily basis. They are discriminated against for a number of intersecting reasons. For example, they demand not to be treated with contempt at school because of their clothes or their work. They defend themselves against racist or sexist slogans, which often turn into violence. Children from Indigenous or Afro-descendant families who have migrated to cities organize or participate in demonstrations against racist police violence. They create interactive web portals or perform self-composed rap songs in streets and squares. Here is an example of young people of Indigenous origin in a marginalized neighbourhood in the south of Buenos Aires:

> The present and the past, the *Las Malvinas* neighbourhood and the province of Chaco, are thus mixed through rhythm, through the so-called *beats*[9] that generate an almost automatic movement of heads moving to the rhythm of the compositions and of the assistants who share, to a greater or lesser degree, emotions and experiences. They are not famous in the Buenos Aires rap scene and have only recorded a few songs in a neighbourhood recording studio, but the group is admired and recognized by children, young people and adults in the *Las Malvinas* neighbourhood and nearby areas. In their performances – more improvised than prepared – they overflow the limits of words in exchange for experimentation with rhythms, musical beats, collective waves of dancing arms and bodies that shudder and vibrate for the same meaning. (Daza Cárdenas, 2018: 215)

Sometimes they also create their own programmes on community radio. Indigenous children participate in their communities' campaigns against tourism megaprojects or the commercialization of their culture as folklore. In neighbourhoods, they call on authorities to protect them from racist and sexist harassment and violence on the streets, whether on the way to school or in their workplaces. Children selling sweets or lottery tickets at traffic lights demand protection from aggressive drivers rather than being thrown out of their workplaces.

Children living in great poverty are very resourceful in their search for income opportunities. They do not like to appeal to the compassion of others, for example, by begging. They have a fine sense of their own dignity and want to experience themselves as assets. They look for work opportunities and sometimes invent certain activities themselves that benefit others. In doing so, they rarely act individually and on their own account, but join forces with other children. Collective action sometimes even leads to self-organized work projects or a kind of cooperative. These organized forms often depend on the support of adults. They are only possible if space and financial resources are available, at least in the beginning. However, when these conditions are fulfilled, children often show remarkable perseverance and a lot of creativity in designing their projects.

The recent COVID-19 pandemic has had a particularly life-threatening impact on children and their families in slums and rural areas. They live in cramped spaces and rarely have access to clean water. In several countries, children use the internet to give advice to other children on how best to protect themselves. They organize campaigns to improve health care or urge shopkeepers and supermarkets to provide food for particularly affected families. They survey other children to find out what they need most and post the results on posters or the internet.

All these activities mainly serve for survival, notwithstanding they are always connected to considerations and ideas of a better life. The focus of children's actions is how their own dignity can be maintained or regained. In doing so, children often invoke the fact that they have rights, without, of course, relying too much on them. The basis for action is, above all, confidence in one's own initiative and cohesion with other children. Adult support is indispensable, but is usually only accepted by children if they do not feel patronized and their self-esteem is not affected.

How resistance develops in children

Questions of resistance are of particular interest for understanding and dealing with life situations that are extremely stressful and threatening to the people concerned. Here we need to keep in mind that I am talking about children whose childhoods do not conform to the Western bourgeois childhood pattern and whom we refer to in this book as children of the Global South and as part of 'popular childhoods'. They are children who are directly affected by the injustice of the postcolonial world order. They include children who live in great poverty, who must struggle to survive, who help to provide for the livelihoods of their families and often undertake co-responsibility in communal contexts. They are migrant children, children of Indigenous and African American minorities. Overall, they are the children whose childhoods are usually rendered invisible or perceived only in a distorted way. They are therefore sometimes referred to as 'children out of place' (Connolly and Ennew, 1996; Invernizzi et al, 2017). Part of the invisibility is that there are hardly any terms in the prevailing discourse for these children that do them justice, that are not associated with discrimination, or that are used in a way that does not devalue them.

The children of the Global South are colonized in many ways. They are so in that they are affected by the aftermath of colonization, which continues in the division of societies into a minority of the privileged and the vast majority of those condemned to a life in poverty. This 'coloniality of power' (Quijano, 2008) results in children, as well as adult women and men, being exposed to objects of racist, sexist and homophobic discrimination and violence. Children are additionally marginalized by adultist structures and practices and are largely excluded from social life. The processes of developing forms of resistance can only be recognized and understood if the children are understood as acting subjects and their own views and interpretations of reality are taken into account.

Under the title 'Colonial mask of silence', Brazilian writer Djamila Ribeiro tells the stories of two young mothers during the COVID-19 pandemic. They clearly express the coloniality of power against today's young women:

The first known death in Brazil from the COVID-19 virus is that of Cleonice Gonçalves. Cleonice, a woman of African descent, worked as a domestic worker. She worked for a landlady who was skiing in the Italian Alps in March. When she returned to her flat in one of the country's most expensive districts, she already knew her diagnosis. However, Cleonice kept her busy over the weekend. Cleonice began to feel weak. When her landlady realised this, she called a taxi to take Cleonice to her family, who live two hours away on the outskirts of Rio de Janeiro. Cleonice died a few hours later. In early June, during the quarantine, landlady Sari Corte Real employed domestic worker Mirtes Souza, also of African descent, in her flat in an upscale neighbourhood of Recife in the northeast of the country. Mirtes is the second generation of her family. Her mother had already fed the family by making other families comfortable with sweaty work. Because Mirtes had to work even during the pandemic, she had nowhere to leave her son Miguel Otávio. She took him with her to work. On this early June noon, the landlady was busy with a manicure. She instructed Mirtes to take the dogs out. Miguel stayed in the flat. When the landlady began to find the 5-year-old tired, she put him in the lift unattended and sent him to the ninth floor, where there was a children's play area. Miguel walked, lost his balance on a parapet and fell from the ninth floor just as his mother was returning from her walk. Sari had to go to the police station, paid a bail of 5,000 euros and was allowed to return home. (Ribeiro, 2020: 12)

The colonial era is not over, it continues covertly. In colonial times, children were enslaved just like adults, often 'dumped' in the sea during slave transports, or their hands were cut off if they did not have enough rubber or coffee beans in their harvesting basket. Today, children are exposed to the structural violence of inhumane housing conditions, kept in poverty and forced to work, which endangers their lives and affects their health. In schools, they are forced to be drenched with content that glorifies colonial history, which has nothing to do with their lives and is mostly useless for their lives. The promised equality before the law turns into an inequality after the law for these children (De Sousa Santos, 2014). It is therefore not surprising that they have little confidence in law and justice, and it is surprising that they do not more often react with violence in the face of the violence they have experienced.

Like the colonized in the past (see Fanon, [1952] 2008; Memmi, [1957] 2016), today's Southern children face the dilemma of having been touched by the humiliations they have experienced. They penetrate the mind of children and bring them into an inner conflict between doubt and indignation. It is not easy for these children to develop the necessary self-confidence and to resist in a way that does not lead them further into marginalization and criminalization. Their strength does not stem from the barrels of rifles, but from cohesion with their equal and mutual trust. When they join forces, this often happens spontaneously, without a clear goal, but with a dream of a better life. When social movements emerge out of spontaneous resistance, they are not usually 'pure' children's movements, because they do not experience their childhood as separate from adult life. It is not their identity as children that is the basis of their actions, but the experience that their lives are as many other people's lives who find themselves in the same difficult situation. The difference is that in addition, they also experience being despised and less valued as children and even more so as girls. Therefore, these children always insist on respect for their specific interests and forms of communication which, in an adultist society, arise from their discrimination and exclusion as children.

Several studies (for instance, Boyden, 2003; Boyden and Mann, 2005) have found that in cultures that emphasize children's autonomy and self-responsibility and allow children to take on responsibility at an early age – such as caring for younger siblings or contributing to the family income – this fosters self-confidence, self-efficacy and social skills. Additional emphasis is placed on cultures where children of young age are encouraged to actively address life's risks and acquire communication, problem-solving and self-help skills, by which they are better equipped to cope with difficult situations. For example, children of the Inuit people in Canada are taught to cope with unpredictable dangers of the Arctic environment, meaning that they experience uncertain and dangerous events. They learn that the world is full of problems to be solved and that the ability to discover them, to actively and accurately observe them and to analyse the risks involved in solving them is highly valued (Briggs, 1991).

In many societies, boys in particular are encouraged to participate in activities that enhance their physical strength and stamina, self-confidence and skills. For example, observations were made where Somali boys who had to leave the country and migrate alone were able to cope with this situation in an unexpectedly sovereign manner. This is explained with the traditional nomadic practices of entrusting young children to supervise distant herds of animals. Long periods of separation from their families and communities allow them to live self-sufficiently and autonomously, accepting and recognizing themselves as responsible persons (Rousseau et al, 1998). The fact that girls are usually denied these experiences in such patriarchal cultures makes it more difficult for them to acquire resistant personalities.

Sealing children off from risks and placing them under the protection of adults is not an appropriate way to foster resistance, especially in crisis situations. This is not to say that very heavy burdens may be associated with far-reaching psychological and emotional consequences and that children may need very special care. At this point, it is worth noting that children are not simply the product of adult beliefs, educational practices, investments and interventions, but actors with their own views and competencies. This is why they often resist being treated as helpless victims and passive recipients of charitable doings by aid organizations and why they seek to find their own solutions to their problems. Jo Boyden (2003: 12) therefore recommends that 'wherever possible, children should be given a constructive role in their own protection and at least some degree of responsibility for their own safety'. This is echoed in more recent concepts of protection that are considered participatory.

Conclusion

A fundamental problem with the resilience paradigm is that it is designed as a reactive action in situations of risk and crisis, aiming to restore an original state. This suggests that risks are inevitable and it is often understood as such in the resilience discourse. The resilience paradigm suggests that individuals (or affected communities) should take on responsibility for their misery and that they are expected to cope with it on their own. Therefore, I believe it is necessary to shift this paradigm and develop concepts that do not see competence to act simply as a matter of individual problem-solving skills. In my view, the concept of resistance seems to be more appropriate for this. Resistance arises primarily from social experience and can most likely be effective in cooperation with others. It can contribute to this, but it also depends on the creation of social conditions in which everyone has the same possibilities to shape their lives in a satisfactory way. As far as children are concerned, this means working for living conditions and generational relations in which children are no longer marginalized and socially disadvantaged, and at the same time enabling and contributing to children's opportunities to participate self-reliantly, with equal rights and in an organized way.

Children's protagonism: considerations for its reconceptualization

Introduction

Since the emergence of youth movements in the second half of the 19th century, it has been pondered to what extent young people can be a force for change of social conditions. Mostly, social change or renewal is referred to in a general way. Such generalizing theories about 'generations' and their relationship to each other were already formulated in the 1920s (see Mannheim, [1928] 1952; Mead, 1970; 1973). The debate eventually extended to young people, who today are subsumed under the life phase of childhood. This is expressed not only in terms such as 'Young Pioneers' (in the communist movement), but in the meantime also in numerous statements by UN bodies in which children and young people are declared to be bearers of hope for a better world. Since the adoption of the UN Convention on the Rights of the Child (CRC) in 1989 at the latest, the debate on children's rights has also gone beyond questions of child protection and aims at greater social and political participation of children. In the 'new sociology of childhood' that emerged since the 1980s and is being newly constructed until today, children are explicitly attributed 'agency' and research approaches are developed in which children are granted an active part as producers of knowledge.

The discovery of the young generations as 'agents of social change', however, was not the same for all children and young people. So far, the understanding of children as agents of social change has been limited to those younger generations who more or less conform to the pattern of bourgeois childhood and youth, even if they rebel against the bourgeois order, as in the case of the first youth movements. Numerous children and young people who deviated from this pattern in their social behaviour, for example by skipping school or, mostly due to precarious living conditions, who lead a 'sub-proletarian' life of their own liking, were branded as 'neglected' and a danger to the existing society or the 'disciplined' class struggle.[1] In Germany, before and after the First World War, some of these children and young people had come together in groups that named themselves 'wild cliques' (see Lessing and Liebel, 1981; Rosenhaft, 1982). With regard to children of the working class or the so-called working-class youth, the question was whether their lifestyle and conspicuous activism was acceptable within the framework of the existing social order or whether they threatened to break it. This is still reflected in today's debate on the agency of children and young people. The discussion revolves around whether this is understood to mean only 'positive' or 'constructive' forms of action (such an assessment is usually tacit) or any kind of independent action.

In this chapter, I will deal with a variant of the agency debate that has arisen in Latin America. This debate, which in Spanish is called '*protagonismo infantil*' (sometimes also '*protagonismo juvenil*'),[2] is interestingly characterized by the fact that it does not revolve around the bourgeois form of childhood and youth, but is related to children and adolescents who are socially marginalized and belong to socially disadvantaged population groups. The discourse emerged in Latin America in the 1970s and has been discussed in various publications, mostly in Spanish, since the late 1980s (for instance, Schibotto, 1988; 1990; Cussiánovich, 1990; 1996; 2001a; 2001b; 2006; 2010; 2013; Liebel, 1994; 2000; 2001; 2007a; Alfageme et al, 2003; Liebel and Martínez Muñoz, 2009; Cussiánovich and Martínez Muñoz, 2017). It emerged in the context of working children and young people's movements (NNATs). Its origins are related to lived practice and attempts to characterize it with a concise term.

After introducing the basic ideas of the concept, I review its history and reflect on the risks, misunderstandings and reinterpretations associated with the term. I then present what I consider to be the main challenges for its reconceptualization and ask to what extent the concept of protagonism can serve as an orientation in education and social work.

Basic ideas of children's protagonism

The basic idea of children's protagonism is that children are social subjects who claim to play an active role in society and to be able to meaningfully influence the decisions that affect their lives. This is understood both as a right and an opportunity that children have and as a praxis they already live. The emphasis is not on individual action, but on collective and organized action, ideally expressed in a social movement or organization that is composed by children and in which children play a leading role.

The term represents a theory of the collective agency of children from popular sectors. It aims to express that children are able to organize and represent themselves and other children in similar circumstances and with similar interests. The concept emerges from a reflection of the practices of children's movements and brings together elements from different moments in their history (see Taft, 2017: 3). It concerns, for example, working children, but also includes all children who feel compelled to resist in conditions of exclusion, subordination and exploitation, and to do so collectively. The concept is not limited to Latin America either, despite its historical origins on the continent. With the movements of working and other children of the popular sectors that have been emerging since the 1990s in Africa and parts of Asia, especially in India, the concept is an expression of a self-determined collective practice of children of the Global South who are in marginalized situations or affected by poverty, for example (see Liebel et al, 2001; Rodgers, 2020).

The underlying assumption of the concept of children's protagonism is the notion of a childhood that is closely interwoven with social life and sees itself as connected to that life. This conception differs from the Western bourgeois idea of childhood as a sphere separate from the adult world which is confined to the private sphere. In terms of the relationship to adults, it is posited that children are not 'less worthy' or 'less competent' than adults, but have or can claim the same weight and influence in social life as adults. 'By emphasizing dignity and subjectivity, the movement's invocation of the concept of protagonismo suggests the full humanity of children, affirming their personhood, in contrast to other, more pervasive paradigms of childhood in which they are primarily passive objects for adults to manage, protect, care for, and invest in' (Taft, 2017: 8; see also Taft, 2019: 45–82). The material and intellectual basis for this is that children are both different and equal in comparison to adults, and that the equal weight accorded to them goes hand in hand with recognition of their diversity. The concept of child agency does not imply opposition to adults, nor does it mark a generational conflict, but rather emphasizes the right to be recognized as ethically equal, without being or having to be equal to adults in all respects.

The diversity of childhood is also related to children themselves. They find themselves in different situations of social life, which, depending on their age, gender and socio-cultural backgrounds, have an impact on their positions with social power structures and are associated with different interests, perceptions of reality and subjectivities. In terms of gender, Chilean psychologists Siu Lay-Lisboa et al note, for example:

> Children's protagonism assumes that boys and girls mostly act according to the binary social boundaries established for men and women. It questions these gender relations because they are based on structures of unequal distribution of power, in other words, on a system that makes use of diverse mechanisms that normalize such a patriarchal imaginary. (Lay-Lisboa et al, 2018: 154)

The term children's protagonism emphasizes that because of the socially produced unequal power relation between adults and children, sometimes referred to as adultism or adultcentrism, children must have special rights and opportunities as well as equal rights to be able to assert their age-, gender- and generation-specific interests and perspectives.

The protagonism of children, as a practice, does not deny the need to protect a social group that is especially vulnerable to the violation of their fundamental rights. It rather affirms that the best way to protect them is by promoting and guaranteeing their right to be the main actors of their existence, both individually and collectively. (Alfageme et al, 2003: 50)

It does not mean distancing oneself from adults or excluding them, but establishing a mutually respectful relationship between them. Adults can fulfil important tasks in the practice of children's protagonism, especially as trusted persons and supportive partners who, with their experience and specific knowledge, are always there at the children's sides wherever they are needed, required and wanted (see Bazán, 2005). Children and the adults they trust relate to each other as co-protagonists in the sense of their own responsibility and each other's responsibility. A central element is the notion of co-responsibility, but not on the basis of coercion, but of voluntariness. This includes that children, as protagonists, can act autonomously and make their own decisions.

The term is similar to what is called *child-led advocacy* (Oliver and Dalrymple, 2008; Liebel, 2012b) or *children's agency* (James, 2011; Oswell, 2013; Esser et al, 2016a), but emphasizes more clearly that children (can) take their own initiatives and play an influential role in social, economic and political life. It represents a bottom-up and democratically conceived form of relating and organizing in which all people (here: children) have the opportunity to contribute with words and deeds and have as much to say and determine as those who sometimes occupy leading positions or have more power. In terms of children's participation, the concept of children's protagonism emphasizes that participation is not limited to a framework provided by adults, but that the framework itself is shaped or at least decisively influenced by children. It is the children themselves who determine and voice the objectives, contents and forms of joint action, thus having 'the last word' in all matters at hand.

Origins of the concept of children's protagonism

Since its discursive emergence in the 1970s, the concept of children's protagonism has shown some shifts in emphasis, without, however, changing in essence. While the initial focus was on children's identity with the working or popular classes, since the 1990s there has been a greater emphasis on children's autonomy and the exercise of their rights. This is expressed, among others, in increasingly frequent talk of *protagonist participation* (Cussiánovich and Márquez, 2002; Alfageme et al, 2003; Cussiánovich and Figueroa, 2009). In this context, greater attention is also paid to the inherent ambivalences of the concepts of subject and subjectivity. The clearer demarcation of neoliberal conceptions of the subject is accompanied by a stronger critique of the colonial legacy (see Chapter 6).

The new focus on childhood, represented by the concept of children's protagonism, is centred on marginalized and exploited children, some of whom have to fend for themselves and survive on their own, and some of whom are economic subjects who contribute significantly to their family's survival and to alleviating their poverty. Instead of lamenting the lack of childhood of these children, as presented from a Eurocentric perspective ('children without childhood'), they are seen as capable and as subjects resisting the authorities, embodying 'an invisible childhood' (Schibotto, 1988) or 'another childhood' (Liebel, 2000). The new perspective on childhood links the remembered reflection on forms of childhood in the cultures of the continent's Indigenous and Afro-descendant peoples.

The discourse on children's protagonism is taken from the concept of popular protagonism (*protagonismo popular*) or social protagonism (*protagonismo social*). This is the name given to the movements in Latin America that play an active role in the struggle for liberation and better living conditions for marginalized and exploited population groups, such as landless peasants, slum dwellers in the cities, minorities and majorities of Indigenous and Afro-descendent people (see Colectivo Situaciones, 2002). The term underlines that it is the people themselves who create better living conditions in an organized way as citizens from below, without waiting for or relying on the state as such. Demands on the state are still present, however there is no longer a focus on conquering state power (see Holloway, 2010). Rather, it is about collective self-determination beyond state institutions, a new definition of one's own territory and one's own right to shape this territory autonomously. The self-understanding behind these approaches is a critique of such powers and is thought of as an alternative to paternalistic and developmentalist approaches (based on the so-called 'modernization theory'). Such 'modernized' approaches and concepts see the 'poor' and 'ethnic minorities' as backward, uncivilized and culturally underdeveloped. Just as popular protagonism emphasizes the sovereignty and creativity of subjected classes and peoples, children's protagonism emphasizes the capacities and demands of children and adolescents for an independent and influential role in society.

The impetus for what is expressed by the term children's protagonism came from children, but the term is rarely used by them. 'The expression protagonism started to become part of their common sense, though not necessarily of their everyday language' (Cussiánovich, 2010: 28). It is found partly in the final declarations of local and international meetings of NNATs movements, but predominantly in publications written by adults. However, it was not invented by them, but responds to what they observed in children. Their story is a story of interactions between children and the adults who accompany them. 'Ideas do not fall from the sky or emerge by spontaneous generation, but are the result of social processes, historical contexts, cultural dynamics, political-economic events, of an imperative need for the development of human beings to name things' (Cussiánovich, 2010: 25).

Certainly, it should not be ignored that adults in their role as educators, parents or neighbours repeatedly influence the children's thinking about their social position and their interests and rights. Nevertheless, of far greater importance for the emergence and spread of protagonism in children are informal encounters, in which they experience self-determined discursive spaces and can freely reflect on their situation and compare their particular experiences with each other. In these meetings, for example, the children think about the requirements that their representatives must meet in order to be able to represent the interests of all members of the movement convincingly and effectively. This includes the development of self-confidence and the ability to speak up and assert oneself even in unusual situations in which adults or state authorities set the tone, for example in the phrase, 'they must not mince their words'. This is also expressed in the fact that children want to be role models for adults, or, as a 15-year-old boy from Colombia said at an international meeting in Guatemala in 1992:

> We must set an example to the adults. We must do what they have not been able to do: to unite. To take joint action, to defend also the right of other children, to become independent from adults, to be respected and to get the right to have a say in our affairs. (Quoted in Liebel, 1994: 142)

Children rarely use the term protagonism, but they have an idea of what it is supposed to express. Alejandro Cussiánovich (2010: 80) quotes a girl activist in the Peruvian children's movement MANTHOC, as an example: 'I don't know what protagonism is, but I'm going to tell you how we live it in the movement, how we act and how we help all the NATs to become what you call protagonism.' The same author also reports other comments made by children in the Peruvian children's movement that correspond to the idea of children's protagonism:

> We do not want a society in which a few have everything and our families have almost nothing. – We do not accept a society of a few powerful and even abusive people. We can all participate and make our contribution without being bent over. – It is not enough for them to listen to us and give us reason with words; we also want to provide solutions. – We do not want a society that does not know or value our organization or that thinks that we allow ourselves to be

manipulated. – We are not willing to be pushed back on the advances we have made in our rights. (Quoted in Cussiánovich, 2013)

In the early 1990s some working children who had organized their own movement in Nicaragua expressed their understanding of children's protagonism:

Always taking the initiative in our work. – Expressing our opinions. – Taking the initiative to defend our rights. – Taking action in our work, home, and city. – Fighting for free education. – Fundraising to help the school. – Sharing the income (from our work on the street) with our families and satisfying our needs. – Being organized and working together. – Organizing ourselves within the Movement. – Having our own elections. – Proposing ideas, giving opinions and participating at home, in school, during projects, and at the Representatives Meeting (of the Movement). – Representing NATs at the community, regional, national and Latin-American levels. – Making concrete proposals during municipal meetings where different children's problems are discussed. – Involving the community in order to receive their support over the issues we encounter. – Proposing activities to improve our neighbourhood and taking the initiative to keep it clean. – Proposing and executing our objectives. – Using the mass media (radio, TV, press, posters[3]). – Helping one another (at home as well as on the street). – Asking for help from educators. (Quoted in Liebel, 2007a: 62–63)

We need to consider that the concept of children's protagonism refers not only to children's autonomy, but also to children's active relationship to the world around them. When children act as protagonists, they do not want to separate themselves from the world (to enter a child's 'own' world), but to play an active role in the whole world surrounding them and contribute to changing it.

So far, little research has been done on how protagonism emerges among children as a specific form of action. The debate mainly refers to the social movements of working children and adolescents and interprets the actions and self-understanding of the children who are organized and are organizing themselves. In order to understand the conditions for its emergence, a thought is that it could be linked to studies on children in social movements (see Rodgers, 2020) and research on children's agency (see, for instance, Oswell, 2013; Esser et al, 2016). This contrasts with the approach chosen in resilience research, where the main references are 'protective factors' in children's life histories and environments. This approach, however, falls short, as it does not focus on a possible protagonism, but only on coping with life crises (for a critique, see Chapter 7).

Dilution and perversion of the concept

Since the concept of children's protagonism emerged in Latin America, much has changed in the world and new experiences have emerged that make it necessary to clarify the concept and its possible applications. It should also be kept in mind that the term itself has become a disputed terrain and the subject of different interpretations and uses, which need to be reflected critically and self-critically. Alejandro Cussiánovich, who contributed substantially to the development of the concept, points out: 'We are witnessing new forms of colonization of consciences, imaginaries, subjectivities, thinking, legal and pedagogical discourses that make not only timely but radically necessary a critical review of how the protagonism referred to children, in particular, has been understood up to now' (Cussiánovich, 2010: 15). The term has thus also been extended to ideological fields and discourses not previously considered. Therefore, there is also a need to refine the concept in order to protect it from misuse and, at the same time, to develop it further so that it is more useful in practice and theory.

The discourse on children's protagonism has become widespread and popular, but it has also provoked fears and rejection among people and institutions concerned with children and even among those explicitly advocating for their rights. The defensive strategies involved proceed in various ways. One way is to naturalize or linguistically reinterpret specific characteristics of children, for example, devaluing spontaneous honesty and sincerity as innocence, sensitivity (to injustice) as naivety and irrationality, the desire for words to be followed by action as actionism. The other way is to appropriate elements of the concept and strip it of its emancipatory political content by formalizing it. In this emptied form, it is even used offensively today to give children the illusion that they belong and have a say. In this sense, childhood researcher Noam Peleg (2018) speaks of the 'illusion of inclusion'.

A distinction must be made between the dilution of discourse (by adults) to legitimize one's own supremacy and the practice based on it (micro perspective) and the perversion of discourse through its embedding in neoliberal techniques of human and governmental management (macro perspective). Based on my own experiences, I will first shed light on the micro perspective.

I still vividly remember the discussions we had in Central America and Mexico in the early 1990s about the then new concept of children's protagonism. Some colleagues feared an inappropriate politicization of children and saw their ideas of child participation, which were based on their understanding of children's rights, threatened. In a book I published in 1994 in Nicaragua under the title *Protagonismo Infantil* (Liebel, 1994), I had processed some experiences that surprised me, that I had made during the emergence of the NNATs movement in Nicaragua that was called NATRAS due to the geographical location (see Liebel, 1996). Contrary to my own experiences and convictions, a scepticism against this strange idea of children's protagonism had developed early on among some directors of non-government organizations (NGOs) and educators there. They probably felt that they were being restricted or marginalized in the dominant role they played in educational projects. A frequent accusation levelled against children who were organizing themselves (usually behind closed doors) was that they were paying homage to short-sighted actionism or that they were even being politically manipulated by some adults.

As the term spread rapidly among children, they tried to defuse it by reinterpreting it as an educational concept, according to which protagonism was understood primarily as a process of learning by children depending exclusively on teaching by educators. A rather technocratic variant of this position argues that children's protagonism itself should be understood as a method of educational work. Thus, protagonism is reduced to a kind of offer to the children to take over responsibility step by step in the educational process itself. Sometimes the children get the opportunity to take their own initiatives and cooperate in the realization of the goal that the educators have previously given. In this case, the concept of protagonism becomes a kind of stimulating motivation (see Liebel, 2007a).

The discourse of children's protagonism, like the discourse of resilience, of the subject and of subjectivity, is in danger of turning against the interests of children.

> What has been produced in Latin America on the protagonism of childhood and youth continues to be a production that we would not hesitate to describe as incipient and of an abductive nature, that is, inferential, hypothetical, and open. Perhaps this is why we should be vigilant about the inevitable attempts to co-opt the term from different ideological matrices. (Cussiánovich and Martínez Muñoz, 2017: 238)

Some discreetly attempt through the adoption of prestige-laden language of the limelight to make it appear as a 'progressive' or 'in keeping with the times' practice, which under other circumstances would have been labelled otherwise. One form of this is when children are flattered into believing that they are called to, and capable of, effecting social change or even renewing the world simply by being young, by nature.

Challenges for reconceptualization

Children's protagonism emerged as a partisan concept of self-assertion in a situation of almost total exclusion. It reflects and takes sides with children's processes of self-liberation. In the 1960s and 1970s, these processes were usually directed against an authoritarian state and an authoritarian education that disregarded any form of subjectivity and turned children into objects of arbitrary measures and forms of treatment. In the North, these processes were largely related to the relationship between adults and children and the institutionalization of this relationship in educational institutions, especially schools. They were labelled 'infantilization'. In the South, initially in Latin America, they were more strongly directed at processes of social marginalization of whole sections of the population and dictatorial forms of governance. Children were not primarily understood as antipodes of adults, but as part of the marginalized and oppressed sectors of the population. Children's protagonism was embedded in popular protagonism, most clearly visible in the understanding of children as working children or children of the working class or subaltern classes.

Changes in the political environment since the 1990s have partly paved the way for a perversion of the discourse and have been begging for its reconceptualization. Authoritarian modes of governance have not disappeared, but their manifestations have changed. Only in exceptional situations ('state of emergency') or in the face of open rebellion is oppression exercised through direct violence. In Latin America, 'democracy' and the 'rule of law' are considered the norm. Even children are declared 'citizens' or 'legal subjects' who have the right to be heard and to participate. Like the discourse of multiculturalism towards minorities with non-Western cultural roots and traditions, children now encounter tolerance and 'understanding'. Participation is propagated and forms of participation are established in various spheres of society, including educational institutions. Nevertheless, these forms of participation are rather symbolic and instrumental in character, and do not eliminate either social inequality or inequality of power. They do not serve to reinforce the social position of children in society, but are intended to convey the feeling that they are no longer excluded. The feeling of 'being heard' should motivate them to 'take part'. So Cussiánovich asks:

> Why, in the context of fragmentation and inequality caused by the market and its effects on the conception and role of the state, does a new kind of discourse emerge? A discourse that asserts autonomy, social visibility, the right to participate, the rejection of exclusion and forced social disappearance precisely when we are called to the market as consumers, that is, when we create a fiction of being protagonists, of being free, of being social subjects? The concept of protagonism is a child of this dynamic insofar as it takes up the agonizing experience of not ceasing to be, and thus the condition of the individual, the

subject, understood as a social movement and not reducible to social roles. (Cussiánovich, 2010: 30–31)

These processes of participation are being prepared in the consumer sphere of capitalist societies. Here, children have long been taught that they are 'important' and 'taken seriously'. Here, as today in the digital media, they even witness a certain prominence by being addressed as 'trendsetters' who can make an 'innovative' contribution. Here they are flattered by the fact that they are 'creative' and can actively contribute to 'renewal'. Their subjectivity is no longer ignored, and even celebrated as a special quality of age. Meanwhile, even beyond the sphere of consumption, children are treated as 'entrepreneurs' who can help keep society going and contribute to social change. Instead of being provided for, as has been the dominant Western model of childhood, they are asked to be active and exercise responsibility for themselves and take their lives into their own hands. The key to a modern childhood is now to develop a 'success mentality', as expressed recently, for example, in a child-entrepreneur school project in Paraguay and Bolivia.[4] Another example is the stylization of children as forward-thinking 'eco-bankers' and entrepreneurs who had begun recycling garbage in Peru and started a credit cooperative to generate much-needed income for themselves and their families.[5] The internet celebrates children as 'kidpreneurs' who initiate million-dollar deals before they turn 15.[6] The discourse of protagonism

is gaining significant space in language and in the modulation of ideas ... the business culture loaded with symbols, with meanings that configure a stereotype or profile of the successful young person who progresses ... discourses on leadership, on successful management, on administrative re-engineering, competitiveness, organizational technology, personnel management, intra-company relations and public relations system, and so on. (Cussiánovich, 2010: 49)

Such a changed environment cannot leave the discourse of children's protagonism unchanged if it is not to dissolve into arbitrariness or be instrumentalized for purposes that no longer have anything to do with the original emancipatory intentions. The discourse must become aware that its abuse and perversion are also inherent to the very idea of protagonism. To imagine people as protagonists is always to consider them as individuals distinct from others who are not or cannot be protagonists. In this context, Cussiánovich (2010: 10) speaks of 'the risks of a liberal understanding of human rights and protagonism', which suggests an individualizing and competitive vision.[7] This makes it all the more important to emphasize the aspect of solidarity and mutual connectedness.

Children's protagonism as an orientation for socio-educational work

The concept of children's protagonism represents a practice of children, but it can also serve as a guideline for social and pedagogical work, similar to children's rights. Since the beginning of the second millennium, various proposals have been developed and teaching materials have been elaborated on the basis of previous experiences. One example is the practice manual *De la participación al protagonismo infantil: propuestas para la acción* (Alfageme et al, 2003). It presents different proposals on how to counteract prejudices and obstacles to children's participation in social and pedagogical practice and how to fight for children's 'protagonist participation'. It also holds a battery of indicators on different dimensions. Other writings (Gaitán, 2014; Piotti, 2019) take up the concept of children's protagonism and reinterpret children's rights in light of this concept and relate it to social work practice. An essay (Lay-Lisboa et al, 2018) offers reflections on how to promote children's protagonism in the institutional setting of school, both inside and outside the classroom. A guide developed in Spain sets out how to advance protagonist participation in processes and presents indicators for a metropolitan municipality (Cabrerizo Sanz et al, 2018). The same authors had previously provided guidance in another guide on how to evaluate experiences of promoting and practising organized protagonism with children (Martínez Muñoz and Cabrerizo Sanz, 2015).

Attempts to promote children's protagonism or protagonist participation within social and educational projects or institutions face the problem that children's opportunities to take their own initiatives and influence decisions within existing institutions are limited. This is the case when forms of participation, such as student councils, are set up according to guidelines or rules by adults. Children's protagonism cannot be created artificially or even from above, because it is based on the children's own initiative and thus also on the conditions that favour such initiatives. Contradictions which are at times not easy to resolve also arise in the actions of the very people who want to promote children's protagonism within the framework of their professional activity.[8] They can go so far that these advocates have to ask themselves whether, in the 'role' they play by virtue of their profession, they can do justice to the basic ideas of children's protagonism at least to a sufficient degree. Instead, they have to ask themselves more what this means in a particular situation, and what the possibilities and limits of their professional performance are. Psychological aspects, such as the internalized habit of controlling or guiding children can also become a barrier, as children's protagonism can only be lived by a redistribution of power between adults and children.

However, the concept of children's protagonism can serve as a kind of sting that challenges educators and social workers – sometimes painfully – to reflect on the meaning and perspectives of their professional action and, if necessary, to rebel against their framework conditions or at least to 'come clean'. This requires a willingness to take risks and not to ignore the political dimensions of all educational and social work. Or to put it positively: they have to ask themselves to what extent their actions can go beyond mere help for the children and turn into solidarity with them, and what is the right place and time for this in each case. Their basic attitude towards children as full subjects of rights is decisive. They must understand children's rights in general and participation in particular as a resource for children which can help to strengthen their social position in society, which up to now has remained subordinate. This requires taking children's own experiences and views seriously and doing everything in their power to assert them in their living environment and in society at large. I will illustrate this with some examples from different time periods and regions.

Fifty years ago, I accompanied young people in Berlin who had fled their homes or institutions to escape abuse or authoritarian control and create a self-determined life for themselves. For this purpose, they had occupied a vacant building. They met me and my colleagues, who wanted to help them, with the statement that they did not want 'social workers' in their new home, but wanted to be accompanied by us as 'collaborators'. While I was employed at the time in an institution where we were developing new participatory concepts for out-of-school education with children and young people (that means, I was relatively independent), three other people from our support group were working as social workers in the municipal administration. To avoid major conflicts, the authorities refrained from violently evicting the occupied building, but wanted to place social workers in the house to keep an eye on the young people and make sure that 'the laws', especially the child protection law, were not breached. At that time, there was no talk of children's rights, nor even of children's protagonism, but in our support group we were convinced that young people had a right to a life determined jointly by them. We believed that the best way to help them was to use pedagogical arguments to mediate between the young people and the state authorities. From the young people's point of view this was an unnecessary 'egg dance'. In this situation, we realized that our own biographical imprint and our professional involvement in the social bureaucracy could undermine the solidarity we were subjectively striving for. For all of us, the experience of this contradiction gave rise to a political learning process that remained with me for many years. In the end, it led to an emancipatory understanding of children's and youth's rights that sees them first and foremost as a resource for children and young people in their everyday lives.

In their professional role, teachers, educators and social workers tend (and I do not exclude myself at all) to let their actions be guided by a paternalistic rationality that pays too little attention to the specific experiences and perspectives of children and young people. They have to learn again and again that the 'truthfulness' of the criteria of a supposedly rational decision depends not only on assumed and objectively measurable facts, but also on the respective perspective and perception of the subjects involved. This can be illustrated by a scene in a German kindergarten in which an educator lets her actions be guided by the principle of understanding and interacting with the children in her care in their diverse subjectivity and with respect for their point of view:

> The educator is cold. She knows that because she often freezes, as she says, 'especially when I'm outside.' She sees a girl who has gone into the garden only in a T-shirt. She then goes to the girl three times and asks if she is okay and if she can feel her temperature. The girl accepts the need for action of the educator and allows her to do so. But when the teacher comes a fourth time and asks again if she is feeling well or if she is cold and if she should feel, the girl turns around and says, 'Are you cold? Then put on your jacket! I'm fine'. The educator takes this hint and thinks for herself: 'Wow! I'm gonna go, then'. (Richter and Lehmann, 2016: 57)

The educator's action is not guided by doubts about the girl's competence, but by the difference between her own perception and the girl's. She admits to herself that her sensation is not the same as the child's and that an adult cannot always easily know what is best for the child. In the study with this example, it reads: 'In this interaction example, not the possible consequences of the girl's decision, but ultimately the arguments of the girl are used to justify pedagogical action. The girl is given the opportunity to "keep the last word" and to assume responsibility independently' (Richter and Lehmann, 2016: 57).

This attitude of the educator could have been inspired by the Polish-Jewish educator Janusz Korczak. Already at the beginning of the 20th century, he conceived children's rights in an emancipatory and vital sense. In the children's homes he directed he practised them in a manner very close to the idea of children's protagonism (although he did not express it in such terms). For Korczak, the central idea was that the adult educator cannot know what is best for the child. He must acquire this knowledge together with the child and question it again and again in his interaction with the child. For him, this also means questioning the constitutive power of pedagogical action and having the will to meet children on an equal footing and to be ready and open to learn from them. Korczak's description of his learning experience at a summer camp is such an example:

I understood then that children represent a force that can be encouraged to collaborate, discouraged by spurning, in any case power to be reckoned with. These truths, by strange coincidence, were driven into me with a stick. – The next day, during a get-together in the forest, for the first time I spoke not to the children but with the children. I spoke not of what I would like them to be but of what they would like to and could be. Perhaps then, for the first time, I found out that one could learn a great deal from children, that they make, and have every right to make demands, conditions, reservations. (Korczak, [1919] 2007: 271)

If we understand children as subjects of full rights, we face the challenge, in particular in educational and social work, to respect children as equals and, whenever possible, to understand their point of view and recognize their will. When I worked with children in Nicaragua in the 1990s as an NGO worker and street educator, I found that this was easier said than done. Together with other colleagues, I supported children to organize their own movement and to collectively defend their interests and rights. While I had relatively wide leeway in my institution, other colleagues were accused of neglecting their duties as 'educators' by their institution when they supported children to create their own organization. Some were asked to exercise solidarity with the children in their 'free time' outside the institution, others were even threatened with dismissal.

These conflicts clearly showed that solidarity with children organized within the framework of an institution can have narrow limits. The task expected of us as 'educators' was obviously different from what we understood as a relationship of solidarity with the children and promoting children's protagonism. Whereas in the institution we were obliged to take responsibility for the children *and* guide them, the now organized children expected us to respect their own will and support them in carrying it out. It was no longer us who made the decisions and had the final say, but the organized children. Although pedagogical considerations always played a role in our relationship with the children, it became clear to us that there was a big difference between our role as educators and that of, as we later said, *advisors* or *collaborators* in the children's movement. I was struck by the parallels with the experience I had had two decades earlier in Berlin.

Conclusion

Children's protagonism did not emerge as abstract discourse, but from the exercise of a new perception of the already existing social reality. This reality consists of the fact that there are children and young people:

- who rebel against living conditions and forms of relationships that they perceive as unjust;

- who demand to be recognized as social, economic and political subjects; and
- who want to change their environment in their own interest and according to their own ideas.

Understood as a theory, the discourse of protagonism must provide answers to the reasons why this specific form of agency was and is possible. This has been discussed only rudimentarily until now. It requires more intensive studies and deeper evidence-based reflections. My hypothesis is that children perceive the marginalized and subordinate childhood status of 'not yet' as a contradiction to their lived reality, in which they already take on vital tasks. They therefore experience the adultist power as hollow. However, this also presupposes that the children can find or create social spaces that are largely self-determined and in which they can reflect on their situation together and come to their own conclusions. In this way, new collective identities can emerge in which children experience themselves as (co-)responsible persons without having to give up their child-specific needs and their relative autonomy as children. Emancipatory social movements in the children's environment can also have a stimulating effect here because they make it easier for the children to feel they belong to other collectives in which they find recognition for their emancipatory interests. The path chosen in resilience research of referring to 'protective factors' in children's life history and environment falls short, in my opinion, because it does not have a possible protagonism in mind, but only the defensive coping with life crises (for criticism, see Chapter 7).

Children's protagonism cannot be created by adults, not even in the context of educational and social work, or in the institutions concerned. If we want to support and promote it, we have to say goodbye to our own power over children, externally and internally, and enter into a different kind of relationship with them, based on equality and respect. We must not dust off our professional expertise and our co-responsibility and neither must we deduct a claim to power from it. The best way to promote children's protagonism is to discover it in children's everyday lives and to advocate for the social conditions that make it more possible in organized ways. We cannot eliminate the contradictions that arise, but we can and must always reflect on them. And we have to always be aware and advocate for the children to have their own social spaces where they can think together freely and unbiasedly about their situation and come to their own conclusions.

'Not about us, but with us!': Perspectives of insurgent research with children of the Global South

Introduction

Since the turn of the millennium, social childhood studies have not only become more interested in children and childhoods of the Global South, but have also critically reflected on the Eurocentric focus of previous childhood studies (see, for instance, Liebel and Budde, 2017). This critical perspective has been taken up recently in a special issue of the international journal *Childhood*, claiming to 'develop perspectives that de-construct northern, dominant scholarships, and facilitate generative thinking on the study of childhood and children using southern epistemologies' (Abebe et al, 2022: 2; see also Kannan et al, 2022). Part of this (self-)critical view is that until now, a large part of research has been characterized by an approach that uses children of the Global South as a source of knowledge without asking what the knowledge generated means for the children themselves (see Ansell, 2019, and Chapter 4). I will discuss this in detail in this chapter. I want to encourage reflection on forms of knowledge production in childhood and children's rights research that benefit children themselves and contribute to recognizing them as equal human beings and to strengthen their social position in society.

I will focus my reflections on the question of what kind of knowledge is required to reach this aim and how it can be generated. It must be knowledge that reveals children's perceptions and perspectives, that is, how they think, feel and deal with everyday experiences. And it must be knowledge in which not only the marginalization, disregard, oppression, exploitation and violence experienced by children become visible, but also their potential to defend themselves against it. In my opinion, such knowledge, sometimes called 'situated knowledges' (Haraway, 1988) or 'liberatory knowledge' (Giri, 2013), can only emerge together with the children concerned. It must be legitimized by them and accessible to them. The generation of such knowledge requires ethnographic methodologies that do not separate the researcher from the researched, but see research as a joint project in which there are horizontal and equal relationships between all participants. And it requires methodologies that do not build on cognitive and linguistic premises usually attributed to adults, but give equal weight to mimetic and emotional skills and ways of communicating. Here, I refer primarily to research approaches that have emerged in Latin American and Indigenous contexts and represent what Argentine semiotician Walter Mignolo (2009) has called 'epistemic disobedience'.

These research approaches have been discussed and practised since the 1970s under the terms *Participatory Action Research (PAR)* and since the 1990s as *Epistemologies of the South, Indigenous Methodologies* or *Horizontal-Dialogical Methodologies*. The core here is not to define certain methods in advance, but to ask ourselves as researchers together with all participants, that is also with children, which methods are appropriate and applicable in a particular context and in what way the cognitive limits of established academic science can be overcome. The choice of methods is itself part of a communication process in which professional researchers and non-academic co-researchers are equally influential and ultimately arrive at decisions together. The research approaches that have emerged under the terms mentioned here have so far rarely taken children into account, but they can also open up new avenues of research with children and on childhoods and children's rights.

This is particularly important in the case of children who are denied basic conditions of a dignified life. While human rights apply to them as they do to all children, they have little opportunity to claim them. As 'children of the Global South' (Diana, 2020) or 'children out of place' (Connolly and Ennew, 1996; Invernizzi et al, 2017), they embody ways of life that are far removed from dominant Western notions of a 'true childhood' and are therefore often even denied having a childhood at all.[1] In order to do justice to these children's life experiences and make them visible, research approaches are needed that are not guided by a predefined pattern of childhood and that contribute to what could be called the decolonization of childhoods (Liebel, 2020; Araneda-Urrutia, 2022). The perspective of decolonization refers primarily to children living in the Southern or postcolonial regions of the world, but it is also relevant for children in other regions of the world who are affected by social inequality and poverty.

I will present different dialogical and action-oriented research approaches, highlight the importance of the research attitude and physicality of those involved in the research and finally discuss pitfalls and possible perspectives in dealing with linguistic diversity and the relationship between rationality and emotions. In the end, I will show why these research approaches are also relevant for emancipatory childhood and children's rights research and how they can be applied in this context.

Dialogical and action-based research approaches

Dialogical and action-based research approaches are seen as a critique of the ideology of scientific universalism. This assumes that only scientific knowledge represents true, valid, representative or objective knowledge and is therefore superior to all other forms of knowledge. The corresponding research defines the researcher as an expert who approaches the people, social conditions or nature to be investigated from the outside and turns them into an object of knowledge. Thus, according to the critique, the reality experienced by people is only expressed in a distorted form. The knowledge contained in it is devalued and rendered invisible. A logic oriented towards an instrumental and mono-cultural rationality is imposed, which turns the produced knowledge into a commercial object. It becomes a commodity in the hands of those who have put knowledge into a scientific form and/ or have the power to use it in their particular interests. In other words, it is an exploitative or 'extractivist' form of knowledge production (see Gaudry, 2011).

In the concept of PAR, which was formulated in the 1960s by the Colombian sociologist Orlando Fals-Borda (1970; 1979; 2009), research, on the other hand, arises from joint action against living conditions that are perceived as unacceptable or, on the other, it serves to empower excluded and oppressed people.[2] Researchers do not limit themselves to participant observation, as in other forms of participatory research, but see themselves as partners acting in solidarity with population groups whose emancipation and liberation are at stake. They see their research as partisan and consciously take the point of view of these population groups. It is obvious that such an attitude is neither easy to win over nor to apply without contradictions, since the life situation of the researchers in the research period does not become identical to that of their co-researchers. However, since research is an integral part of transformative practice, the knowledge gained is not separated from action, but can be used by oppressed and marginalized population groups in their struggles to improve living conditions. In this sense, there is also talk of 'insurgent research' (Gaudry, 2011; Corntassel and Gaudry, 2014; Strega and Brown, 2015).

The theoretical outline of *Epistemologies of the South*, which was introduced by the Portuguese sociologist Boaventura de Sousa Santos (2014; 2018), considers it essential to bring to light the knowledges that have been made invisible in the course of colonization. De Sousa Santos calls this a 'sociology of absences' and strives for an 'ecology of knowledges'. By this he means that 'the logic of the monoculture of scientific knowledge and rigor must be confronted with the identification of other knowledges and criteria of rigor and validity' (De Sousa Santos, 2014: 176). The ecology of knowledges 'aims to create a new kind of relation, a pragmatic relation, between scientific knowledge and other kinds of knowledge' (De Sousa Santos, 2014: 190). According to De Sousa Santos (2018: 43), two basic kinds of knowledge are included: 'knowledges that are born in struggle and knowledges, while not born in struggle, (that) may be useful in the struggle'. Every form of knowledge that participates in the conversation of humanity brings along the notion of 'another possible world' (De Sousa Santos, 2014: 190). According to De Sousa Santos, 'throughout the world, there are not only diverse forms of knowledge of matter, society, life and spirit, but also many and very diverse concepts of what counts as knowledge and the criteria that may be used to validate it' (De Sousa Santos, 2014: 192). This does call for 'a deeper reflection on the difference between science as monopolistic knowledge and science as a part of an ecology of knowledges' (De Sousa Santos, 2014: 193).

However, according to De Sousa Santos, the revalorization of non-scientific forms of knowledge does not mean a total rejection of scientific forms of knowledge. Rather, it is about their 'counter-hegemonic use' (De Sousa Santos, 2014: 207), or 'its pretention to being the only valid kind of knowledge' (De Sousa Santos, 2018: 45). In this sense, the ecology of knowledges 'focuses on the relations among knowledges, on the hierarchies and power emerging among them' (De Sousa Santos, 2014: 207). In the same circumstances, preference shall be given to knowledge 'that guarantees more participation to the social groups involved in the conception, execution, control, and function of the intervention' (De Sousa Santos, 2014: 208). As De Sousa Santos consequently advocates for a 'polyphonic epistemology involving poetry and science' (De Sousa Santos, 2014: 208), new possibilities are also opened to establish relations with and give recognition to children's knowledges and modes of articulation.[3] In this sense, the ecology of knowledges could also be understood as 'a precondition for achieving cognitive justice' (De Sousa Santos, 2014: 212), from which children are no longer excluded.

Indigenous methodologies are understood as research approaches devised and practised by the people directly affected or under their direction. They emerged as a critique of research methods, particularly in anthropology and ethnology. These had regarded Indigenous peoples primarily as a source of knowledge and were conducted according to standards based exclusively on Western assumptions of scientific truth ('truth regime'). On the other hand, Indigenous methodologies are understood as a way for Indigenous individuals and peoples to reappropriate the knowledge embedded in their cultures. In this way, they oppose research practices that are understood as a continuation of colonial subjugation or the coloniality of power and knowledge, and thus have a decolonial perspective.

The concept of Indigenous methodologies can be traced back to, among others, Shawn Wilson (2008), Margaret Kovach (2010; 2015), Linda Tuhiwai Smith (2005; 2012) and Bagele Chilisa (2012; 2020), feminist-oriented social researchers of Indigenous origin from Canada, New Zealand/Aotearoa and Botswana. This has since given rise to a broad movement of researchers in the continents of the South who are themselves of Indigenous origin, and some of whom work in a kind of diaspora in 'Western' universities. These authors do not claim a monopoly on the study of their cultures, but insist that their non-Indigenous allies in academia reflect self-critically on their own privileged status and traditional ways of thinking and researching, question them and adopt a decolonial perspective.

Indigenous methodologies should not only contribute to bringing Indigenous knowledge systems and epistemologies to light, but also to overcome the 'positional superiority' of Western knowledge (Tuhiwai Smith, 2012: 62, with reference to Said, [1978] 2013). Her starting point is the critique that the 'knowledge gained through our colonization has been used ... to colonize us' (Tuhiwai Smith, 2012: 62). This corresponds to what the African writer Ngugi wa Thiong'o (1986) has called the 'colonisation of the mind'. According to Tuhiwai Smith, 'the globalization of knowledge and Western culture constantly reaffirms the West's view of itself as the centre of legitimate knowledge, the arbiter of what counts as knowledge and the source of "civilised" knowledge' (Tuhiwai Smith, 2012: 66). The author therefore stresses:

> For Indigenous peoples universities are regarded as rather elite institutions, which reproduce themselves through various systems of privilege. Even those universities, which are state-funded are considered major bastions of Western elitism. It is not surprising, then, that many Indigenous students find little space for Indigenous perspectives in most academic disciplines and most research approaches. (Tuhiwai Smith, 2012: 132)

Margaret Kovach highlights the emancipatory and decolonizing intention of Indigenous methodologies in the following words: 'Indigenous researchers make research political simply by being who we are' (Kovach, 2015: 46). She locates the beginning of research based on Indigenous methodologies in the 1990s. At this time, Indigenous knowledge systems began to be considered as part of the discourse of qualitative research that saw itself as transformative. 'As a result of decolonization efforts exposing extractive research practices involving indigenous peoples, there was a focus on the recognition and protection of indigenous knowledges' (Kovach, 2015: 48). In Indigenous knowledge systems, Kovach sees the 'heartbeat' of Indigenous methodologies. It is not possible to practice Indigenous methodologies without understanding Indigenous knowledge systems from the ground up.

> In applying Indigenous methodologies, researchers are putting force an identity standpoint (whether they desire or not) and there is an expectation for them to engage in anti-colonial work. ... There must be a deep, abiding respect for Indigenous knowledge systems and Indigenous experience. This often requires unpacking one's

understanding of what respect means in this context. (Kovach, 2015: 57)

Kovach believes that 'non-Indigenous allies' have a responsibility to accommodate Indigenous methodologies in research practice, especially in universities, and to enable researchers of Indigenous origin to apply their own research criteria and standards and to gain control over the use of the results. 'Research is a tool that has become so entangled with haughty theories of what is "truth" that it's easy to forget that research is simply "about learning and so is a way of finding out things"' (Kovach, 2015: 59, referring to Hampton, 1995: 48). Shawn Wilson emphasizes the difference between the prevailing academic research paradigms and the Indigenous research paradigm in the following way:

> The major difference between those dominant paradigms and an Indigenous paradigm is that those dominant paradigms are built on the fundamental belief that knowledge is an individual entity: the researcher is an individual in search of knowledge, knowledge is something that is gained and therefore knowledge may be owned by an individual. An Indigenous paradigm comes from the fundamental belief that knowledge is relational. Knowledge is shared with all of creation. It is not just interpersonal relationships, or just with the research subjects I may be working with, but it is a relationship with all of creation. It is with the cosmos; it is with the animals, with plants, with the earth that we share this knowledge. It goes beyond the individual's knowledge to the concept of relational knowledge. ... You are answerable to all your relations when you are doing research. (Wilson, 2008: 56)

Bagele Chilisa highlights the need for a decolonial perspective and looks at the Indigenous research paradigm 'as a framework of belief systems that emanate from the lived experiences, values, and histories of those belittled and marginalized by Euro-Western research paradigms' (Chilisa, 2020: 23).[4] The Indigenous research paradigm does not only focus on individuals, but also on the 'communal forms of living'. It creates a space 'for inquiries based on relational realities and forms of knowing that are predominant among the non-Western Other/s still being colonized' (Chilisa, 2020: 2). For Indigenous methodologies, narrative methods are important but, according to Chilisa, they go beyond standard qualitative research approaches by 'employing Indigenous languages, metaphors, spirituality, and relations with the cosmos, symbolism, and art as in dance, song, poetry, and artifacts. Research questions asked are guided by Indigenous worldviews' (Chilisa, 2020: 21). Elsewhere, she describes what she understands as Indigenous knowledge in the following terms: 'Indigenous knowledge is embodied in languages, legends, folktales, stories, and cultural experiences of the formerly colonized and historically oppressed; it is symbolized in cultural artifacts such as sculpture, weaving, and painting and embodied in music, dance, rituals, and ceremonies such as weddings and worshipping' (Chilisa, 2020: 92).

Chilisa also refers to Indigenous methodologies as 'third-space methodologies' with reference to Homi Bhabha's (1994) concept of 'the space in-between'. 'Thus, in the third space, indigenousness is interrogated to include the voices of those disadvantaged on the basis of gender, race, ethnicity, ableness, health, socioeconomic status, sexual orientation, age, and so on' (Chilisa, 2020: 32). With this enumeration, Chilisa gives an indication that 'Indigenous' is not understood, at least by her, in an essentialist way as an ethnic category, but tends to include all people who are discriminated against, disregarded, marginalized and socially disadvantaged, or, in other words, who 'have no place' in a social system or world order based on domination and social inequality.[5]

Researchers who advocate and apply *dialogic and horizontal methodologies* in their research share similar principles with representatives of Indigenous methodologies. However, they are rarely of Indigenous origin and can be understood, in a sense, as the 'non-Indigenous allies' of Indigenous researchers. Like the latter, they have a decolonial perspective, but their critique of the Western-influenced system of academic science is not based on ethnic classifications. Instead they reject any form of authoritarian monopoly claim to scientific truth in a radically democratic way. They see such claim as rooted primarily in the dominance of White masculinity and the instrumental reason it embodies. They see horizontal methodologies as closely linked to political activism for a socially just society that strives for social equality with respect for cultural diversity and corresponding ways of life. The differences between the claim to academic superiority and the emancipatory aims of research 'do not always arise from a gap between Western academic culture and the radical otherness of the researcher/ indigenous person, but rather from the gap between the academic and the activist' (Rappaport and Ramos Pacho, 2005: 61–62). In this they are similar to PAR.

Research based on horizontal methodologies cannot avoid questioning the institutionalized hierarchies of the academic enterprise. These make it difficult to conduct research that is not based on hierarchical relationships between researchers and researched. Horizontal methodologies are based on the principle of overcoming this separation and of creating communities in which all participants equally shape and control the research process (see Corona and Kaltmeier, 2012a; 2012b; Cornejo and Rufer, 2020; Corona Berkin, 2020a; 2020b). In this context, it would be of particular importance to maintain equitable relations with population groups that are particularly affected by the consequences of colonization and the current postcolonial constellation. Olaf Kaltmeier, a German historian of Latin American history, points out:

> Horizontal methodologies emerge at this juncture of decolonization and democratization, based on dialogue with groups of subaltern actors who, despite racism, discrimination and lack of recognition, are bearers of multiple knowledges. Several researches working with horizontal methodologies enter into dialogue with indigenous ... or Afro-American peoples promoting 'a critical and decolonial collaborative narrative methodology' (Cortés-Gonzales, Leite-Méndez & Rivas-Flores, 2020: 96). At the intersections between the Global South and the Global North, horizontal methodologies have also been applied in the *multi-sited ethnography* of migration processes. (Kaltmeier, 2020: 95; emphasis in original)

In the dialogically designed research process, these researchers do not necessarily see a new 'we' emerging between researchers and co-researchers, but new social ties of a 'with'. This 'with' requires a self-critical reflection by academic researchers on their own privileges and their own dominance in the research process. Horizontal relations in this process cannot be established by goodwill alone, but also require structural changes in the academic system. Moreover, it must be kept in mind that in the relationships between researchers and co-researchers, affections are always at stake.

> Beyond this horizontal knowledge production, research implies an affective and social act. It establishes a corridor inhabited by researchers and co-researchers that forms a bridge between subaltern and marginalized communities, as well as instances within the academic field that still enjoy a high generalized social reputation. On the eve of the blocking of many communication channels and public spaces, it is a challenge for researchers to create platforms for the exchange and dissemination of knowledge produced in dialogue. This implies finding formats beyond the academic monograph and peer-reviewed article. (Kaltmeier, 2020: 107–108)

It also seems important to ask what attitude horizontal relations have in the research process.

Research attitudes and corporeality

Having said this, Mexican social researcher David Bak Geler (2020), for example, distinguishes between 'a conception of tolerant horizontality', which he associates with the ideology of liberalism, and an 'agonistic horizontality', which he locates in the history of republicanism. 'Unlike tolerant horizontality, the agonistic variety does not start from the supreme rule of respecting the conceptions of others, but is open to the criticism and debate of such principles and doctrines' (Bak Geler, 2020: 142). In the sense of the latter conception, he always understands horizontality as provisional or improvised, that is, open to self-critical reflection and change.

> Improvising horizontality would insist on the radical impossibility of finding anything but provisional solutions to political conflicts or disagreements. It would also insist that the accumulation and fragmentary visibility of examples, where conflict has been provisionally resolved, establishes precedents and exemplary figures of the political: that is, reminders, inspirations or models that the work of practical improvisation need not always start from nothing. (Bak Geler, 2020: 142–143)

In the debate on horizontal and Indigenous methodologies, the connection between knowledge production and the body is also significant. Researchers with a tendency to feminism, in particular, point out that the recognition of knowledge as scientific knowledge depends to a large extent on whether it originates from and is represented by White men.

> Scientific authority is almost immediately associated with White, male, heterosexual bodies, which must be recognized as bodies. This does not imply that 'feminized', 'non-heterosexual' and 'disadvantaged racialized' bodies are totally oppressed by the logics of science: there is heterogeneity among people who produce science, even official science, just as there is heterogeneity in colonial bodies. (Nogueira Beltrão, 2020: 246)

According to this author, some bodies are recognized as producers of science, while others are not. There is also a corresponding hierarchy within universities and in the academic writing market.

> It is enough to check the curricula of universities considered as recognized to corroborate that most of the knowledge identified as indispensable and classical refers to books and theories written by men, White and heterosexual ... and preferably European. Assuming a 'body-to-body' knowledge could be a way of 'provincializing' (Chakrabarty, 2009) knowledge and understanding that any and all science, made by bodies, has limited scope, and could not solve all the world's problems. (Nogueira Beltrão, 2020: 246–247)

Nigerian sociologist of Yoruba origin, Oyèrónké Oyěwùmí (1997; 2016) also stresses that the recognition of knowledge is largely dependent on the visual perception of bodies. She therefore speaks of a 'bio-logic' in which the body is essentialized in binary categories of gender and race, which privileges the knowledge of White men over that of Black women.

Argentinean social scientists Rosana Rodríguez and Sofía da Costa (2019) consider that the hierarchy of forms of knowledge represents an unequal social order that, in the name of neutrality, objectivity and universality, excludes multiple forms of knowledge, especially the knowledge of women of the Global South. Their interest is to promote the debate on the epistemic decolonial turn in its multiple aspects. They advocate research from a feminist perspective from the South, the production of situated knowledges, the relationship between research and political action, and the sensitive selection of methods and techniques, and ethical engagement in research. This requires a methodological strategy that transcends the separation of knower and researched, as well as the separation of mind/thought and body or rationality and emotion. Rodriguez and da Costa call the methodology they seek 'bodily biographies' or 'corpo-biographies': 'The corpo-biographies are senti-corpo-perspective reconstructions of the life trajectories and bodily itineraries of women based on their lived bodily experiences. They are conceptual re-elaborations of the experience of corporeality, which implies the subjectivity and the vital trajectory of the lived experience of the body' (Rodríguez and da Costa, 2019: 14).

The authors define their methodological proposal as 'research-action-creation', which they understand as a creative activity 'that comes from social, cultural and subjective experience and allows us to know aspects of lived and perceived reality, through sensations, emotions and feelings. Knowing by knowing oneself' (Rodríguez and da Costa, 2019: 15). It is a methodological strategy that is nourished by the desires of the subjects, 'it includes sensitive criteria that involve the experience of the body, combining rational intelligence with perception, emotion, intuition and imagination' (Rodríguez and da Costa, 2019: 16). When the authors speak of intuition they refer to an action that engages the interior, the subjectivity, which is installed in the 'mythical capacity' of the subjects, 'which is woven with memory, activating all the layers of the body' (Rodríguez and da Costa, 2019: 16). According to them, their proposal coincides with what is understood by 'PAR' and especially by 'feminist activist research' (FAR).

With their proposal, Rodríguez and da Costa explicitly oppose the practice of 'hegemonic academic feminists who define other women as marginal, poor, illiterate, victims, without recognising their valuable contributions to scientific productions' (Rodríguez and da Costa, 2019: 25). According to them, these 'logics of appropriation are sustained by strategies of depoliticisation and decontextualisation, of a profoundly racist matrix, whose purpose is to strengthen the hierarchization of knowledge and the bodies that produce it' (Rodríguez and da Costa, 2019: 25). In this way, they see a geopolitics of control and domination of knowledge, through the unequal number of citations of scholars of the Global South, which erases the right to authorship of its true producers.

All the earlier-mentioned authors see a Eurocentric and colonial construction in the claim to scientific authority, as both the term science and the emergence of universities as we know them today have their origins in colonizing countries (see, from an autobiographical perspective, Perrin, 2020).

Reactionary and emancipatory translations

'Cognitive injustice' (De Sousa Santos, 2010) or the 'coloniality of knowledge' (Lander, 2000; Quijano, 2008) is also expressed in the fact that only knowledge formulated in one of the dominant written languages of today's world, especially English, is recognized and disseminated as scientific knowledge.[6] This renders invisible and devalues a huge body of knowledge articulated in 'local' or 'Indigenous' languages and oral narratives. Margaret Kovach points to the 'fundamental barrier' this creates between Indigenous and Western knowledge systems and epistemologies:

> The stronghold of language, written, and worldview in generating 'truth' creates difficulties for Indigenous people, whose traditional philosophies are held deep within constructs that are neither written, nor consistent with the patterns of dominant language. Most Indigenous languages are verb-based and tell us of the world in motion, interacting with humans and nature. This is in contrast to the noun-based nature of the English language, which accentuates an outcome orientation to the world. Language is a central system for how cultures code, create and transmit meaning. Cultural values remain alive and are reflective of a worldview found in their native language. Values that honour relationships are important for cultures that value the journey as much as the destination. Written language adds additional complexity in transmitting Indigenous ways of knowing, given that most Indigenous cultures are oral. (Kovach, 2015: 52–53)

Even when knowledge generated in Indigenous cultures and articulated in their languages is taken up and translated into a written language, its meaning changes. This is also true when it is presented in a narrative style ('storytelling').[7] Writing brings out the fact that Indigenous forms of knowledge are 'fluid, non-linear and relational' (Kovach, 2015: 53) and always have a close relationship with the person or persons who express them. Moreover, the 'mother tongue' in a colonial or postcolonial situation is always the language of 'the others', 'the language of the host' (Rufer, 2020: 282; see also De la Peza, 2017). Mario Rufer illustrates the dilemma this poses using the example of the Indigenous peoples of Mexico. According to him, the imposition of the colonial language Spanish onto the Indigenous peoples without recognizing their cultures and associated languages, is not discussed (critically).

> The logic of the host implies a risk: that one's own territory will be modified. A risk that the multicultural state is not willing to take. Hence, the hospitality it offers is on its own terms of power and management (of identities, languages, territories), concealing the fact that the will it receives is not that of the guest who opens up, but that of the sovereign who concedes. (Rufer, 2020: 283)

The devaluation and marginalization of Indigenous languages and the knowledge they contain is further exacerbated by their exclusion from scientific knowledge. Knowledge can be expressed and communicated in all languages of the world and in all genres of text. But only knowledge that is recognized by academic institutions and disseminated in journals and books is considered scientific knowledge. This knowledge 'is mainly based on traditional literacy skills. Those who do not master literacy are not considered scientists, even if they teach/practise/learn theories and methods, and reflect on it' (Nogueira Beltrão, 2020: 246). It is argued that the writing system is the most complex form of knowledge production. With it, colonial languages have established themselves as world languages, while Indigenous languages and modes of communication are degraded to local phenomena that are special but never universal. 'Today, an imposed hierarchy of languages continues to inform in whose language the discipline of research is conducted and debated and its findings disseminated' (Chilisa, 2020: 205). Even when the social sciences pursue an intercultural approach, they remain trapped in this system.

> It is urgent to recognize the people involved in the production of knowledge, and not just to mention the books that are authorized as scientific by universities. This is a first step towards provincializing the knowledge produced and legitimized as superior by centres that represent and are represented by mostly White and/or heterosexual and/or male bodies. It would also make explicit that much of the knowledge that becomes books is not exclusive to writing, and that it was apprehended, elaborated, reflected upon, theorized, tested and dialogued in other languages, by many bodies, racialized in advantage or disadvantage. The above would allow us to demonstrate that both

scientific historiography and the production of new intellectuals who are today extremely valued and considered indispensable for the production of knowledge are the result of processes of epistemic racism/sexism. (Nogueira Beltrão, 2020: 248)

To recover knowledge excluded and devalued by the coloniality of power, and to give it an influence beyond the narrow local context, Boaventura de Sousa Santos proposes an 'intercultural translation from different perspectives' (De Sousa Santos, 2014: 213; see also De Sousa Santos, 2018: 32–34). This task, however, is not easy, as it is complicated by the continued dominance of colonial languages and the compulsion to put everything in writing. The question and possibilities of translation bear more difficulties for a dominated culture than for a dominant culture. 'Authors in a dominated culture who dream of reaching a larger audience will tend to write while having in mind their translation into a hegemonic language, and this will require some degree of compliance with stereotypes' (De Sousa Santos, 2014: 230).

This coercion to adapt has been taken up in the concepts of multiculturalism that have emerged since the 1990s in the context of neoliberal policies. Therefore, De Sousa Santos speaks of 'reactionary multiculturalism' (De Sousa Santos, 2014: 231). It must be countered by an 'emancipatory interculturality', that aims to focus not only on hegemonic forms of knowledge and interpretations of the world and strives for equality with the recognition of difference. 'Emancipatory interculturality presupposes recognition of a plurality of knowledges and distinct conceptions of the world and human dignity' (De Sousa Santos, 2014: 200). The Ecuadorian educationalist Catherine Walsh (2005; 2007; 2009; 2012; 2013; 2018) speaks in a similar vein of 'critical interculturality', which she distinguishes from 'functional interculturality'. Even more clearly than De Sousa Santos, she attributes to critical interculturality a transformative task aimed at decolonization. This kind of interculturality

signifies more than an interrelation or dialogue among cultures. More critically, it points toward the building of radically different societies, of an 'other' social ordering, and of structural economic, social, political and cultural transformations. ... Interculturality, from this perspective, is not an existing condition or a done deal. It is a process and project in continuous insurgence, movement, and construction, a conscious action, a radical activity, and praxis-based tool of affirmation, correlation, and transformation. (Walsh, 2018: 57 and 59)

Future research with children and for children's rights will need to be guided by these considerations if it is to understand children's realities as lived realities and their knowledge as situated and liberatory knowledge.

Sensing-thinking

In order to produce situated or liberatory knowledge, the divisions between the apparently objective and the subjective, rationality and sense, body and soul, thinking and feeling and similar opposites, which are deeply rooted in the universalist understanding of science, must be questioned without, however, ignoring the binary distinctions that are made in life and in the dominant languages. In Latin American Spanish, a term has come to express this claim well: the verb *sentipensar* and the noun *sentipensamiento*, an integral combination of being sensitive and thinking.

The term, or what it presumes to express, has a long history in different parts of the world. One might think, for instance, of the cognitive theories of emotion formulated by the psychologist Magda Arnold (1960) in the 1960s and the philosopher Martha Nussbaum (2001) four decades later. These are about how cognitive processes are influenced by emotions. The connection between emotions and thinking has been discussed in the Western tradition since Greek antiquity, especially by Aristotle. Here, however, I refer mainly to the reflections of the Colombian anthropologist Arturo Escobar (2014). The author takes up this concept proposed by the Colombian sociologist Orlando Fals Borda (1970; 1979; 2009) already in the 1970s, to underline that the 'lived life' of people cannot be conceived with the category of rationality on which modern Western science is based, but that the senses, the 'heart', also play an important role. By his own admission, Fals Borda had encountered the word *sentipensante* with a peasant on the Caribbean coast of Colombia.

In the book *Libro de los abrazos* (Book of Embraces) by Uruguayan writer Eduardo Galeano, published in English with the title *Celebration of the Marriage of Reason and Heart*, we find the following sentence:

> Why does one write, if not to put one's pieces together? From the moment we enter school or church, education chops us into pieces: it teaches us to divorce soul from body and mind from heart. The fishermen of the Colombian coast must be learned doctors of ethics and morality, for they invented the word *sentipensante*, feeling-thinking, to define language that speaks the truth. (Galeano, 1991: 121)

Patricio Guerrero Arias (2010; 2016) introduced the term *corazonar* (synthesis of heart and reasoning) with a similar meaning. According to this author, *corazonar* or *corazonamiento* represents 'the affective, epistemic and ethical-political potential of the insurgent wisdoms of all the diverse peoples that inhabit the continent' (Guerrero Arias, 2010: 17). De Sousa Santos (2018: 99–102) takes up this term in his theoretical outline of 'Epistemologies of the South' and translates it as 'warming up the reason'.[8]

The verb *sentipensar*, as Escobar (2014) understands it, refers not only to feelings, but to all bodily emotions such as love, affection, concern or intuitions.[9] He understands *sentipensar* as a term that comes from below, from the community, and is directed against those who believe to be superior and claim power over others. In this sense, it is a 'subaltern' way of making oneself felt. We find it in the narratives of various non-modern worlds, such as Indigenous peoples, Afro-descendants or, in a broader sense, in people and populations subjugated and excluded by power. According to Escobar, the meaning of *sentipensamiento* is always situational. It is also present in social movements that claim their rights within their territory and the disposition of it. Space or territory in this sense includes not only the earth and its ecosystems, but also the processes of 'territorialization' that generate identities and appropriations. Escobar conceives of territory as a 'life project' in which the socio-political project, autonomy and future perspectives combine.

The concept of sensing-thinking is opposed to the Western model of rationality, in which concepts such as economy, body, mind, individual, culture and nature are separated from each other, with the now widely observed consequence of ecological and socio-political crises and catastrophes. The ways of perceiving and thinking of Indigenous and Black peoples, on the other hand, are relational. From their perspective, the human is not separate from the non-human, nor is culture separate from nature, nor is the mind separate from the body. In this perspective, an object, person or situation cannot be understood isolated from its context, as it does not exist in itself. Similar concepts can be found in the ontologies and ethics of *Ubuntu* in southern Africa, *Sumak Kawsay* or *Buen Vivir/ Vivir Bien* of Indigenous peoples in the Andes, and *mino-bimaadiziwin* of First Nations in Canada (see Mawere and van Stam, 2016; Pérez, 2016; Gruner, 2018: 269–274). Similar ideas have been taken up in feminist thought, according to which no individual can exist on his or her own, all depend on each other in mutual care. However, while the feminist-inspired ethic of care emphasizes compassionate care for others who are perceived as vulnerable (particularly infants), the concept of *sentipensar* emphasizes the aspect of ownership and liberation from imposed and one-sided dependencies. The aim is an intersubjective encounter of equal weight and value between people with different personal characteristics who understand themselves as connected to and responsible for each other.

I return here to the concept of sensing-thinking because it allows us to take seriously children's specific modes of existence and subjectivities and to recognize them as differently equal. In the dominating Western model of thinking or reasoning, which makes the rationality of emotion and the body appear separate, children's specific abilities are denied or devalued as irrational and subordinated to the supposedly more developed, matured and perfected abilities of adults. The concept of *sentipensar*, on the other hand, is open to recognition of the diversity of capacities children have. It allows them to be recognized and made visible at all. This applies especially to children who are excluded and discriminated against in several and many ways.

Conclusion

The research approaches, methodologies and ethical concepts presented here have hardly been taken up in childhood and children's rights studies so far. Although they repeatedly emphasize the necessity of not only using children as objects of research or as sources of information, but also of involving them as partners or actors in the research process, this is rarely done with the intention of empowering children as actors and supporting them in their daily lives (see Budde and Markowska-Manista, 2020). Also, participatory research with children usually produces knowledge for those persons or institutions that have access to children – with whatever intentions. Thus, in the sense presented earlier, these are 'extractivist' varieties of research that do not question the subordinate or colonized status of children and childhoods.

Basically, childhood and children's rights studies must be reconceptualized by freeing themselves from their academic corset and opening themselves to a knowledge production that includes all who can contribute to this production. The process of gaining knowledge must be oriented to questions, modes of perception and modes of articulation that are interesting and useful for all research participants. Thus, it is not just a matter of professional adult researchers trying to do research 'from the perspective of children', as was already discussed in the late 1990s (James and Prout, 1997; Honig et al, 1999). Instead, scientific research must be transformed into research processes that create equal opportunities for all participants, including children, to engage with their own questions, ways of knowing and ways of expressing themselves (for current examples see Afroze, 2022; Amigó et al, 2022; Jirata, 2022). This also includes the perspective of recognizing children themselves as independent researchers and, if necessary, advising and supporting them in their research (see, for instance, Alderson, 2008; Kellett, 2005; Mason and Watson, 2014).

The research methodologies presented here enable taking the specific modes of existence and subjectivities of children seriously and to recognize children as different but equal. Under the dominance of the Western model of thinking, which makes rationality appear separate from emotion and body, the specific abilities of children are denied or devalued as irrational and subordinated to the supposedly more developed, matured and perfected abilities of adults. In contrast, the methodological concepts of dialogic and action-oriented research, namely the concept of *sentipensar/sensing-thinking*, are open to recognizing the diversity of abilities found in children. They can help to make visible and better understand the lived realities of children, especially those children who are marginalized and discriminated against in many ways. This is indispensable for a children's rights practice of solidarity with these children that strives for social justice and a life in dignity.

Epilogue: Children's rights as counter-rights

With this book, we hope to have provided numerous reasons to rethink the prevailing discourse and practice of children's rights. As such, we believe it is indispensable to transform the hitherto dominant concepts of (state) law and (subjective) rights. In the international human rights system, the principle of formal equality of legal subjects, which has repeatedly led to 'paradoxes' (Brown, 2002) in the enjoyment of rights, has been expanded by the introduction of specific rights (women's rights, children's rights, rights of persons with disabilities, rights of Indigenous peoples, and others) in the sense of powerless and disadvantaged groups of people. But it cannot stop there.

With regard to children's rights, we believe that an essential element of this transformation is to connect these rights with children's concrete experiences. This mediation is envisioned in the concept of *Living Rights* (Hanson and Nieuwenhuys, 2013; 2020). However, this concept is limited to 'translating' the legal rights, that is, those authorized by the state, into children's everyday lives and making visible the contradictions and conflicts of interest that arise. Instead, children, like other subaltern groups of people, would have to be enabled to formulate their own rights and to facilitate their use to shape the reality that surrounds them, without having to rely on or trust state authority ('state power').

Where this is done, rights are not formulated in an abstract way as 'general rights' that apply and are meaningful to all children in the world in the same way. In fact, they refer to specific life situations and indicate what needs to change in these distinct contexts in order to achieve a safe, dignified and satisfying life. Similarly, they are formulated in a language that does not require expert knowledge or legal experts to understand these rights. In existing legal language, these are understood as 'moral rights'. In order for them to be understood as being more than moral admonitions that ultimately have no consequences, they rely on processes of self-empowerment that emerge from society and the collective action of young people. Since they have to deal with overcoming unequal distribution of power, they only have a chance if they see themselves as a 'counter-hegemonic democratic project' (Buckel, 2021: 270) or as 'social and political counter-rights' (Menke, 2018) that not only have their 'own' freedom in mind, but want to achieve a different society and world order. This would evoke a society and 'globalization from below' (Brecher et al, 2000; De Sousa Santos and Rodriguez-Garavito, 2005; Della Porta et al, 2006) in which freedom and equality are essentially defined as expressions of the communal existence of people and institutions, coined by Balibar (2014) as 'equaliberty'.

Counter-rights in the sense we understand them do not distance themselves from the idea of subjective rights, as Christoph Menke (2018) suggests, but rather expand, modify and specify them. They are not derived from human nature and are not fixed only to individual human beings, but arise in connection with other human beings living together. Counter-rights consider the 'sociality of human subjectivity' (Loick, 2017: 305). As such, they are social as well as political rights that are dependent on a society in which people do not compete with each other and prioritize what is their own. Instead, the focus is put on what is common for all and what is done for each other as characteristics of intersubjective relations. Such a society and world order require a minimum of social and political equality and mutual recognition of individuals with their own life histories and everyone's particular characteristics and thoughts. Equality and diversity are not opposites in this society and world order, but are mutually dependent.

Understood in this sense rights do not require state authority to guarantee and enforce them with power, but are based on the communal self-government of people in the places where they live. They embody a new 'concept of right(s) that overcomes etatistic reductionism' (Fischer–Lescano, 2018: 383) and abandons the 'ideology of the free person that underlies conventional subjective right' (Fischer–Lescano, 2018: 385). These rights are necessarily counter-rights, since such self-government must first be enforced against existing unequal power and, if necessary, state violence. They require not only a fundamental democratization of decision-making and rights enforcement, but a democratization of the national and international legal systems themselves (Buckel, 2021: 275–276). This poses a particular challenge with regard to children, as they have so far been systematically excluded from law-making and jurisdiction.

Likewise, these rights must further be conceived as counter-rights, because people who are socially and politically marginalized, oppressed and disadvantaged are particularly dependent on them. This is true both within nation-state territories and in the relationship between the Global North and Global South ('coloniality'). In the case of children, the unequal power is embodied by 'adults' who presume to rule over the 'not-yet-adults', as they see fit ('adultism'). However, children's rights as counter-rights are not directed against adults as persons or generations, but against dominant social habits, rules, laws and structures that subordinate children to adults and that extend and prolong children's dependence on care and protection beyond what is anthropologically required. In order to make them a reality, young people are dependent on joining forces with other young people and becoming a countervailing force in the places where they live and, where possible, beyond them. In doing so, their subordinate and relatively powerless position makes them dependent on adults in solidarity and offers a minimum of opportunities to take their lives into their own hands in collective action.

Children's rights understood in this sense arise and have their best chance of realization in the places where children live. Nevertheless, they are not necessarily limited to the local level. They gain in importance and power when young people can network beyond their localities and express their common interests. As rights that emphasize what young people have in common, they are more than subjective rights in the individual sense. They are *inter-subjective* or *trans-subjective* rights that emerge from young people's communication and awareness in social spaces determined by themselves and claim validity beyond these spaces. Such processes can be observed wherever children come together in their own movements and organizations to remind adults and, in particular, those with political responsibility of their obligations to young and future generations, as is expressed today, for example, in the climate justice movements Fridays for Future or The Last Generation and, particularly in the Global South, in social movements of working and Indigenous children. Such aspirations can be seen wherever children from subaltern and Indigenous sectors gather to resist the silence imposed on them, their stigmatization and social contempt as 'poor', 'underdeveloped', 'retarded', 'naughty' or 'minor'. In this way, young people reaffirm themselves as collective subjects of rights against every form of social injustice, racism, sexism and adultism at once.

Notes

Introduction

[1] Short self-designation of the working children (*niños, niñas y adolescentes trabajadores*) in Latin America organized in movements of their own (see https://molacnats.com/).

Chapter 1

[1] Boaventura de Sousa Santos is accused by several women of having pressured them to perform sexual acts, taking advantage of his privileged status as a prominent university professor (see https://en.wikipedia.org/wiki/Boaventura_de_Sousa_Santos). Like my co-authors, I strongly criticize this inexcusable sexist behaviour, but I believe that it does not render his writings worthless. On the issue of sexual harassment in academia, see Pritchard and Edwards (2023).

[2] 'Eugenic theories served as a pretext for racist and supremacist positions, as was the case with Nazism in Germany, and identified peoples and social groups as inferior, weak or backward who should not reproduce or who deserved to die, as well as trying to prevent the miscegenation of races they considered inferior' (Valenzuela Arce, 2020: 41).

[3] Confronted with the fact that many of the affected children lost their lives, Pope Francis recently had to admit that it was genocide (www.cbc.ca/news/indigenous/pope-fran cis-residential-schools-genocide-1.6537203). On the American Indian relocation and resistance see Jacobs (2021).

Chapter 2

[1] Today this idea is mainly connected to the idea of children's 'citizenship' which goes beyond singular and temporal projects of child participation (see, for example, Invernizzi and Williams, 2008; Cordero Arce, 2015a).

[2] Relevant descriptions are, among others: Veerman (1992); Detrick (1992); Verhellen (1994); van Bueren (1995); Freeman and Veerman (1997); Alston and Tobin (2005); Dillon (2010); Invernizzi and Williams (2016); Freeman (2020).

[3] Philosopher Hans Joas (2015: 46 and 61–62) recalls that slavery is not a pre-modern relic, but an integral part of colonial rule until after the Second World War. Liberal fathers of human rights, such as John Locke, also invested in slave trading companies and made themselves rich with them (see also Losurdo, 2014).

[4] This process, described by Karl Marx in his main work *Capital* (1869: vol 1, chapter 26) as 'primitive accumulation', was the beginning of capitalistic production. It is now nearly omnipresent in the Global South, where multinational corporations and large landowners are forcing small farmers to leave their ancestral lands to grow monocultures (for example, soya or oil palms) for export, with state approval. This process, known as 'land grabbing', is often accompanied by the transformation of community property into private property and is driven by free trade agreements.

[5] The quite different motives and justifications in the history of compulsory education in different countries cannot be dealt with here.

[6] Submission from Manchester's Factory Children Committee sent to the House of Commons in 1836 (https://spartacus-educational.com/IRmanchester.htm).

[7] Further examples can be found in the internet archive of the Children's History Society (www.histchild.org).

8   In his epochal study on the history of children's rights, Philip Veerman (1992) described this as a previously neglected task of children's rights research more than 30 years ago. In it, he referred to an article in a paediatric journal in which, as early as the beginning of the 20th century, children's rights were called to be examined from the children's perspective (Barnes, 1900).

9   Already in 1892, the US American feminist Kate Douglas Wiggin ([1892] 1971) fought for respect for the child as an autonomous individual.

10   Korczak together with the children and adult collaborators of the orphanage he directed, was murdered in the Treblinka II Extermination Camp by the Nazis.

11   In the biography on Korczak, *The King of Children*, Betty Jean Lifton (1989) depicts all rights Korczak formulated in his works.

12   Korczak referred to the 'Declaration on the Rights of the Child' adopted 1924 by the League of Nations in Geneva.

13   On this see Adams et al (1971); Gottlieb (1973); Gross and Gross (1977); Boulding (1979); Cohen (1980); Hawes (1991); Veerman (1992).

14   This applies only to a limited extent to Farson, who, as is expressed in the title of his book, has at least partially understood children's rights as natural rights or birthrights.

15   Referring to the 1980s, Cantwell (2011) mentions also the creation of Working Groups for Children within Amnesty International national sections.

16   The following presentation refers mainly to Latin America. The descriptions are based, if sources are not indicated, on my own observations and conversations with children and children's rights activists between October 2019 and March 2020.

17   This was manifested mainly in activities of so-called non-governmental organizations which had come together internationally in the 1980s specifically to influence the elaboration of the CRC.

18   The right to work under dignified conditions, as demanded by the working children's movements, is similar to ideas expressed in the Moscow Declaration on the Rights of the Child and the Children's Liberation Movement, without explicitly referring to these lines of tradition (see Liebel, 2013; 2016).

19   In this respect, Galvis Ortiz looks to the meaningfulness of toddlers' body language and reminds of the French philosopher Jean-Jacques Rousseau, who had declared the latter to be the 'universal language' in his main work *Emile, or on Education* ([1762] 1979).

20   In the CRC, however, children are denied some rights that are granted to 'all people' in international covenants on human rights, for example, the right to work or to organize in trade unions.

21   The concept of democratic states is based on the idea that 'civil society' (generally limited to adults with voting rights) also participates in state decisions.

22   For these distinctions in the legal-philosophical discussion about children's rights, in which the so-called *will theory* and the so-called *interest theory* face each other, see Liebel (2018b).

23   If 'welfare rights' were understood as children's rights it would be more suitable to speak of *responsibility rights* or *rights for recognition*.

24   Therefore, the children's rights activist Richard Farson (1974) demanded not to protect the children but their rights.

Chapter 3

1   The question of the history of the origin of children's rights is still dominated by an approach based on the history of ideas (for example, Veerman, 1992), while in human rights research the emergence of these rights is now mainly seen as a result of the emancipation struggles of disadvantaged population groups subject to power (for example, Mutua, 2002; Stammers, 2009). In a broader sense, this also applies to the

various critical approaches to international law (for an overview see Altwicker and Diggelmann, 2014).

2   Matías Cordero Arce (2018) localizes his research on children's rights as 'legal studies' within the interdisciplinary field of childhood studies. Elsewhere, Cordero Arce (2015a) points out that jurisprudence in the sense of the interpretation of legal documents, the sociology of law and political theories of law are often mixed up, and therefore speaks of 'disciplined interdisciplinary'. Brian Gran (2021) drafts a 'sociology of children's rights'. On the debates within French sociology, see Poretti (2018).

3   Hanson (2012) distinguishes four schools of thought, which he assigns the terms 'paternalism', 'welfare', 'emancipation' and 'liberation'. In a review article on the discussion in Spanish (Bácares Jara, 2020), three tendencies are distinguished with regard to Latin America. First, a tendency that refuses to grant children their own rights ('*negacionista*'); second, an 'official' tendency that limits itself to a dogmatic application of the CRC and understands it essentially as state or substitutional action ('*oficialista*'); and, third, a counter-mainstream tendency that emphasizes children's agency and participation in claiming their rights ('*contraoficialista*').

4   According to Cordero Arce (2015b), the emancipatory goal of children's rights studies is based on the assumption that children are an 'oppressed minority', just as feminist-oriented jurisprudence conceives of women as an oppressed social group. We prefer to say that children, like women, belong to the subaltern classes, albeit mediated and influenced by their position in the economically determined class and power structures.

5   See also the reflections of Nelson Maldonado-Torres (2016; 2017). Following Frantz Fanon ([1952] 2008; [1966] 2004) and Aimé Césaire ([1950] 2000) he points out that the claim to universality of human rights is based on an understanding of humanity that creates 'zones of sub-humanity' and degrades the colonized to mere addressees of a civilizing mission. Human rights themselves must therefore be decolonized. Similarly, Boaventura de Sousa Santos (2010: 83 and 87) advocates for 'an intercultural conception of human rights … as a form of subaltern and insurgent cosmopolitanism'.

6   Magistris (2012; 2016) speaks of the 'magnetism of rights' to critically point out the supposed self-efficacy of children's rights solely due to their codification.

7   In the Latin American discussion, this problem is placed in the context of neoliberal policies that shift the state's responsibility for decent living conditions onto individuals without renouncing authoritarian interventions in daily life. In this way, the living conditions of many children are worsened (see Vergara del Solar et al, 2021). On the state of the discussion in Latin America 30 years after the adoption of the UN Convention on the Rights of the Child, see Grinberg and Isacovich (2020); Magistris (2020).

8   The concept of situated knowledges refers to the fact that no knowledge is detached from its context or from the subjectivity of the person who expresses it. The social position of the person is also considered, as viewpoints are never neutral in ethical terms. The concept was first formulated by Simone de Beauvoir ([1949] 2010) in relation to women's knowledges and expanded by Donna Haraway (1988; 2005). According to Haraway, it applies to the knowledges of all subaltern groups. She proposes to examine the interactions between the 'axes of inequality' (gender, class, 'race'). In relation to these axes, we think it is necessary to also include the social positioning associated with age, which is usually not considered in intersectional analyses. In this way, the essentialist views of childhood, which do not consider its diversity, are questioned. Only in this way can children's knowledges be made visible and adequately understood.

9   This is emphasized in the concept of 'children's rights from below' (Liebel, 2012a), in contrast to the concept of 'living rights'.

10 Examples of this perspective are found, for example, in Vandenhole (2012; 2020); Sinervo and Cheney (2019); Howard and Okyere (2021); in Spanish: Barna (2012); Ruz Carrera (2012); Cordero Arce (2015b); Szulc et al (2016).

[11] In the following lines we refer to a paper by Elizabeth Dieckermann, a former student of the master's in 'Childhood Studies and Children's Rights' at Potsdam University of Applied Sciences (Dieckermann, 2018).

[12] For the discussion on universalism and cultural relativism and the inclusion of children in research on children's rights, see also Wall (2017: 25–39).

[13] The article by Nieuwenhuys and Hanson (2020) was triggered by an experience they had at an International Forum with working children in October 2017 in La Paz, Bolivia. They had been invited to this forum, together with other researchers, to meet and exchange views with organized children who work to defend their rights, other than in a research project. They had the irritating experience that children, who most likely never experience a university from the inside, had precise expectations of the scientists.

[14] This is now regarded as a basic ethical principle for all research involving children and is expressed, for example, in a charter that goes back to an initiative of the Innocenti Research Institute of UNICEF in Florence (see Graham et al, 2013). The question whether research benefits children is particularly acute for children of the Global South, especially when it is conducted by researchers who are far removed from the social reality of children.

[15] The relationship between researchers and children as research participants may be different if the research is carried out in the framework of social movements or self-organized groups of children. With regard to Indigenous groups or other minorities, Linda Tuhiwai Smith (2012: 138–142) distinguishes between research constellations in which the researchers come from outside or are an integral part of movements or groups ('outsider/insider research'). For approaches that understand research as part of the acts of resistance of oppressed and marginalized population groups, see the contributions in Strega and Brown (2015).

Chapter 4

[1] Childhood researchers from different parts of the world were involved in drafting the Charter. It is continuously discussed on a separate website (https://childethics.com/).

[2] We do not address this aspect. For the complications that may arise with regard to the mandatory consent of guardians, see the newly conceived second edition of the handbook *Ethics in Research with Children* (Alderson and Morrow, 2020: 139). This book provides a practical overview of the ethical challenges and risks at various stages of research.

[3] In a seminal paper in the journal *Childhood*, Pia Christensen and Alan Prout (2002) had argued for 'ethical symmetry' in research with children, drawing attention to some of the dilemmas that repeatedly arise.

[4] This also includes the Western-influenced universities in the former settler colonies of Australia and New Zealand.

[5] On the need to free ourselves from dependence on the 'monoculture of scientific knowledge' of the Global North, to overcome 'global cognitive injustice' and to discover and become aware of the ways of knowing and cognition of the Global South, see De Sousa Santos (2014: 188–211).

Chapter 5

[1] The chapter is based on a text the authors first wrote in German for a book on adultism (Liebel and Meade, 2023).

[2] The information is based on Manfred Liebel's own experience.

[3] Meanwhile, the UN Committee on the Rights of the Child edited the General Comment No. 25 on children's rights in relation to the digital environment (UNCRC, 2021), and is working on the new General Comment No 26 on children's rights and the environment with a special focus on climate change (UNCRC, forthcoming).

4   In a similar vein, Jørgensen and Wyness (2021) conceptualize a multidimensional model of 'kids power' and intergenerational relations.

5   An important consideration is also the extent to which the economy is shaped democratically.

6   Child-led groups such as We Want to Vote and the National Youth Rights Association in the United States have been actively campaigning for decades for voting for all, regardless of age. They are joined by adult-led groups such as Amnesty International in the UK, the Children's Voice Association and the Freechild Institute in the US and the Foundation for the Rights of Future Generations in Germany. Some of these groups now collaborate through a global network called the Children's Voting Colloquium (www.childrenvoting.org), in which around 100 activists and academics are aiming at abolishing the minimum voting age worldwide.

7   In some countries, for example in the United States, also adults have to register to vote.

8   A comprehensive study by Mexican legal scholar Luis Gabriel Ferrer Ortega (2014) and an essay by Peruvian legal scholar Pierre Foy Valencia (2019) provide an overview of the previous international debate on intergenerational justice and proposals and agreements on the rights of future generations. On intergenerational justice in the context of the climate crisis, see also the study by Tracey Skillington (2019).

9   In the context of the COVID-19 pandemic and its effects on children, sociologist Leena Alanen (2020) reflects on the need for a relational perspective in childhood studies. She points out that the pandemic is not simply a transmission from animals to humans, but the result of the manipulation of non-human living beings by humans themselves. However, in the suggestive plea for a transdisciplinary cosmology, she only refers to the critique of the Anthropocene, without reference to the cosmologies of non-Western pre-colonial cultures where, for example, the responsibility of humans for 'Mother Earth' has been emphasized for centuries (see Mancuso, 2019).

Chapter 6

1   Chapter 7 is devoted to the controversial discussion on the concept of resilience.

2   'Juridism blocks a good human life as coexistence because it represents a specific regime of subjectivation: It produces modes of existence and coexistence that are not conducive to human flourishing' (Loick, 2017: 289). In the legal and social philosophical debate on subjective rights, however, children are very rarely referred to. In a recent German anthology on the idea of subjective rights (Hilgendorf and Zabel, 2021a), there is a lot of talk about 'all human beings' or human beings in general, but the specific conditions and challenges that arise for children as bearers of subjective rights are not addressed in a single word.

3   For discussion, see the contributions in the anthology *Gegenrechte: Recht jenseits des Subjekts* (Counter-rights: Right beyond the Subject) (Fischer-Lescano et al, 2018). In this volume, too, however, children and their rights are not discussed at any point.

4   On this, see the reflections on a 'citizenship from below' that emerges from self-organized children's movements and is not content with a formal legal status, in Liebel (2020: 191–215). On the idea of an 'insurgent' or 'rebellious' citizenship, see Balibar (2014).

5   This problem arises from the liberal understanding of subjective rights, since in it subjects are not conceived in their life contexts and as people dependent on social relations, but as isolated monads. In order to release the 'emancipatory potential inherent in legality', therefore, 'the sociality of human subjectivity' must be taken into account (Loick, 2017: 332–333; see also Douzinas, 2019).

6   They were my academic teachers and I owe them a lot.

7   They begin their book *Dialectic of Enlightenment*, written in exile in the United States during the Second World War and first published in Amsterdam in 1947, with the sentences: 'Enlightenment, understood in the widest sense as the advance of thought,

has always aimed at liberating human beings from fear and installing them as masters. Yet the wholly enlightened earth is radiant with triumphant calamity' (Horkheimer and Adorno, [1947] 2002: 1).

[8] See, for example, the studies by Proyecto Andino de Tecnologías Campesinas (PRATEC) (2005; 2008; 2013; 2020).

[9] This issue has received particular attention in feminist theories (see, for instance, Bordo, 1993; Brown, 1995; Buckel, 2021).

[10] Argentinian anthropologist Rita Segato situates this rationality, which she calls 'instrumental Eurocentric reason', in the 'coloniality of power' (Quijano) and calls for the 'epistemic subversion of power' (Segato, 2013: 31–32). It is noteworthy that as early as in the 1920s the Italian philosopher and political activist Antonio Gramsci (2011) conceptually shifted from the language of subjects to that of persons and a theory of personality (for discussion see Thomas, 2009; Jackson, 2017).

[11] The disregard or devaluation of the subjective is also expressed in the following adjectives: influenced, unobjective, biased, unjust, unfair or irrational. Example: the jury assessed the case *subjectively*, that is unobjectively. In contrast, the objective is associated with the following adjectives understood as positive: uninfluenced, neutral, impartial, impersonal, objective or rational.

[12] Foucault (1982) has drawn attention to the double meaning of the discourse of the subject: on the one hand, the sovereign and self-confident subject, who is the origin of action and control of his conditions of life and the other (the ideal subject of the philosophy of the subject, identical to himself); on the other hand, the subject as the product of a subjection, called by Foucault 'subjectivation' (in analogy with the meaning of the Latin words *subiectum* and *subiacere*). This latter understanding is also expressed in the phrase 'to be subjected to something'. By contrast, French philosopher Jacques Rancière (1998) understands 'subjectification' as meaning that a person who does not yet 'count' at all 'comes into consideration' to be taken seriously, that is, literally becomes visible and audible. To underline this meaning, he explicitly speaks of 'political subjectivation'.

[13] Other authors have previously spoken of 'labour entrepreneurs' in a similar sense and associated them with processes of the 'subjectification of labour' (Voß and Pongratz, 1998; Voß and Moldaschl, 2002).

[14] For further examples, see www.opinion.com.bo/articulo/cochabamba/primera-escuela-sudamerica-ninos-empresarios-llega-llajta/20210109113256803045.html or www.negociosyemprendimiento.org/2013/05/ideas-de-negocios-para-ninos-emprendedores.html.

[15] So far, International Labour Organization programmes for entrepreneurship development have targeted young people aged 15 and older, to the extent that they have completed their compulsory education.

[16] See the debate on so-called liberal eugenics as part of a 'genetic supermarket': Robertson (1996); Habermas (2003); Sandel (2007).

[17] In a recent anthology edited by Gavin Rae and Emma Ingala (2017), the relationship between subjectivity and the political is discussed, in particular with regard to authors in the European philosophical tradition. Some contributions (Marciniak, 2017; Rae, 2017; Singh, 2017) refer particularly to the Global South.

Chapter 7

[1] In some of the cities participating in the network, the participation of children and young people is also planned. The limitations and difficulties that have become apparent during implementation are being investigated in some studies (Derr et al, 2017a; 2017b; 2018). However, they do not address the ambivalences of the resilience concept on which the network is based. On 'resilient cities' and 'resilient regions' see also Deppisch (2016); Fekete et al (2016).

[2] See: www.gfdrr.org/en/crp.

[3] Individualizing and pathologizing patterns of thought are still very dominant, especially in the German-speaking resilience discourse. In Lösel and Bender (2007), for example, 'behavioural disorders', 'antisocial developments', 'aggressive behaviour', and so on, are repeatedly mentioned in order to identify personality traits in which risk factors dominate and which stand in the way of developing resilience.

[4] See the contributions in Kotliarenco et al (1996); Silva (1999); Melillo and Suárez Ojeda (2001); Melillo et al, 2004.

[5] In reference to Malinche, the Indigenous translator and lover of Hernán Cortés, the Spanish conquistador of Mexico, this is an attitude that submits to imperial interests and influences from abroad and exposes its own cultural roots (see Kay Jager, 2015: 29–36).

[6] Voss (2008) explicitly draws attention to the fact that the opportunities for participation of local populations in the Global South are affected by the dominance of Western ways of thinking and former colonial languages and may force them to remain without voice.

[7] Salazar does not clarify whether they are children of Indigenous origin. But as many Indigenous families in the barrios have migrated from rural areas, it can be assumed that this is also the case for the children he is talking about. For these children, integration into the communities and early co-responsibility play an important role. It may stimulate children's action in the sense that they insist on being taken seriously and that they play an important role in community life (see, with reference to Mapuche children, Ruz Carrera, 2012; Szulc, 2015; 2018).

[8] In the following examples, I refer to my own observations in the years 2017 to 2021.

[9] The *beat* is the musical track that accompanies the singers of the genre in their performances; it is the instrumental, the rhythm in which the 'beats' of the track and the harmony in general are also included.

Chapter 8

[1] The rhetorical figure of the 'street child' also arose in this context.

[2] One difficulty of the presentation is that the term *protagonismo infantil*, which is widely used in Latin America, cannot be easily translated into other languages. An English-language author who has worked intensively on the topic therefore retains the Spanish term (Taft, 2017; 2019). Here I translate the term as 'children's protagonism'. When the discourse speaks of *protagonismo infantil*, not only children but also adolescents are included, insofar as they are still minors in the legal sense, that is younger than 18 years old. In the following, I mainly speak of children, but also include adolescents.

[3] There was no internet at the time. Today they use also digital social media.

[4] See www.opinion.com.bo/articulo/cochabamba/primera-escuela-sudamerica-ninos-empresarios-llega-llajta/20210109113256803045.html.

[5] See www.facebook.com/watch/?v=1389116324949698.

[6] See www.entrepreneur.com/leadership/11-successful-kid-entrepreneurs-keeping-their-eyes-on-the/273222 or www.surveycrest.com/blog/kidpreneurs-in-business-world/.

[7] This immanent problem is also expressed in the fact that the term '*protagonismo infantil*' cannot be translated into any of the Indigenous languages. Even where movements or networks of Indigenous children emerge, the term is rarely used.

[8] Using the working children's movement in Peru as an example, Jessica Taft (2015; 2019: 151–182) sensitively and accurately explored how even people who see themselves as collaborators, and who see children's protagonism as guiding their practice, 'talk too much', undermining their own intentions. Because dominance as an adult is so deeply embedded in their own psyche and is repeatedly reinforced by the adultism that prevails in society, they find it difficult to restrain themselves and let children speak and make the decisions.

Chapter 9

[1] Aitken (2001) speaks of the 'unchildlike child'.

[2] Earlier approaches to action research can be traced back to the social psychologist Kurt Lewin (1946) and have been further developed since the late 1960s in the United States, Australia and some Western European countries. They had a socio-critical intention, above all to generate an alternative to research standards such as objectivity and neutrality within the social sciences. It was criticized that by claiming neutrality, the social sciences entered into an implicit alliance with the ruling social powers and definitional monopolies, which did not change social structures but affirmed and reproduced them (see Kemmis and McTaggart, 2005).

[3] This is also true for so-called *artistic research* (see Boeck, 2021).

[4] I quote from the second edition of her book, which has been significantly expanded from the first edition published in 2012.

[5] Nevertheless, the term Indigenous always implies the danger of attributing certain characteristics to people in an essentialist way or of assigning them to an ethnically defined group. It should therefore be recalled that here the term Indigenous is understood in the context of decolonial critique as a collective self-designation of persons and peoples who were and are particularly affected by colonial and postcolonial violence and exclusion. Their ways of life and worldviews are by no means homogeneous and they speak different languages.

[6] Also, all writings cited here were written in the colonial languages of English and Spanish.

[7] On 'storytelling methods' in the context of Indigenous methodologies, see Chilisa (2020: 193–204), in detail.

[8] For an illustrative example of connecting 'hearts and minds' in research practice with Aboriginal people in Australia, see Wright et al (2013).

[9] In an abridged English publication of Escobar's text, *sentipensar* is translated as 'thinking-feeling' (Escobar, 2016). I find it more appropriate to translate the term as *sensing-thinking*, since it is not rational thinking that is in the foreground, but rather sensing or empathizing.

References

100 Resilient Cities (2018) 'Frequently asked questions about 100 Resilient Cities', available at: https://resilientcitiesnetwork.org/FAQ

Abebe, Tatek (2019) 'Reconceptualising children's agency as continuum and interdependence', *Social Sciences*, 8(3): 1–16.

Abebe, Tarek and Bessell, Sharon (2014) 'Advancing ethical research with children: Critical reflections on ethical guidelines', *Children Geographies*, 12(1): 126–133.

Abebe, Tatek, Tar, Anandini and Lyså, Ida M. (2022) 'Southern theories and decolonial childhood studies', *Childhood*, 29(3): 255–275.

Adams, Paul, Berg, Lelia, Berger, Nan, Duane, Michael, Neill, Alexander S. and Ollendorf, Robert (1971) *Children's Rights: Towards the Liberation of the Child*, London: Elek.

Adorno, Theodor W. (1970) *Aufsätze zur Gesellschaftstheorie und Methodologie*, Frankfurt: Suhrkamp.

Afroze, Jiniya (2022) 'Decolonizing children's agency: Perspectives of children in an Urdu-speaking Bihari camp in Bangladesh', *Childhood*, 29(3): 276–291.

Aguilar Morales, Silvia and Ocampo Carapia, Luis Arturo (eds) (2018) *De emprendedor a empresario. Haga que su negocio ¡sea negocio!*, Mexico City: Patria Educación.

Aitken, Stuart C. (2001) 'Global crisis of childhood: Rights, justice and the unchildlike child', *Area*, 33(2): 119–127.

Alaimo, Kathleen (2002) 'Historical roots of children's rights in Europe and the United States', in K. Alaimo and B. Klug (eds) *Children as Equals: Exploring the Rights of the Child*, Lanham, New York: University Press of America, pp 1–23.

Alanen, Leena (2020) 'A relational challenge to post-corona childhood studies', *Childhood*, 27(4): 431–434.

Alderson, Priscilla (2008) 'Children as researchers: The effects of participation rights on research methodology', in P. Christensen and A. James (eds) *Research with Children: Perspectives and Practices* (2nd edn), London: Routledge, pp 241–257.

Alderson, Priscilla and Morrow, Virginia (2020) *The Ethics of Research with Children and Young People: A Practical Handbook* (2nd edn), Los Angeles: SAGE.

Alfageme, Erika, Cantos, Raquel and Martínez Muñoz, Marta (2003) *De la participación al protagonismo infantil: propuestas para la acción*, Madrid: Plataforma de Organizaciones de Infancia.

Alston, Philip and Tobin, John (2005) *Laying the Foundations for Children's Rights: An Independent Study of some Key Legal and Institutional Aspects of the Impact of the Convention on the Rights of the Child*, Florence: UNICEF Innocenti Research Centre.

Altwicker, Tilmann and Diggelmann, Oliver (2014) 'What should remain of the critical approaches to international law? International legal theory as critique', *Swiss Review of International and European Law*, 24: 69–92.

Alvarado, Sara Victoria (2014) 'Ampliación de la comprensión de los procesos de configuración de subjetividades políticas de niños, niñas y jóvenes en Colombia desde una perspectiva alternativa de desarrollo humano: tránsitos y aprendizajes', in C.E. Vasco (ed) *Socialización política y configuración de subjetividades. Construcción social de niños, niñas y jóvenes como sujetos políticos*, Bogotá: Siglo del Hombre Editores, pp 17–53.

Amigó, María Florencia, García Palacios, Mariana, Enriz, Noelia and Hecht, Ana Carolina (2022) 'Indigenous epistemologies of childhood in contexts of inequality: Three case studies from the Global South', *Childhood*, 29(3): 307–321.

Ansell, Nicola (2019) 'Global south research in children's geographies: From useful illustration to conceptual challenge', in T. Skelton and S. Aitken (eds) *Establishing Geographies of Children and Young People: Geographies of Children and Young People 1*, Singapore: Springer Nature, pp 51–70.

Antimil Caniupan, Jaime (2015) 'Pu püchi kona. La vida de niñas y niños alquilados en el Gülu Mapu', in E. Antileo Baeza, L. Cárcamo-Huechante, M. Calfío Montalva and H. Huinca-Piutrin (eds) *Awukan ka kuxankan zugu wajmapu mew. Violencias coloniales en Wajmapu*, Temuco: Ediciones Comunidad de Historia Mapuche. Centro de Estudios e Investigaciones Mapuche, pp 159–188.

Araneda-Urrutia, Carlos (2022) 'The invention of the "weird" Southern child: Mapping coloniality in the political problematization of disadvantaged children's lives in the global South', *Childhood*, 29(3): 292–306.

Archard, David (2015) *Children: Rights and Childhood* (3rd edn), London: Routledge.

Archard, David and Macleod, Colin M. (eds) (2002) *The Moral and Political Status of Children*, Oxford: Oxford University Press.

Arias Vargas, Viviana, González López, Luis Eduardo and Hernández Guevara, Nohema (2009) 'Constitución de sujeto político: historias de vida política de mujeres líderes afrocolombianas', *Universitas Psychologica*, 8(3): 639–652.

Arnold, Magda B. (1960) *Emotion and Personality*, vols 1 and 2, New York: Columbia University Press.

Atkinson, Catherine (2019) 'Ethical complexities in participatory childhood research: Rethinking the "least adult role"', *Childhood*, 26(2): 186–201.

Bácares Jara, Camilo (2020) 'Un estado del arte analítico de las publicaciones sobre los derechos del niño en español. A propósito de tres tendencias bibliográficas: la negacionista, la oficial y la contraoficial', *Derecho por PUCP – Revista de la Facultad de Derecho de la Universidad del País Vasco (España)*, 85: 473–515.

Bailón Vásquez, Fabiola (2012) 'La Escuela Correccional de Artes y Oficios de Oaxaca, 1889–1901', *Estudios de Historia Moderna y Contemporánea de México*, 44: 137–173.

Bak Geler, David (2020) 'Alternativas de lo plural: pluralismo liberal, pluralidad republicana e improvisación práctica', in I. Cornejo and M. Rufer (eds) *Horizontalidad. Hacia una crítica de la metodología*, Buenos Aires: CLACSO and Guadalajara: CALAS, pp 123–143.

Balagopalan, Sarada (2013) 'The politics of failure: Street children and the circulation of rights discourses in Kolkata (Calcutta), India', in K. Hanson and O. Nieuwenhuys (eds) *Reconceptualizing Children's Rights in International Development: Living Rights, Social Justice, Translations*, New York: Cambridge University Press, pp 133–151.

Balagopalan, Sarada (2019) 'Teaching "global childhoods": From a cultural mapping of "them" to a diagnostic reading of "Us/US"', in A. Twum-Danso Imoh, M. Bourdillon and S. Meichsner (eds) *Global Childhoods beyond the North-South Divide*, Basingstoke: Palgrave Macmillan, pp 13–33.

Balibar, Étienne (2014) *Equaliberty: Political Essays*, Durham, NC: Duke University Press.

Ball, Jessica (2005) 'Restorative research partnerships in Indigenous communities', in A. Farrell (ed) *Ethical Research with Children*, Maidenhead: Open University Press, pp 81–96.

Barna, Agustín (2012) 'Convención Internacional de los Derechos del Niño. Hacia un abordaje desacralizado', *KAIROS. Revista de Temas Sociales*, 16(29): 1–19.

Barnes, Earl (1900) 'Study of children's rights as seen by themselves', *The Paedologist*, 2(3): 142–144.

Barnes, Marian, Brannelly, Tula, Ward, Lizzie and Ward, Nicki (eds) (2015) *Ethics of Care: Critical Advances in International Perspective*, Bristol: Bristol University Press.

Barranco Avilés, Maria del Carmen (2007) 'Globalización y Derechos de la infancia y la adolescencia', in M.C. García and J. Guilló Jiménez (eds) *Globalización y derechos de la infancia y la adolescencia*, Madrid: Save the Children. Centro de Investigación y Documentación sobre Derechos de la Infancia y la Adolescencia, pp 11–24.

Bartoletti, Susan Campbell (1999) *Kids on Strike*, Boston: Houghton Mifflin.

Bastian, Johannes and Rolff, Hans-Günter (2002) *Abschlussevaluation des Projektes 'Schule & Co.'*, Gütersloh: Bertelsmann-Stiftung and Universität Hamburg.

Bazán, Juan Enrique (2005) *Ser colaborador. Anotaciones preliminares para un ensayo*, Lima: Save the Children.

Beazley, Harriot, Bessell, Sharon, Ennew, Judith and Waterson, Roxana (2009) 'The right to be properly researched: Research with children in a messy, real world', *Children's Geographies*, 7(4): 365–378.

Beckman, Ericka (2009) 'The creolization of imperial reason: Chilean state racism in the War of the Pacific', *Journal of Latin American Cultural Studies*, 18(1): 73–90.

Beier, J. Marshall (2020) 'Subjects in peril: Childhoods between security and resilience', in J.M. Beier (ed) *Discovering Childhood in International Relations*, Cham: Palgrave Macmillan, pp 219–242.

Bell, John (1995) *Understanding Adultism: A Major Obstacle to Developing Positive Youth-Adult Relationships*, Somerville, MA: YouthBuild USA.

Bell, John (2018) 'Adultism', in B. Frey (ed) *The SAGE Encyclopedia of Educational Research, Measurement, and Evaluation*, Thousand Oaks, CA: SAGE.

Bendo, Daniella (2020) 'Parallel lines? Childhood discourses emphasized by the children's rights movement and the emerging field of children's rights studies', *Childhood*, 27(2): 173–187.

Benedikter, Roland and Fathi, Karim (2017) 'What is a resilient society?', available at: https://intpolicydigest.org/2017/09/17/what-is-a-resilient-society/

Bent, Emily (2013) 'A different girl effect producing political girlhoods in the #invest in girls' climate', in S.K. Nenga and J.K. Taft (eds) *Youth Engagement: The Civic-Political Lives of Children and Youth*, Bingley: Emerald, pp 3–20.

Bergman, Carla (ed) (2022) *Trust Kids! Stories on Youth Autonomy and Confronting Adult Supremacy*, Chico, CA and Edinburgh: AK Press.

Bessell, Sharon, Beazley, Harriot and Waterson, Roxana (2017) 'The methodology and ethics of rights-based research with children', in A. Invernizzi, M. Liebel, B. Milne and R. Budde (eds) *'Children Out of Place' and Human Rights: In Memory of Judith Ennew*, Cham: Springer International, pp 211–231.

Bhabha, Homi K. (1994) *The Location of Culture*, London: Routledge.

Bhambra, Gurminder K. (2014) 'Postcolonial and decolonial dialogues', *Postcolonial Studies*, 17(2): 115–121.

Blum, Sabine, Endreß, Martin, Kaumann, Stefan and Rampp, Benjamin (2016) 'Soziologische Perspektiven', in R. Wink (ed) *Multidisziplinäre Perspektiven der Resilienzforschung*, Wiesbaden: Springer VS, pp 151–177.

Bobbio, Norberto (1996) *The Age of Rights*, Cambridge: Polity.

Boeck, Angelika (2021) 'What is artistic research?', *w/k – Between Science & Art*, available at: https://doi.org/10.55597/e6798

Bolados García, Paola (2017) *Orígenes versus Originarios. La disputa por el control de la salud indígena atacameña*, Valparaíso: Editorial UV de la Universidad de Valparaíso.

Bolin, Inge (2006) *Growing Up in a Culture of Respect: Child Rearing in Highland Peru*, Austin, TX: Texas University Press.

Bonvillani, Andrea (2012) 'Hacia la construcción de la categoría subjetividad política: una posible caja de herramientas y algunas líneas de significación emergentes', in C. Piedrahita Echandía, Á. Díaz Gómez and P. Vommaro (eds) *Subjetividades políticas: desafíos y debates latinoamericanos*, Buenos Aires: CLACSO, pp 191–202.

Bordo, Susan (1993) *Unbearable Weight: Feminism, Western Culture, and the Body*, Berkeley, CA: University of California Press.

Boulding, Elise (1979) *Children's Rights and the Wheel of Life*, New Brunswick, NJ: Transaction Books.

Bourdillon, Michael, Levison, Deborah, Myers, William and White, Ben (2010) *Rights and Wrongs of Children's Work*, New Brunswick, NJ: Rutgers University Press.

Bourdillon, Michael, Meichsner, Sylvia and Twum-Danso Imoh, Afua (2019) 'Reflections on binary thinking', in A. Twum-Danso Imoh, M. Bourdillon and S. Meichsner (eds) *Global Childhoods beyond the North-South Divide*, Basingstoke: Palgrave Macmillan, pp 255–263.

Boyden, Jo ([1990] 1997) 'Childhood and the policy makers: A comparative perspective on the globalization of childhood', in A. James and A. Prout (eds) *Constructing and Reconstructing Childhood*, London: Falmer Press, pp 190–229.

Boyden, Jo (2003) 'Children under fire: Challenging assumptions about children's resilience', *Children, Youth and Environments*, 13(1): 1–29.

Boyden, Jo and Howard, Neil (2013) 'Why does child trafficking policy need to be reformed? The moral economy of children's movement in Benin and Ethiopia', *Children's Geographies*, 11(3): 354–368.

Boyden, Jo and Mann, Gillian (2005) 'Children's risk, resilience, and coping in extreme situations', in M. Ungar (ed) *Handbook for Working with Children and Youth: Pathways to Resilience across Cultures and Contexts*, Thousand Oaks, CA: SAGE, pp 3–25.

Brand, Ulrich and Wissen, Markus (2017) *Imperiale Lebensweise: Zur Ausbeutung von Mensch und Natur im globalen Kapitalismus*, Munich: Oekom.

Brand, Ulrich, Fried, Barbara, Koch, Rhonda, Schurian, Hannah and Wissen, Markus (2022) 'Deiche bauen reicht nicht. Wie eine linke Anpassungspolitik aussehen kann', *Luxemburg – Gesellschaftsanalyse und linke Praxis*, 2(22): 32–41.

Brecher, Jeremy, Costello, Tim and Smith, Brendan (2000) *Globalization from Below: The Power of Solidarity*, West Cornwall: Stone Soup Books.

Briggs, Jean L. (1991) 'Expecting the unexpected: Canadian Inuit training for an experimental lifestyle', *Ethos*, 19(3), DOI: 10.2307/640523

Brighouse, Harry (2002) 'What rights (if any) do children have?', in D. Archard and C.M. Macleod (eds) *The Moral and Political Status of Children*, Oxford: Oxford University Press, pp 31–52.

Briones, Claudia (2020) 'La horizontalidad como horizonte de trabajo', in I. Cornejo and M. Rufer (eds) *Horizontalidad. Hacia una crítica de la metodología*, Buenos Aires: CLACSO, pp 59–92.

Bröckling, Ulrich (2015) *The Entrepreneurial Self: Fabricating a New Type of Subject*, Los Angeles and London: SAGE.

Bröckling, Ulrich (2017) *Gute Hirten führen sanft. Über Menschenregierungskünste*, Berlin: Suhrkamp.

Brown, Nicholas J.M. (2015) 'A critical examination of the U.S. Army's comprehensive soldier fitness program', *The Winnower*, 2: e143751.17496, DOI: 10.15200/winn.143751.17496

Brown, Wendy (1995) *States of Injury: Power and Freedom in Late Modernity*, Princeton, NJ: Princeton University Press.

Brown, Wendy (2002) 'Suffering the paradoxes of rights', in W. Brown and J. Halley (eds) *Left Legalism/Left Critique*, Durham, NC: Duke University Press, pp 420–434.

Brown Weiss, Edith (1989) *In Fairness to Future Generations: International Law, Common Patrimony and Intergenerational Equity*, New York: Transnational Publishers and the United Nations University.

Brown Weiss, Edith (1990) *Our Rights and Obligations to Future Generations for the Environment*, Washington, DC: Georgetown University Law Center.

Brown Weiss, Edith (1992) *Intergenerational Equity: A Legal Framework for Global Environmental Change. Environmental Change and International Law: New Challenges and Dimensions*, Tokyo: United Nations University Press.

Brumlik, Micha (1999) 'Freiheit, Gleichheit, Nachhaltigkeit. Zur Kritik eines neuen Grundwerts', *Blätter für deutsche und internationale Politik*, 12: 1460–1466.

Buckel, Sonja (2008) 'Zwischen Schutz und Maskerade. Kritik(en) des Rechts', in A. Demirovic (ed) *Kritik und Materialität*, Münster: Westfälisches Dampfboot, pp 110–131.

Buckel, Sonja (2021) *Subjectivation and Cohesion: Towards the Reconstruction of a Materialist Theory of Law*, Leiden: Brill.

Budde, Rebecca and Markowska-Manista, Urszula (eds) (2020) *Childhood and Children's Rights between Research and Activism*, Wiesbaden: Springer VS.

Bundesministerium der Verteidigung (2016) *Weißbuch 2016. Grundlagen deutscher Sicherheitspolitik*, Berlin; available at: www.bmvg.de/de/themen/weissbuch

Burghardt, Daniel (2019) 'Von Charaktermasken zum unternehmerischen Selbst? Fragen der kritischen Pädagogik an die kritische Soziologie', in N. Ricken, R. Casale and C. Thompson (eds) *Subjektivierung. Erziehungswissenschaftliche Theorieperspektiven*, Weinheim: Beltz-Juventa, pp 179–198.

Burke, Ronald (2010) *Decolonization and the Evolution of International Human Rights*, Philadelphia, PA: University of Pennsylvania Press.

Burman, Erica (1994) 'Innocents abroad: Western fantasies of childhood and the iconography of emergencies', *Disasters*, 18(3): 238–253.

Butler, Judith (1997) *The Psychic Life of Power: Theories in Subjection*, Stanford, CA: Stanford University Press.

Butler, Judith (2015) *Notes Toward a Performative Theory of Assembly*, Cambridge, MA and London: Harvard University Press.

Butler, Judith (2016) 'Rethinking vulnerability and resistance', in J. Butler, Z. Gambetti and L. Sabsay (eds) *Vulnerability in Resistance*, Durham, NC: Duke University Press, pp 12–27.

Cabrerizo Sanz, Lorena, Martínez Muñoz, Marta, Zelaya Paredes, Maureen, García López de Rodas, Mercedes and Andrés-Candelas, Mario (2018) *Guía para promover la Participación Infantil y Adolescente en la Ciudad de Madrid*, Madrid: Ayuntamiento de Madrid & Enclave de Evaluación.

Cannella, Gaile S. and Viruru, Radhika (2004) *Childhood and Postcolonization: Power Education, and Contemporary Practice*, New York: Routledge-Falmer.

Cantwell, Nigel (2011) 'Are children's rights still human?', in A. Invernizzi and J. Williams (eds) *The Human Rights of Children: From Visions to Implementation*, London: Routledge, pp 37–59.

Caparrós, Martín (2020) *Hunger: The Oldest Problem*, Brooklyn, NY: Melville House.

Cárcamo Solís, María de Lourdes, Arroyo-López, María del Pilar, Álvarez-Castañon, Lorena del Carmen and García-López, Elvia (2017) 'Developing entrepreneurship in primary schools. The Mexican experience of "my first enterprise": entrepreneurship by playing', *Teaching and Teacher Education*, 64: 291–304.

Cardinal, Pierre-Alexandre (2016) 'Resistance and international law: De-coloniality and pluritopic hermeneutics', *Inter Gentes*, 1(1): 40–52.

Césaire, Aimé ([1950] 2000) *Discourse on Colonialism*, New York: Monthly Review Press.

Chakrabarty, Dipesh (2009) *Provincializing Europe: Postcolonial Thought and Historical Difference*, Princeton, NJ: Princeton University Press.

Cheney, Kristen E. (2014) 'Conflicting protectionist and participation models of children's rights: Their consequences for orphans and vulnerable children in Uganda', in A. Twum-Danso and N. Ansell (eds) *Children's Lives in an Era of Children's Rights: The Progress of the Convention on the Rights of the Child in Africa*, London: Routledge, pp 17–33.

Cheney, Kristen E. and Sinervo, Aviva (eds) (2019) *Disadvantaged Childhoods and Humanitarian Intervention: Processes of Affective Commodification and Objectification*, Basingstoke: Palgrave Macmillan.

Cheney, Kristen and Ucembe, Stephen (2019) 'The orphan industrial complex: The charitable commodification of children and its consequences for child protection', in K. Cheney and A. Sinervo (eds) *Disadvantaged Childhoods and Humanitarian Intervention*, Basingstoke: Palgrave Macmillan, pp 37–61.

Children vs Climate Crisis (2019) *Communication to the Committee on the Rights of the Child. Submitted under Article 5 of the Third Optional Protocol to the United Nations Convention on the Rights of the Child*, 23 September, available at: https://childrenvsclimatecrisis.org

Chilisa, Bagele (2012) *Indigenous Research Methodologies*, Los Angeles: SAGE.

Chilisa, Bagele (2020) *Indigenous Research Methodologies* (2nd edn), Los Angeles: SAGE.

Christensen, Pia and Prout, Alan (2002) 'Working with ethical symmetry in social research with children', *Childhood*, 9(4): 477–497.

Clark, Jill (2004) 'Participatory research with children and young people: Philosophy, possibilities and perils', *Action Research Expeditions*, 4(11): 1–18.

Cockburn, Tom (2006) 'Global childhood?', in A. Carling (ed) *Globalization and Identity: Development and Integration in a Changing World*, London: Taurus, pp 77–88.

Cohen, Howard (1980) *Equal Rights for Children*, Totowa: Rowman & Littlefield.

Colectivo Situaciones (2002) *A puntes para el nuevo protagonismo social*, Buenos Aires: Ediciones de mano en mano.

Collins, Patricia H. (2000) *Black Feminist Thought: Knowledge, Consciousness, and the Politics of Empowerment*, New York: Routledge.

Connolly, Mark and Ennew, Judith (1996) 'Introduction: Children out of place', *Childhood*, 3(2): 131–147.

Cordero Arce, Matias (2012) 'Towards an emancipatory discourse of children's rights', *International Journal of Children's Rights*, 20: 365–421.

Cordero Arce, Matias (2015a) 'Maturing children's rights theory: From children, with children, of children', *International Journal of Children's Rights*, 23: 283–331.

Cordero Arce, Matías (2015b) *Hacia un Discurso Emancipador de los Derechos de las Niñas y los Niños*, Lima: Ifejant.

Cordero Arce, Matias (2018) 'Why is (to be) the subject of children's rights?', in S. Spyrou, R. Rosen and D.T. Cook (eds) *Reimagining Childhood Studies*, London: Bloomsbury Academic, pp 169–182.

Cornejo, Inés and Rufer, Mario (eds) (2020) *Horizontalidad. Hacia una crítica de la metodología*, Buenos Aires: CLACSO and Guadalajara: CALAS.

Corntassel, Jeff and Gaudry, Adam (2014) 'Insurgent education and Indigenous-centred research: Opening new pathways to community resurgence', in C. Etmanski, B.L. Hall and T. Dawson (eds) *Learning and Teaching Community-Based Research: Linking Pedagogy to Practice*, Toronto: University of Toronto Press, pp 167–185.

Corona, Sarah and Kaltmeier, Olaf (eds) (2012a) *Methoden dekolonialisieren. Eine Werkzeugkiste zur Demokratisierung der Sozial- und Kulturwissenschaften*, Münster: Westfälisches Dampfboot.

Corona, Sarah and Kaltmeier, Olaf (eds) (2012b) *En diálogo. Métodos horizontales en Ciencias Sociales y Culturales*, Barcelona: Gedisa.

Corona Berkin, Sarah (2020a) *Producción horizontal del conocimiento*, Guadalajara: Bielefeld University Press.

Corona Berkin, Sarah (2020b) 'Investigar en el lado oscuro de la horizontalidad', in I. Cornejo and M. Rufer (eds) *Horizontalidad. Hacia una crítica de la metodología*, Buenos Aires: CLACSO and Guadalajara: CALAS, pp 27–58.

Corona Caraveo, Yolanda (2003) 'Diversidad de infancias. Retos y compromisos', in Y. Corona Caraveo and R.R. Villamil Uriarte (eds) *Tramas. Subjetividad y procesos sociales. Diversidad de infancias*, Mexico City: Universidad Autónoma Metropolitana, pp 13–31.

Crawley, Heaven and Skleparis, Dimitris (2018) 'Refugees, migrants, neither both', *Journal of Ethnic and Migrant Studies*, 4: 48–64.

Cregan, Kate and Cuthbert, Denise (2014) *Global Childhoods: Issues and Debates*, London: SAGE.

Crenshaw, Kimberlé W., Ocen, Priscilla and Nanda, Jyoti (2015) *Black Girls Matter: Pushed Out, Overpoliced, and Underprotected*, New York: Center for Intersectionality and Social Policy Studies.

Cronin-Furmann, Kate and Lake, Milli (2018) 'Ethics abroad: Fieldwork in fragile and violent contexts', *PS: Political Science and Politics*, 51(3): 607–614.

Crouch, Colin (2005) *Post-Democracy*, Cambridge: Polity Press.

Cupples, Julie and Grosfoguel, Ramón (eds) (2019) *Unsettling Eurocentrism in the Westernized University*, London: Routledge.

Cussiánovich, Alejandro (1990) 'Cuando los Nats se organizan ... es porque piedras traen. ¿Hacia un movimiento social de y en favor de los niños?', in G. Schibotto (ed) *Niños Trabajadores. Construyendo una identidad*, Lima: MANTHOC, pp 359–414.

Cussiánovich, Alejandro (1996) *Some Premises for Reflection and Social Practices with Working Children and Adolescents*, Lima: Save the Children Suecia.

Cussiánovich, Alejandro (2001a) 'What does protagonism mean?', in M. Liebel, B. Overwien and A. Recknagel (eds) *Working Children's Protagonism: Social Movements and Empowerment in Latin America, Africa and India*, Frankfurt: IKO, pp 57–70.

Cussiánovich, Alejandro (2001b) 'The paradigm of integral protagonism's promotion', in M. Liebel, B. Overwien and A. Recknagel (eds) *Working Children's Protagonism: Social Movements and Empowerment in Latin America, Africa and India*, Frankfurt: IKO, pp 309–319.

Cussiánovich, Alejandro (2006) *Ensayos sobre Infancia. Sujeto de Derechos y Protagonista*, Lima: Ifejant.

Cussiánovich, Alejandro (2007) *Aprender la condición humana. Ensayo sobre Pedagogía de la ternura*, Lima: Ifejant.

Cussiánovich, Alejandro (2010) *Paradigma del Protagonismo*, Lima: INFANT.

Cussiánovich, Alejandro (2013) 'Protagonismo, participación y ciudadanía como componente de la educación y ejercicio de los derechos de la infancia', in A. Cussiánovich (ed) *Historia del pensamiento social sobre la infancia*, Lima: Universidad Nacional Mayor de San Marcos, pp 86–102.

Cussiánovich, Alejandro (2022) *Pedagogía de la Ternura – componente del Paradigma del Protagonismo*, Lima: Ifejant.

Cussiánovich, Alejandro and Figueroa, Elvira (2009) 'Participación protagónica: ¿ideología o cambio de paradigma?', in M. Liebel and M. Martínez Muñoz (eds) *Infancia y derechos humanos: hacia una ciudadanía participante y protagónica*, Lima: Ifejant, pp 23–40.

Cussiánovich, Alejandro and Márquez, Ana María (2002) *Hacia una participación protagónica de los niños, niñas y adolescentes*, Lima: Save the Children Suecia.

Cussiánovich, Alejandro and Martínez Muñoz, Marta (2017) 'La participación de los niños y niñas como factor constitutivo del bienestar de la comunidad', in A. Cussiánovich, *Ensayos sobre Infancia III*, Lima: Ifejant, pp 214–256.

Cyrulnik, Boris (2011) *Resilience: How Your Inner Strength Can Set You Free from the Past*, London: Penguin.

Daly, Aoife, Thorburn Stern, Rebecca and Leviner, Pernilla (2022) 'UN Convention on the Rights of the Child, and Article 2 discrimination on the basis of childhood: The CRC paradox?', *Nordic Journal of International Law*, 91(3): 419–452.

Darian Smith, Kate (2013) 'Children, colonialism and commemoration', in K. Darian Smith and C. Pasceo (eds) *Children, Childhood and Cultural Heritage*, London: Routledge, pp 159–174.

Därmann, Iris (2021) *Widerstände. Gewaltenteilung in statu nascendi*, Berlin: Matthes & Seitz.

Daza Cárdenas, Giovanny (2018) 'Jóvenes indígenas en la ciudad. Espacialidades híbridas y nuevas sensibilidades', in P. López and L. García Guerreiro (eds) *Movimientos Indígenas y Autonomías en América Latina: Escenarios de Disputa y Horizontes de Posibilidad*, Buenos Aires: El Colectivo and CLACSO, pp 207–228.

De Beauvoir, Simone ([1949] 2010) *The Second Sex*, New York: Vintage.

De Castro, Lucia Rabello (2020a) 'Why global? Children and childhood from a decolonial perspective', *Childhood*, 27(1): 48–62.

De Castro, Lucia Rabello (2020b) 'Age epistemology and the politics of age', in C. Baraldi and L.R. de Castro (eds) *Global Childhoods in International Perspective: Universality, Diversity and Inequalities*, Los Angeles: SAGE, pp 33–50.

De Castro, Lucia Rabello (2021) 'Decolonising child studies: Development and globalism as orientalist perspectives', *Third World Quarterly*, 42(11): 2487–2504.

De la Peza, María del Carmen (2017) 'Is Spanish our language? Alfonso Reyes and the policies of language in Mexico', in O. Kaltmeier and M. Rufer (eds) *Entangled Heritages: Postcolonial Perspectives on the Uses of the Past in Latin America*, London: Routledge, pp 69–85.

De Sousa Santos, Boaventura (2010) *Para descolonizar occidente: más allá del pensamiento abismal*, Buenos Aires: CLACSO and Prometeo libros.

De Sousa Santos, Boaventura (2014) *Epistemologies of the South: Justice against Epistemicide*, Boulder, CO: Paradigm Publishers.

De Sousa Santos, Boaventura (2018) *The End of the Cognitive Empire: The Coming of Age of Epistemologies of the South*, Durham, NC: Duke University Press.

De Sousa Santos, Boaventura and Rodríguez, César A. (eds) (2005) *Law and Globalization from Below: Towards a Cosmopolitan Legality*, Cambridge: Cambridge University Press.

Dekker, Jeroen H. (2000) 'The century of the child revisited', *International Journal of Children's Rights*, 8: 133–150.

Della Porta, Donatella, Andretta, Massimiliano, Mosca, Lorenzo and Reiter, Herbert (2006) *Globalization from Below: Transnational Activists and Protest Networks*, Minneapolis: University of Minnesota Press.

Dembour, Marie-Bénédicte (2001) 'Following the movement of the pendulum: Between universalism and relativism', in J.K. Cowan, M.-B. Dembour and R.A. Wilson (eds) *Culture and Rights: Anthropological Perspectives*, Cambridge: Cambridge University Press, pp 56–79.

Deppisch, Sonja (2016) 'Urbane sozial-ökologische Resilienz', in R. Wink (ed) *Multidisziplinäre Perspektiven der Resilienzforschung*, Wiesbaden: Springer VS, pp 199–213.

Derr, Victoria, Chawla, Louise and van Vliet, Willem (2017a) 'Children as natural change agents: Child-friendly cities as resilient cities', in K. Bishop and L. Corkery (eds) *Designing Cities with Children and Young People: Beyond Playgrounds and Skate Parks*, New York: Routledge, pp 24–35.

Derr, Victoria, Corona, Yolanda and Gülgönen, Tuline (2017b) 'Children's perceptions of and engagement in urban resilience in the United States and Mexico', *Journal of Planning Education and Research*, available at: http:// doi: 0739456X17723436

Derr, Victoria, Sitzoglou, Maria, Gülgönen, Tuline and Corona, Yolanda (2018) 'Integrating children and youth participation into resilience planning: Lessons from three resilient cities', *Canadian Journal of Children's Rights*, 5(1): 116–149.

Desmet, Ellen, Lembrechts, Sara, Reynaert, Didier and Vandenhole, Wouter (2015) 'Conclusions: Towards a field of critical children's rights studies', in W. Vandenhole, E. Desmet, D. Reynaert and S. Lembrechts (eds) *Routledge International Handbook of Children's Rights Studies*, London: Routledge, pp 412–429.

Detrick, Sharon (ed) (1992) *The United Nations Convention on the Rights of the Child: A Guide to the 'Travaux Preparatoires'*, Dordrecht: Martin Nijhoff.

Deutsche Bundesregierung (2017) *Globale Nachhaltigkeitsstrategie. Neuauflage 2016*, available at: www.bundesregierung.de/resource/blob/975292/730 844/3d30c6c2875a9a08d364620ab7916af6/deutsche-nachhaltigkeitsstrate gie-neuauflage-2016-download-bpa-data.pdf?download=1

Diana, Chiara (2020) 'Global South childhoods', in D.T. Cook (ed) *The SAGE Encyclopedia of Children and Childhood Studies*, Los Angeles: SAGE, pp 867–870.

Dias, José, Gallego, Francisco A. and Lafortune, Jeanne (2016) 'Nacimientos fuera del matrimonio en la historia de Chile: Algunos echos estilizados', *Estudios Públicos*, 142: 37–79.

Díaz Barriga, Frida and Reséndiz, Ana María (2017) 'Factores de resiliencia y vulnerabilidad en jóvenes afectados por la violencia en Ciudad Juárez, Chihuahua', *Argumentos – Estudios Críticos de la Sociedad*, 84: 147–168.

Díaz Gómez, Álvaro and Alvarado Salgado, Sara Victoria (2012) 'Subjetividad política encorpada', *Revista Colombiana de Educación*, 63: 111–128.

Dieckermann, Elizabeth (2018) 'The best interests principle and its relationship to subjectivity, culture and historical injustice', unpublished paper, Potsdam University of Applied Sciences, MA Childhood Studies and Children's Rights.

DiGirolamo, Vincent (2022) *Crying the News: A History of America's Newsboys*, New York: Oxford University Press.

Dillon, Sara (2010) *International Children's Rights*, Durham, NC: Carolina Academic Press.

Dörre, Klaus (2009) 'Die neue Landnahme. Dynamiken und Grenzen des Finanzmarktkapitalismus', in K. Dörre, S. Lessenich and H. Rosa (eds) *Soziologie – Kapitalismus – Kritik. Eine Debatte*, Frankfurt/M.: Suhrkamp, pp 21–86.

Douzinas, Costas (2019) *The Radical Philosophy of Rights*, London: Routledge.

Duque Monsalve, Luisa Fernanda, Patiño Gaviría, Carlos Dario, Muñoz Gaviría, Diego Alejandro, Villa Holguín, Edison Eduardo and Cardona Estrada, Jhon Jairo (2016) 'La subjetividad política en el contexto latinoamericano. Una revisión y una propuesta', *Revista CES Psicología*, 9(2): 128–151.

Durkheim, Émile (1934) *L'éducation morale*, Paris: Presses Universitaires de Paris.

Dussel, Enrique (1980) *Philosophy of Liberation*, London: Wipf and Stock Publishers.

Eichsteller, Gabriel (2009) 'Janusz Korczak: His legacy and its relevance for children's rights today', *International Journal of Children's Rights*, 17: 377–391.

Endreß, Martin and Maurer, Andrea (eds) (2015) *Resilienz im Sozialen. Theoretische und empirische Analysen*, Wiesbaden: Springer VS.

Engler, Wolfgang (2005) *Bürger, ohne Arbeit. Für eine radikale Neugestaltung der Gesellschaft*, Berlin: Aufbau.

Ennew, Judith (2009) *The Right to be Properly Researched: How to Do Rights-based Scientific Research with Children*, 10-manual boxed set, Bangkok: Knowing Children, Norwegian Centre for Child Research and World Vision International.

Ennew, Judith, Myers, William E. and Plateau, Dominique Pierre (2005) 'Defining child labor as if human rights really matter', in B.H. Weston (ed) *Child Labor and Human Rights*, Boulder, CO: Lynne Rienner Publishers, pp 27–54.

Enriz, Noelia, Hecht, Ana Carolina and García Palacios, Mariana (2020) 'Niñas y niños indígenas, entre derechos universales y particulares', in P. Isacovich and J. Grinberg (eds) *Infancias y juventudes a 30 años de la Convención sobre los Derechos del Niño*, José C. Paz: Edunpaz, pp 215–242.

Escobar, Arturo (2014) *Sentipensar con la tierra: Nuevas lecturas sobre desarrollo, territorio y diferencia*, Medellin: UNAULA.

Escobar, Arturo (2016) 'Thinking-feeling with the earth: Territorial struggles and the ontological dimension of the epistemologies of the south', *Revista de Antropologia Iberoamericana*, 11(1): 11–32.

Esser, Florian (2016) 'Neither "thick" nor "thin": Reconceptualising agency and childhood relationally', in F. Esser, M.S. Baader, T. Betz and B. Hungerland (eds) *Reconceptualising Agency and Childhood: New Perspectives in Childhood Studies*, London: Routledge, pp 48–60.

Esser, Florian, Baader, Meike S., Betz, Tanja and Hungerland, Beatrice (eds) (2016) *Reconceptualising Agency and Childhood: New Perspectives in Childhood Studies*, London: Routledge.

European Commission (2005) *Best Procedure Project: 'Mini-Companies in Secondary Education'. Final Report of the Expert Group*, Brussels: European Commission, Directorate-General for Enterprise and Industry.

European Commission (2013) *Action Plan for Resilience in Crisis-prone Countries 2013–2020*, available at: https://ec.europa.eu/echo/files/polic ies/resilience/com_2013_227_ap_crisis_prone_countries_en.pdf

European Commission (2016) 'Building resilience. The EU's approach. EU factsheet – resilience', available at: https://ec.europa.eu/echo/files/aid/ countries/factsheets/thematic/EU_building_resilience_en.pdf

European Union (2016) *Shared Vision, Common Action: A Stronger Europe. A Global Strategy for the European Union's Foreign and Security Policy*, available at: http://eeas.europa.eu/archives/docs/top_stories/pdf/eugs_review_web.pdf

Evans, Brad and Reid, Julian (2014) *Resilient Life: The Art of Living Dangerously*, Cambridge: Polity.

Fals Borda, Orlando (1970) *Ciencia propia y colonialismo intelectual*, México: Nuestro Tiempo (new edition: Bogotá: Punta de Lanza y Carlos Valencia Editores, 1981).

Fals Borda, Orlando (1979) *El problema de cómo investigar la realidad para transformarla*, Bogotá: Tercer Mundo.

Fals Borda, Orlando (2009) *Una sociología sentipensante para América Latina*, Compilado por Victor Manuel Moncayo, Bogotá: Siglo del Hombre Editores and CLACSO.

Fanon, Frantz ([1952] 2008) *Black Skin, White Masks*, New York: Grove Press.

Fanon, Frantz ([1966] 2004) *The Wretched of the Earth*, New York: Grove Press.

Färber, Corina (2019) 'Subjektivierung in der Pädagogik. Das Subjekt zwischen Ent- und Ermächtigung', in N. Ricken, R. Casale and C. Thompson (eds) *Subjektivierung. Erziehungswissenschaftliche Theorieperspektiven*, Weinheim: Beltz-Juventa, pp 75–94.

Farson, Richard (1974) *Birthrights: A Bill of Rights for Children*, New York: Macmillan.

Faulkner, Elizabeth A. and Nyamutata, Conrad (2020) 'The decolonisation of children's rights and the colonial contours of the Convention on the Rights of the Child', *International Journal of Children's Rights*, 28: 66–88.

Faulkner, Joanne (2020) 'Colonialism and childhood', in D.T. Cook (ed) *The SAGE Encyclopedia of Children and Childhood Studies*, Thousand Oaks, CA: SAGE, pp 538–542.

Federle, Katherine Hunt (1994) 'Rights flow downhill', *International Journal of Children's Rights*, 2: 343–368.

Fekete, Alexander, Grinda, Christiane and Norf, Celia (2016) 'Resilienz in der Risiko- und Katastrophenforschung: Perspektiven für disziplinübergreifende Arbeitsfelder', in R. Wink (ed) *Multidisziplinäre Perspektiven der Resilienzforschung*, Wiesbaden: Springer VS, pp 215–231.

Felsman, J. Kirk (1989) 'Risk and resiliency in childhood: The lives of street children', in T.F. Dugan and R. Coles (eds) *The Child in Our Times: Studies in the Development of Resiliency*, New York: Brunner and Mazel, pp 56–80.

Ferguson, Lucinda (2013) 'Not merely rights for children but children's rights: The theory gap and the assumption of the importance of children's rights', *International Journal of Children's Rights*, 21: 177–208.

Ferrer Ortega, Luis Gabriel (2014) *Los derechos de las futuras generaciones desde la perspectiva del derecho internacional. El principio de equidad intergeneracional*, Mexico City: Universidad Nacional Autónoma de México, Instituto de Investigaciones Jurídicas.

Fiedler, Julia and Posch, Christian (eds) (2009) *Yes, They Can! Children Researching Their Lives*, Baltmannsweiler: Schneider Verlag Hohengehren.

Fischer-Lescano, Andreas (2018) 'Subjektlose Rechte', in A. Fischer-Lescano, H. Franzki and J. Horst (eds) *Gegenrechte*, Tübingen: Mohr Siebeck, pp 377–420.

Fischer-Lescano, Andreas, Franzki, Hannah and Horst, Johan (eds) (2018) *Gegenrechte. Recht jenseits des Subjekts*, Tübingen: Mohr Siebeck.

Flasher, Jack (1978) 'Adultism', *Adolescence*, 13(51): 517–523.

Fletcher, Adam F.C. (2015) *Facing Adultism*, Olympia: CommonAction Books.

Folke, Carl, Carpenter, Stephen, Walker, Brian, Scheffer, Marten, Chapin, Terry and Rockström, Johan (2010) 'Resilience thinking: Integrating resilience, adaptability and transformability', *Ecology and Society*, 15(4): Art. 20.

Foucault, Michel (1978) *The History of Sexuality. Volume 1: An Introduction*, New York: Pantheon Books.

Foucault, Michel (1982) 'The subject and the power', *Critical Inquiry*, 8(4): 777–795.

Foy Valencia, Pierre (2019) 'Bases conceptuales para el estudio interdisciplinario del sistema juridico y las futuras generaciones: perspecitiva teórica y empírica desde el derecho ambiental', *THÉMIS – Revista de Derecho*, 74: 20–26.

Fraser, Nancy (2013) *Scales of Justice: Reimagining Political Space in a Globalizing World*, Cambridge: Polity.

Freeman, Michael (2002) *Human Rights: An Interdisciplinary Approach*, London: Wiley.

Freeman, Michael (2007) 'Why it remains important to take children's rights seriously', *International Journal of Children's Rights*, 15: 5–23.

Freeman, Michael (2009) 'Children's rights as human rights: Reading the UNCRC', in J. Qvortrup, W.A. Corsaro and M.-S. Honig (eds) *The Palgrave Handbook of Childhood Studies*, Basingstoke: Palgrave Macmillan, pp 377–393.

Freeman, Michael (2020) *A Magna Carta for Children? Rethinking Children's Rights*, Cambridge: Cambridge University Press.

Freeman, Michael and Veerman, Philip E. (eds) (1997) *The Moral Status of Children: Essays on the Rights of the Child*, Dordrecht: Martinus Nijhoff.

Freire, Paulo ([1968] 2000) *Pedagogy of the Oppressed*, New York: The Continuum International Publishing Group.

Freud, Sigmund ([1915] 1963) 'The unconscious', in *General Psychological Theory: Papers on Metapsychology*, New York: Collier Books Macmillan, pp 116–150.

Freud, Sigmund ([1923] 1957) 'The ego and the id', in J. Rickman (ed) *A General Selection from the Works of Sigmund Freud*, New York: Liveright Publishing Corporation, pp 5–22.

Gaitán, Lourdes (2014) *De 'menores' a protagonistas. Los derechos de los niños en el trabajo social*, Barcelona: Impulso a la Acción Social, Colección Libros A Punto and Madrid: Consejo General del Trabajo Social.

Galeano, Eduardo (1991) *The Book of Embraces*, New York and London: W.W. Norton & Company.

Galvis Ortiz, Ligia (2006) *Las niñas, los niños y los adolescentes – titulares activos de derechos*, Bogotá: Ediciones Aurora.

Galvis Ortiz, Ligia (2007) 'Reflexiones en torno a la titularidad de derechos', in E. Durán and M.C. Torrado (eds) *Derechos de los niños y las niñas. Debates, realidades y perspectivas*, Bogotá: Universidad Nacional de Colombia, pp 57–64.

García Canclini, Néstor (1990) *Culturas híbridas. Estrategias para entrar y salir de la modernidad*, Mexico City: Grijalbo (English edition: *Hybrid Cultures: Strategies for Entering and Leaving Modernity*, Minneapolis: University of Minnesota Press, 2005).

García Canclini, Néstor (2002) *Culturas populares en el capitalismo*, Mexico City: Grijalbo.

García Rodríguez, Raúl Ernesto (2013) 'La carnavalización del mundo como crítica: risa, acción política y subjetividad en la vida social y en el hablar', *Athenea Digital*, 13(2): 121–130.

Garmezy, Norman (1981) 'Children under stress: Perspectives on antecedents and correlates of vulnerability and resistance to psychopathology', in I.A. Rabin, J. Aronoff, A.M. Barclay and R.A. Zucker (eds) *Further Explorations in Personality*, New York: Wiley, pp 196–269.

Gaudry, Adam J.P. (2011) 'Insurgent research', *Wicazo Sa Review*, 26(1): 113–136.

Gebauer, Thomas (2015) 'Paradox der Resilienz', *medico international – Rundschreiben 02/15*: 4–7.

Gebauer, Thomas (2017) 'Fit für die Katastrophe. Ein neues entwicklungspolitisches Modewort verhindert Ursachenbekämpfung', in medico international (ed) *Fit für die Katastrophe? Kritische Anmerkungen zum Resilienzdiskurs im aktuellen Krisenmanagement* , Gießen: Psychosozial-Verlag, pp 13–22.

Gilmore, Amir A. and Bettis, Pamela J. (2021) 'Antiblackness and the adultification of Black children in a US prison nation', in *Oxford Research Encyclopedias, Education*, Oxford: Oxford University Press, pp 1–32.

Giri, Ananta Kumar (2013) *Knowledge and Human Liberation: Towards Planetary Realizations*, London: Anthem Press.

Goff, Phillip A., Jackson, Matthew C., Lewis Di Leone, Brooke A., Culotta, Carmen M. and DiTomasso, Natalie A. (2014). 'The essence of innocence: Consequences of dehumanizing Black children', *Journal of Personality and Social Psychology*, 106(4): 526–544.

Goldsmith, Edward (2002) 'Development as colonialism', *World Affairs*, 6(2): 18–36.

González-Muzzio, Claudia (2013) 'El rol del lugar y el capital social en la resiliencia comunitaria posdesastre. Aproximaciones mediante un estudio de caso después del terremoto del 27/F', *EURE* (Santiago de Chile), 39(117): 25–48.

Gottlieb, David (1973) *Children's Liberation*, Englewood Cliffs, NJ: Prentice Hall.

Graefe, Stefanie (2019) *Resilienz im Krisenkapitalismus. Wider das Lob der Anpassungsfähigkeit*, Bielefeld: transcript.

Graham, Anne, Powell, Mary Ann, Taylor, Nicola, Anderson, Donnah and Fitzgerald, Robyn (2013) *Ethical Research Involving Children*, Florence: UNICEF Innocenti Office of Research.

Gramsci, Antonio (2011) *Prison Notebooks*, 3 volumes, edited and translated by Joseph Buttigieg, New York: Columbia University Press.

Gran, Brian (2021) *The Sociology of Children's Rights*, Cambridge: Polity.

Griffin, James (2002) 'Do children have rights?', in D. Archard and C.M. Macleod (eds) *The Moral and Political Status of Children*, Oxford: Oxford University Press, pp 19–30.

Grinberg, Paula and Isacovich, Julieta (2020) 'Introducción. Los derechos de las infancias y las juventudes: debates e interrogantes a la luz del 30 aniversario de la Convención de los Derechos del Nino', in P. Isacovich and J. Grinberg (eds) *Infancias y juventudes a 30 años de la Convención sobre los Derechos del Niño*, Buenos Aires: EDUNPAZ – Editorial Universitaria, pp 41–84.

Gross, Beatrice and Gross, Ronald (eds) (1977) *The Children's Rights Movement: Overcoming the Oppression of Young People*, Garden City, NY: Anchor Books.

Gruner, Sheila (2018) 'Territorio y el ser decolonial: Pervivencia de las mujeres y los pueblos en tiempos de conflicto, paz y desarrollo', in P. López and L. García Guerreiro (eds) *Movimientos Indígenas y Autonomías en Anmérica Latina: Escenarios de Disputa y Horizontes de Posibilidad*, Buenos Aires: El Colectivo and CLACSO, pp 259–283.

Gstettner, Peter (1981) *Die Eroberung des Kindes durch die Wissenschaft. Aus der Geschichte der Disziplinierung*, Reinbek: Rowohlt.

Gu, Xiaorong (2022) '"Save the children!": Governing left-behind children through family in China's great migration', *Current Sociology*, 70(4): 513–538.

Guerrero Arias, Patricio (2010) *Corazonar. Una Antropología Comprometida con la Vida. Miradas otras desde Abya-Yala para la descolonización del poder, del saber y del ser*, Quito: Ediciones Abya-Yala.

Guerrero Arias, Patricio (2016) *Colonialidad del saber e insurgencia de las sabidurías otras: Corazonar las epistemologías hegemónicas, como respuesta de insurgencia (de)colonial*, Quito: Universidad Andina Simón Bolívar, Sede Ecuador, Área de Letras y Estudios Culturales.

Habermas, Jürgen (1981) *The Theory of Communicative Action, Vol. 2. Lifeworld and System: The Critique of Functionalist Reason*, Boston, MA: Beacon.

Habermas, Jürgen (1996) *Between Facts and Norms: Contributions to a Discourse Theory of Law and Democracy*, Cambridge: Polity.

Habermas, Jürgen (2003) *The Future of Human Nature*, Cambridge: Polity.

Häkli, Jouni and Kallio, Kirsi Pauliina (2018) 'On becoming political: The political in subjectivity', *Subjectivity*, 11: 57–73.

Hall, Stuart (1981) 'Notes on deconstructing "the popular"', in R. Samuel (ed) *People's History and Socialist Theory*, London: Routledge and Kegan Paul, pp 227–240.

Hammersley, Martyn and Kim, Chae-Young (2021) 'Child-led research, children's rights and childhood studies: A reply to Thomas', *Childhood*, 28(2): 200–202.

Hampton, Eber (1995) 'Memory comes before knowledge: Research may improve if researchers remember their motives', paper presented at the First Biannual Indigenous Scholars' Conference, University of Alberta, Edmonton.

Hanisch, Michael (2017) 'Vorwärts, Resilienz! Vorschläge zum Resilienzausbau in Deutschland', *Arbeitspapier Sicherheitspolitik*, No 16/2017, Berlin: Bundesakademie für Sicherheitspolitik, available at: www.baks.bund.de/sites/baks010/files/arbeitspapier_sicherheitspolitik_2017_16.pdf

Hanson, Karl (2012) 'Schools of thought in children's rights', in M. Liebel, K. Hanson, I. Saadi and W. Vandenhole, *Children's Rights from Below: Cross-cultural Perspectives*, Basingstoke: Palgrave Macmillan, pp 63–79.

Hanson, Karl (2014) 'Editorial: "Killed by charity" – towards interdisciplinary children's rights studies', *Childhood*, 21(4): 441–446.

Hanson, Karl and Nieuwenhuys, Olga (eds) (2013) *Reconceptualizing Children's Rights in International Development: Living Rights, Social Justice, Translations*, Cambridge: Cambridge University Press.

Hanson, Karl and Nieuwenhuys, Olga (2020) 'A child-centred approach to children's rights law: Living rights and translations', in J. Todres and S.M. King (eds) *The Oxford Handbook of Children's Rights Law*, Oxford: Oxford University Press, pp 101–120.

Hanson, Karl and Peleg, Noam (2020) 'Waiting for children's rights theory', *International Journal of Children's Rights*, 28(1): 15–35.

Haraway, Donna (1988) 'Situated knowledges: The science question in feminism and the privilege of partial perspective', *Feminist Studies*, 14(3): 575–599.

Haraway, Donna J. (2005) 'Conversations with Donna Haraway', in J. Schneider (ed) *Live Theory*, New York: MPG books, pp 114–157.

Harcourt, Deborah and Hägglund, Solveig (2013) 'Turning the UNCRC upside down: A bottom-up perspective on children's rights', *International Journal of Early Years Education*, 21(4): 286–299.

Harris-Short, Sonia (2003) 'International human rights law: Imperialist, inept and ineffective? Cultural relativism and the UN Convention on the Rights of the Child', *Human Rights Quarterly*, 3: 130–181.

Harsin, Jayson and Hayward, Mark (2013) 'Stuart Hall's "deconstructing the popular": Reconsiderations 30 years later', *Communication, Culture & Critique*, 6: 201–207.

Hawes, Joseph (1991) *The Children's Rights Movement: A History of Advocacy and Protection*, Boston, MA: Twayne.

Hefner, Keith (1979) *Children's Rights Handbook*, Ann Arbor, MI: Youth Liberation Press.

Held, Virginia (2006) *The Ethics of Care: Personal, Political, and Global*, Oxford: Oxford University Press.

Hilgendorf, Eric and Zabel, Benno (eds) (2021a) *Die Idee subjektiver Rechte*, Berlin: De Gruyter.

Hilgendorf, Eric and Zabel, Benno (2021b) 'Die Idee subjektiver Rechte', in E. Hilgendorf and B. Zabel (eds) *Die Idee subjektiver Rechte*, Berlin: De Gruyter, pp 1–16.

Hinkelammert, Franz, J. (1999) 'La inversión de los derechos humanos: el caso de John Locke', *Pasos 85*, DEI, San José, Costa Rica, September–October, pp 20–35.

Hobbes, Thomas (1651) *Leviathan*, London.

Hollander, Jocelyn A. and Einwohner, Rachel L. (2004) 'Conceptualizing resistance', *Sociological Forum*, 19(4): 533–554.

Holling, Crawford S. (1973) 'Resilience and stability in ecological systems', *Annual Review of Ecology and Systematics*, 4(1): 1–23.

Holling, Crawford S. (2001) 'Understanding the complexity of economic, ecological, and social systems', *Ecosystems*, 4: 390–403.

Holloway, John (2010) *Change the World Without Taking Power: The Meaning of Revolution Today*, London: Pluto Press.

Holmberg, Arita and Alvinius, Aida (2019) 'Children's protest in relation to the climate emergency: A qualitative study on a new form of resistance promoting political and social change', *Childhood*, 27(1): 78–92.

Holt, John (1974) *Escape from Childhood*, New York: Dutton.

Honig, Michael-Sebastian, Lange, Andreas and Leu, Hans Rudolf (eds) (1999) *Aus der Perspektive von Kindern? Zur Methodologie der Kindheitsforschung*, Weinheim: Juventa.

Horkheimer, Max (2013) *Critique of Instrumental Reason*, London: Verso.

Horkheimer, Max and Adorno, Theodor W. ([1947] 2002) *Dialectic of Enlightenment: Philosophical Fragments*, Stanford: Stanford University Press.

Howard, Neil and Okyere, Samuel (eds) (2021) *International Child Protection: Towards Politics and Participation*, Cham: Springer International Publishing.

Hungerland, Beatrice, Liebel, Manfred, Liesecke, Anja and Wihstutz, Anne (2007) 'Paths to participatory autonomy: The meanings of work by children in Germany', *Childhood*, 14(2): 257–277.

Hunner-Kreisel, Christine, Ben-Arieh, Asher and Lee, Bong Jo (2022) 'Do children have a transnational age? Representation and epistemic violence as research-ethical challenges in child well-being (indicator) research', in M. Joos and L. Alberth (eds) *Forschungsethik in der Kindheitsforschung*, Weinheim: Beltz-Juventa, pp 140–154.

Hutcheson, Francis (1755) *A System of Moral Philosophy*, Glasgow: University of Glasgow.

IFRC (2018) *Road Map to Community Resilience: Operationalizing the Framework for Community Resilience*, Geneva: International Federation of Red Cross and Red Crescent Societies, available at: https://media.ifrc.org/ifrc/wp-content/uploads/sites/5/2018/03/1310403-Road-Map-to-Community-Resilience-Final-Version_EN-08.pdf

ILO (1989) *Indigenous and Tribal Peoples Convention* (C 169), Geneva: International Labour Organization, available at: www.ilo.org/dyn/normlex/en/f?p=NORMLEXPUB:55:0::NO::P55_TYPE,P55_LANG,P55_DOCUMENT,P55_NODE:REV,en,C169,/Document

Instituto de Defensa Legal (2019) 'Niños y niñas presentan demanda de amparo ambiental contra el Estado peruano', available at: www.idl.org.pe/ninos-presentan-demanda-de-amparo-ambiental-contrael-estado-peruano/?fbclid=IwAR0rzkF2od085sNWm69Tq_E27hwABcQy_ZDKFr2bsn7_QgBKpKk X7lm

International Monetary Fund (2019) 'Building resilience in developing countries vulnerable to large natural disasters', *Policy Paper No. 19/020*, available at: www.imf.org/en/Publications/Policy-Papers/Issues/2019/06/24/Building-Resilience-in-Developing-Countries-Vulnerable-to-Large-Natural-Disasters-47020

Invernizzi, Antonella and Williams, Jane (eds) (2008) *Children and Citizenship*, Los Angeles: SAGE.

Invernizzi, Antonella and Williams, Jane (eds) (2016) *The Human Rights of Children: From Visions to Implementation*, London: Routledge.

Invernizzi, Antonella, Liebel, Manfred, Milne, Brian and Budde, Rebecca (eds) (2017) *'Children Out of Place' and Human Rights: In Memory of Judith Ennew*, Cham: Springer International Switzerland.

Jackson, Robert P. (2017) 'Antonio Gramsci: Persons, subjectivity, and the political', in G. Rae and E. Ingala (eds) *Subjectivity and the Political: Contemporary Perspectives*, New York: Routledge, pp 135–157.

Jacobs, Margaret D. (2009) *White Mother to a Dark Race: Settler Colonialism, Maternalism, and the Removal of Indigenous Children in the American West and Australia, 1880–1940*, Lincoln, NE: University of Nebraska Press.

Jacobs, Margaret D. (2021) *After One Hundred Winters: In Search of Reconciliation on America's Stolen Lands*, Princeton, NJ: Princeton University Press.

James, Allison (2011) 'Agency', in J. Qvortrup, W. Corsaro and M. Honig (eds) *The Palgrave Handbook of Childhood Studies*, Basingstoke: Palgrave Macmillan, pp 34–45.

James, Allison and Prout, Alan (eds) (1997) *Constructing and Reconstructing Childhood: Contemporary Issues in the Sociological Study of Childhood*, London: Falmer Press.

Jay, Martin (ed) (1987) *An Unmastered Past: The Autobiographical Reflections of Leo Löwenthal*, Berkeley, CA: University of California Press.

Jiménez García, Marco Antonio (2015) 'Lo Popular en la educación: Entre mito e imaginario', *Praxis & Saber*, 6(12): 31–52.

Jirata, Tadesse Jaleta (2022) 'Indigenous conceptualization of children's rights among agropastoral societies in southern Ethiopia', *Childhood*, 29(3): 389–405.

Joas, Hans (2015) *Sind Menschenrechte westlich?* Munich: Kösel.

Joos, Magdalena and Alberth, Lars (eds) (2022) *Forschungsethik in der Kindheitsforschung*, Weinheim: Beltz-Juventa.

Jørgensen, Clara R. and Wyness, Michael (2021) *Kid Power, Inequalities and Intergenerational Relations*, London: Anthem Press.

Kaltmeier, Olaf (2012) 'Methoden dekolonialisieren: Reziprozität und Dialog in der herrschenden Geopolitik des Wissens', in S. Corona and O. Kaltmeier (eds) *Methoden dekolonialisieren. Eine Werkzeugkiste zur Demokratisierung der Sozial- und Kulturwissenschaften*, Münster: Westfälisches Dampfboot, pp 18–44.

Kaltmeier, Olaf (2019) *Refeudalización. Desiqualdad social, economía y cultura política en América Latina en el temprano siglo XXI*, Bielefeld: Bielefeld University Press.

Kaltmeier, Olaf (2020) 'Horizontal en lo vertical. ¿O cómo descolonizar las metodologías en contextos de extrema desigualdad y de la crisis planetaria', in I. Cornejo and M. Rufer (eds) *Horizontalidad. Hacia una crítica de la metodologí*, Buenos Aires: CLACSO and Guadalajara: CALAS, pp 93–122.

Kämpfe, Karin, Menzel, Britta and Eunicke, Nicoletta (2022) 'Kinder als Gegenspieler*innen – Widerständiges Handeln von Kindern in Gruppendiskussionen', in M. Joos and L. Alberth (eds) *Forschungsethik in der Kindheitsforschung*, Weinheim: Beltz-Juventa, pp 88–104.

Kannan, Divya, Dar, Anandini, Duff, Sarah E., Sen, Hia, Nag, Shivani and Bergère, Clovis (2022) 'Childhood, youth, and identity: A roundtable conversation from the global south', *Journal of Childhood Studies*, 47(2): 20–31.

Kaplan, Howard B. (1999) 'Toward an understanding of resilience: A critical review of definitions and models', in M.D. Glantz and J.L. Johnson (eds) *Resilience and Development: Positive Life Adaptations*, New York: Kluwer Plenum, pp 17–84.

Kay Jager, Rebecca (2015) *Malinche, Pocahontas, and Sacagawea: Indian Women as Cultural Intermediaries and National Symbols*, Norman, OK: University of Oklahoma Press.

Kellett, Mary (2005) *How to Develop Children as Researchers: A Step by Step Guide to the Research Process*, London: Paul Chapman.

Kellett, Mary (2010) *Rethinking Children and Research: Attitudes in Contemporary Society*, London: Continuum.

Kelly, Mark G.E. (2013) 'Foucault, subjectivity and technologies of the self', in C. Falzon, T. O'Leary and J. Sawick (eds) *A Companion to Foucault*, Hoboken, NJ: Blackwell, pp 510–525.

Kemmis, Stephen and McTaggart, Robin (2005) 'Participatory action research: Communicative action and the public sphere', in N. Denzin and Y. Lincoln (eds) *Handbook of Qualitative Research* (3rd edn), Thousand Oaks, CA: SAGE, pp 559–603.

Kim, Chae-Young (2016) 'Why research "by" children? Rethinking the assumptions underlying the facilitation of children as researchers', *Children & Society*, 30(3): 230–240.

Kim, Chae-Young (2017) 'Participation or pedagogy? Ambiguities and tensions surrounding the facilitation of children as researchers', *Childhood*, 24(1): 84–98.

Kipling, Rudyard (1899) 'The white man's burden' (poem), available at: https://ux1.eiu.edu/nekey/syllabi/british/kipling1899.pdf

Kirby, Perpetua (1999) *Involving Young Researchers*, York: York Publishing Services.

Kleibl, Tanja, Lutz, Ronald, Noyoo, Ndangwa, Bunk, Benjamin, Dittmann, Annika and Seepamore, Boitumelo (eds) (2020) *The Routledge Handbook of Postcolonial Social Work*, London: Routledge.

Klocker, Natascha (2007) 'An example of "thin" agency: Child domestic workers in Tanzania', in R. Panelli, S. Punch and E. Robson (eds) *Global Perspectives on Rural Childhood and Youth*, New York: Routledge, pp 83–93.

Komulainen, Sirkka (2007) 'The ambiguity of the child's "voice" in social research', *Childhood*, 14(1): 11-28.

Komulainen, Sirkka Liisa (2020) 'Children's voices', in D.T. Cook (ed) *The SAGE Encyclopedia of Children and Childhood Studies*, Thousand Oaks, CA: SAGE, pp 507–510.

Korczak, Janusz ([1919] 2007) *How to Love a Child*, in *Selected Works of Janusz Korczak*, digital reprint by University of Michigan, pp 93–354.

Korczak, Janusz (2007) *Selected Works of Janusz Korczak*, edited by Martin Wolins, digital reprint by University of Michigan, available at: www.januszkorczak.ca/legacy/CombinedMaterials.pdf

Korczak, Janusz (2009) *The Child's Right to Respect* (first edition in Polish 1929), Strasbourg: Council of Europe, Commissioner for Human Rights.

Korczak, Janusz (2018) *How to Love a Child and Other Selected Works*, vol 1, London: Vallentine Mitchell.

Kotliarenco, María Angélica, Cáveres, Irma and Álvarez, Catalina (eds) (1996) *Resiliencia: construyendo en adversidad*, Santiago de Chile: CEANIM – Centro de Estudios y Atención del Niño y la Mujer.

Kovach, Margaret (2010) *Indigenous Methodologies: Characteristics, Conversations and Contexts*, Toronto: Toronto University Press.

Kovach, Margaret (2015) 'Emerging from the margins: Indigenous methodologies', in S. Strega and L. Brown (eds) *Research as Resistance: Revisiting Critical, Indigenous and Anti-Oppressive Approaches*, Toronto: Canadian Scholars' Press and Women's Press, pp 43–64.

Krause, Kristine and Schramm, Katharina (2011) 'Thinking through political subjectivity', *African Diaspora*, 4: 115–134.

Kupffer, Heinrich (1974) *Jugend und Herrschaft. Eine Analyse der pädagogischen Entfremdung*, Heidelberg: Quelle & Meyer.

Kusch, Rodolfo (1977) *El pensamiento indígena y popular en América*, Buenos Aires: Hachette.

Laclau, Ernesto (2005) *On Populist Reason*, London: Verso.

Lahti, Sara E. (2019) 'A tale of two NGO discourses: NGO stories of suffering Qur'anic school children in Senegal', in K. Cheney and A. Sinervo (eds) *Disadvantaged Childhoods and Humanitarian Intervention*, Basingstoke: Palgrave Macmillan, pp 113–134.

Lander, Ernesto (ed) (2000) *La colonialidad del saber: eurocentrismo y ciencias sociales. Perspectivas latinoamericanas*, Buenos Aires: CLACSO.

Lay-Lisboa, Siu, Araya-Bolvarán, Evelyn, Marabolí-Garay, Camila, Olivero-Tapia, Gabriela and Santander-Andrade, Carolina (2018) 'Protagonismo infantil en la escuela. Las relaciones pedagógicas en la construcción de ciudadanía', *Sociedad e Infancias*, 2: 147–170.

Lee-Treweek, Geraldine and Linkogle, Stephanie (eds) (2000) *Danger in the Field: Risk and Ethics in Social Research*, London: Routledge.

LeFrançois, Brenda A. (2014) 'Adultism', in T. Teo (ed) *Encyclopedia of Critical Psychology*, New York: Springer, pp 47–49.

Lessenich, Stephan (2009) 'Mobilität und Kontrolle. Zur Dialektik der Aktivgesellschaft', in K. Dörre, S. Lessenich and H. Rosa (eds) *Soziologie – Kapitalismus – Kritik. Eine Debatte*, Frankfurt: Suhrkamp, pp 126–177.

Lessing, Hellmut and Liebel, Manfred (1981) *Wilde Cliquen. Szenen einer anderen Arbeiterjugendbewegung*, Bensheim: päd.extra buchverlag.

Lewin, Kurt (1946) 'Action research and minority problems', *Journal of Social Issues*, 2(4): 34–46.

Liebel, Manfred (1994) *Protagonismo Infantil. Movimientos de Niños Trabajadores en América Latina*, Managua: Nueva Nicaragua.

Liebel, Manfred (ed) (1996) *Somos NATRAS. Testimonios de Niños, Niñas y Adolescentes Trabajadores de Nicaragua*, Managua: Nueva Nicaragua.

Liebel, Manfred (2000) *La Otra Infancia. Niñez trabajadora y acción social*, Lima: Ifejant.

Liebel, Manfred (2001) 'Working children's protagonism, children's rights and the outline of a different childhood: A comparative reflection on the discourses in Latin America and the "First World"', in M. Liebel, B. Overwien and A. Recknagel (eds) *Working Children's Protagonism: Social Movements and Empowerment in Latin America, Africa and India*, Frankfurt: IKO, pp 321–348.

Liebel, Manfred (2004) *A Will of Their Own: Cross-cultural Perspectives on Working Children*, London: Zed Books.

Liebel, Manfred (2007a) 'Paternalism, participation and children's protagonism', *Children, Youth and Environments*, 17(3): 56–73.

Liebel, Manfred (2007b) 'Between prohibition and praise: Some hidden aspects of children's work in affluent societies', in B. Hungerland, M. Liebel, B. Milne and A. Wihstutz (eds) *Working to be Someone: Child Focused Research and Practice with Working Children*, London: Jessica Kingsley, pp 123–132.

Liebel, Manfred (2012a), with Karl Hanson, Iven Saadi and Wouter Vandenhole, *Children's Rights from Below: Cross-cultural Perspectives*, Basingstoke: Palgrave Macmillan.

Liebel, Manfred (2012b) 'Child-led organizations and the advocacy of adults: Experiences from Bangladesh and Nicaragua', in M. Freeman (ed) *Law and Childhood Studies: Current Legal Issues 2011*, vol 14, Oxford: Oxford University Press, pp 92–103.

Liebel, Manfred (2013) 'Do children have the right to work? Working children's movements in the struggle for social justice', in K. Hanson and O. Nieuwenhuys (eds) *Reconceptualizing Children's Rights in International Development: Living Rights, Social Justice, Translations*, Cambridge: Cambridge University Press, pp 225–249.

Liebel, Manfred (2014a) 'Adultism and age-based discrimination against children', in D. Kutsar and H. Warming (eds) *Children and Non-Discrimination: Interdisciplinary Textbook*, Tartu: University Press of Estonia, pp 119–143.

Liebel, Manfred (2014b) 'From evolving capacities to evolving capabilities: Contextualizing children's rights', in D. Stoecklin and J.-M. Bonvin (eds) *Children's Rights and the Capability Approach*, Dordrecht: Springer, pp 67–84.

Liebel, Manfred (2016) 'The Moscow Declaration on the Rights of the Child (1918): A contribution from the hidden history of children's rights', *International Journal of Children's Rights*, 24(1): 3–28.

Liebel, Manfred (2017) ' "Children without childhood?" Against the postcolonial capture of childhoods in the global south', in A. Invernizzi, M. Liebel, B. Milne and R. Budde (eds) *'Children Out of Place' and Human Rights: In Memory of Judith Ennew*, Cham: Springer International Switzerland, pp 99–117.

Liebel, Manfred (2018a) 'Janusz Korczak's understanding of children's rights as agency rights', in M. Michalak (ed) *The Rights of the Child Yesterday, Today and Tomorrow – the Korczak Perspective, Part I*, Warsaw: Office of the Ombudsman for Children – Poland, pp 204–239.

Liebel, Manfred (2018b) 'Welfare of agency? Children's interests as foundation of children's rights', *International Journal of Children's Rights*, 26: 597–625.

Liebel, Manfred (2020) *Decolonizing Childhoods: From Exclusion to Dignity*, Bristol: Policy Press.

Liebel, Manfred (2021) *La Niñez Popular. Intereses, derechos y protagonismos de los niños y niñas*, Madrid: Los Libros de la Catarata.

Liebel, Manfred and Budde, Rebecca (2017) 'Other children, other youth: Against Eurocentrism in childhood and youth research', in A. Invernizzi, M. Liebel, B. Milne and R. Budde (eds) *'Children Out of Place' and Human Rights: In Memory of Judith Ennew*, Cham: Springer International Switzerland, pp 119–136.

Liebel, Manfred and Martínez Muñoz, Marta (eds) (2009) *Infancia y Derechos Humanos. Hacia una ciudadanía participante y protagónica*, Lima: Ifejant.

Liebel, Manfred and Meade, Philip (2023) *Adultismus. Die Macht der Erwachsenen über die Kinder. Eine kritische Einführung*, Berlin: Bertz + Fischer.

Liebel, Manfred, Overwien, Bernd and Recknagel, Albert (eds) (2001) *Working Children's Protagonism: Social Movements and Empowerment in Latin America, Africa and India*, Frankfurt: IKO.

Lifton, Betty Jean (1989) *The King of Children: The Life and Death of Janusz Korczak*, London: Pan Books.

Lilja, Mona, Baaz, Mikael, Schultz, Michael and Vinthagen, Stellan (2017) 'How resistance encourages resistance: Theorizing the nexus between power, "organised resistance" and "everyday resistance"', *Journal of Political Power*, 10(1): 40–54.

Llobet, Valeria (2021) 'Las regulaciones del cuidado y los derechos de niños y niñas: un debate situado', in L.R. de Castro (ed) *Infâncias do Sul Global. Experiências, Pesquisa e Teoria desde a Argentina e o Brasil*, Salvador: Ebufa, pp 433–460.

Llobet, Valeria and Milanich, Nara (2018) 'Stratified maternity in the barrio: Mothers and children in Argentine social programs', in R. Rosen and K. Twamley (eds) *Feminism and the Politics of Childhood: Friends or Foes?*, London: UCL Press, pp 172–190.

Locke, John (1689–1690) *Two Treatises of Government*, available at: www.yorku.ca/comninel/courses/3025pdf/Locke.pdf

Locke, John ([1690] 1995) *An Essay Concerning Human Understanding*, Amherst: Prometheus Books.

Loick, Daniel (2017) *Juridismus. Konturen einer kritischen Theorie des Rechts*, Berlin: Suhrkamp.

López, Luis Enrique (ed) (2009) *Interculturalidad, educación y ciudadanía. Perspectivas lationamericanas*, La Paz–Bolivia: Plural Editores.

López, Pavel and García Guerrero, Luciana (eds) (2018) *Movimientos Indígenas y Autonomías en América Latina: Escenarios de Disputa y Horizontes de Posibilidad*, Buenos Aires: El Colectivo and CLACSO.

López Bracamonte, Fabiola Manyari and Limón Aguirre, Fernando (2017) 'Componentes del proceso de resiliencia comunitaria: conocimientos culturales, capacidades sociales y estrategias organizativas', *PSIENCIA – Revista Latinoamericana de Ciencia Psicológica*, 9, doi: 10.5872/psiencia/9.3.61

López Jaramillo, Olga Lucía (2007) 'La resiliencia de las familias en el desplazamiento forzado', in Y. Puyana and M.H. Ramírez (eds) *Familia, Cambios y Estrategias*, Bogotá: Universidad Nacional de Colombia, Facultad de Ciencias Humanas, pp 227–252.

Lorde, Audre (2007) *Sister Outsider: Essays and Speeches*, Berkeley, CA: Crossing Press.

Lorenz, Daniel F. (2013) 'The diversity of resilience: Contributions from a social science perspective', *Natural Hazards*, 67(1): 7–24.

Lösel, Friedrich and Bender, Doris (2007) 'Von generellen Schutzfaktoren zu spezifischen protektiven Prozessen. Konzeptionelle Grundlagen und Ergebnisse der Resilienzforschung', in G. Opp and M. Fingerle (eds) *Was Kinder stärkt. Erziehung zwischen Risiko und Resilienz*, Munich: Ernst Reinhardt, pp 57–78.

Losurdo, Domenico (2014) *Liberalism: A Counter-History*, London: Verso.

Löwenthal, Leo (1989) 'Das kleine Ich und das große Ich. Einspruch gegen die Postmoderne. Rede zur Verleihung des Theodor W. Adorno-Preises 1989 in Frankfurt', *Frankfurter Rundschau*, 2 October, p 17.

Löwy, Michael (2015) *Ecosocialism: A Radical Alternative to Capitalist Catastrophe*, Chicago, IL: Haymarket Books.

Luciani, Leandro (2010) 'La protección social de la niñez: subjetividad y posderechos en la segunda modernidad', *Revista Latinoamericana de Ciencias Sociales, Niñez y Juventud*, 8(2): 885–899.

Lundy, Laura (2007) '"Voice" is not enough: Conceptualising Article 12 of the United Nations Convention on the Rights of the Child', *British Educational Research Journal*, 33: 927–942.

Lundy, Laura and McEvoy, Lesley (2011) 'Children's rights and research processes: Assisting children to (in) formed views', *Childhood*, 19(1): 129–144.

Luthar, Suniya S. (2003) *Resilience and Vulnerability: Adaptation in the Context of Childhood Adversities*, Cambridge: Cambridge University Press.

Maconachie, Roy, Howard, Neil and Bock, Rosilin (2023) 'Theorizing "harm" in relation to children's work', in J. Sumberg and R. Sabates-Wheeler (eds) *Children's Work in African Agriculture: The Harmful and the Harmless*, Bristol: Bristol University Press, pp 24–51.

Magistris, Gabriela (2012) *El magnetismo de los derechos. Narrativas y tensiones en la institucionalización de los Sistemas de Protección de Derechos de los niños, niñas y adolescentes en la provincia de Buenos Aires (2005–2011)*, Tesis por el título de Magister de la Universidad Nacional de San Martín en Derechos Humanos y Políticas Sociales, Buenos Aires.

Magistris, Gabriela (2016) *El Gobierno de la Infancia en la Era de los Derechos. Prácticas locales de 'protección y restitución de derechos de Niños, Niñas y Adolescentes' en dos municipios del conurbano bonaerense*, Tesis para optar por el título de doctora de la Universidad de Buenos Aires en Ciencias Sociales.

Magistris, Gabriela (2020) 'La(s) infancia(s) en la era de los derechos. Balances y desafíos a 30 años de la Convención Internacional sobre los Derechos del Niño', in P. Isacovich and J. Grinberg (eds) *Infancias y juventudes a 30 años de la Convención sobre los Derechos del Niño*, Buenos Aires: EDUNPAZ – Editorial Universitaria, pp 87–120.

Magnat, Virginie (2020) 'Towards a performative ethics of reciprocity', in N.K. Denzin and M.D. Giardina (eds) *Qualitative Inquiry and the Politics of Resistance*, New York: Routledge, pp 115–129.

Maldonado, Ana Lucía and González Gaudiano, Edgar Javier (2013) 'De la resiliencia comunitaria a la ciudadanía ambiental. El caso de tres localidades en Veracruz, México', *Integra Educativa*, 6(3): 13–28.

Maldonado-Torres, Nelson (2007) 'On the coloniality of being: Contributions to the development of a concept', *Cultural Studies*, 21(2–3): 240–270.

Maldonado-Torres, Nelson (2016) 'Outline of ten theses on coloniality and decoloniality', Frantz Fanon Foundation, available at: https://fondat ion-frantzfanon.com/wp-content/uploads/2018/10/maldonado-torres_ outline_of_ten_theses-10.23.16.pdf

Maldonado-Torres, Nelson (2017) 'On the coloniality of human rights', *Revista Crítica de Ciências Sociais*, 114: 117–136.

Mancuso, Stefano (2019) *La nazione delle piante*, Bari: Gius. Laterza & Figli.

Mandell, Nancy (1988) 'The least-adult role in studying children', *Journal of Contemporary Ethnography*, 16(4): 433–468.

Mannheim, Karl ([1928] 1952) 'The problem of generations', in *Essays on the Sociology of Knowledge*, London: Routledge and Kegan Paul, pp 276–320.

Marciniak, Katarzyna (2017) 'Aporias of foreignness: Transnational encounters through cinema', in G. Rae and E. Ingala (eds) *Subjectivity and the Political: Contemporary Perspectives*, New York: Routledge, pp 91–109.

Markowska-Manista, Urszula (2017) 'The dilemmas and passions in intercultural field research: A female pedagogue's ethnographic notes', in U. Markowska-Manista and J. Pilarska (eds) *An Introspective Approach to Women's Intercultural Fieldwork*, Warsaw: Wyd. Akademii Pedagogiki Specjalnej, pp 126–147.

Markowska-Manista, Urszula (2018) 'The ethical dilemmas of research with children from the countries of the global south: Whose participation?', *Polish Journal of Educational Studies*, 71(1): 51–65.

Markowska-Manista, Urszula (2019) '"Bad children": International stigmatisation of children trained to kill during war and armed conflict', in N. von Benzon and C. Wilkinson (eds) *Intersectionality and Difference in Childhood and Youth: Global Perspectives*, London: Routledge, pp 61–75.

Markowska-Manista, Urszula (2020) 'Clarity about the purpose of research', in P. Alderson and V. Morrow (eds) *The Ethics of Research with Children and Young People*, Los Angeles: SAGE, pp 22–23.

Markowska-Manista, Urszula and Liebel, Manfred (2023) 'Research with migrant children from countries of the global south: From ethical challenges to the decolonisation of research in the sensitive contexts of modernity', in S. Arun, K. Badwan, H. Taibi and F. Batool (eds) *Global Migration and Diversity of Educational Experiences in the Global South and North*, London: Routledge, pp 19–34.

Martineau, Sheila (1999) *Rewriting Resilience: A Critical Discourse Analysis of Childhood Resilience and the Politics of Teaching Resilience to 'Kids at Risk'*, Vancouver: University of British Columbia Press.

Martínez Muñoz, Marta and Cabrerizo Sanz, Lorena (2015) *Guía para la Evaluación. Herramienta Prota-Estela*, Lima: Enclave and Save the Children.

Marx, Karl (1869) *Capital: A Critique of Political Economy*, vol I, available at: www.marxists.org/archive/marx/works/download/pdf/Capital-Volume-I.pdf

Marx, Karl and Engels, Friedrich ([1844/1845] 1932) *The German Ideology*, available at: www.marxists.org/archive/marx/works/download/Marx_The_German_Ideology.pdf

Mason, Jan and Watson, Elizabeth (2014) 'Researching children: Research on, with, and by children', in A. Ben-Arieh, F. Casas, I. Frønes and J.E. Corbin (eds) *Handbook of Child Well-Being*, Dordrecht: Springer, pp 2757–2796.

Masten, Ann S. (2014) 'Global perspectives on resilience in children and youth', *Child Development*, 85(1): 6–20.

Mawere, Munyaradzi and van Stam, Gertjan (2016) 'Ubuntu/Unhu as communal love: Critical reflections on the sociology of Ubuntu and communal life in Sub-Saharan Africa', in M. Mawere and N. Marongwe (eds) *Violence, Politics and Conflict Management in Africa: Envisioning Transformation, Peace and Unity in the Twenty-First Century*, Bamenda: Langaa Research and Publishing Common Initiative Group, pp 287–304.

McLeod, Alison (2008) *Listening to Children: A Practitioner's Guide*, London: Jessica Kingsley.

Mead, Margaret (1970) *Culture and Commitment: A Study of the Generation Gap*, New York: Doubleday (Natural History Press).

Mead, Margaret (1973) 'Prefigurative cultures and unknown children', in P.K. Manning (ed) *Youth: Divergent Perspectives*, New York: John Wiley and Sons, pp 193–206.

Meintjes, Helen and Giese, Sonja (2006) 'Spinning the epidemic: The making of mythologies of orphanhood in the context of AIDS', *Childhood*, 13(3): 407–430.

Melillo, Aldo and Suárez Ojeda, Elbio Néstor (eds) (2001) *Resiliencia. Descubriendo las propias fortalezas*, Buenos Aires: Paidós.

Melillo, Aldo, Suárez Ojeda, Elbio Néstor and Rodríguez, Daniel (eds) (2004) *Resiliencia y subjetividad. Los ciclos de la vida*, Buenos Aires: Paidós.

Memmi, Albert ([1957] 2016) *The Colonizer and the Colonized*, London: Souvenir Press.

Menke, Christoph (2018) *Kritik der Rechte*, Berlin: Suhrkamp.

Merasty, Joseph Auguste and Carpenter, David (2017) *The Education of Augie Merasty: A Residential School Memoir*, Saskatchewan: University of Regina Press.

Merk, Usche (2017) '"Crisis is the new normal": Überleben in der Dauerkrise', in medico international (ed) *Fit für die Katastrophe? Kritische Anmerkungen zum Resilienzdiskurs im aktuellen Krisenmanagement*, Gießen: Psychosozial-Verlag, pp 125–149.

Meueler, Erhard (1993) *Die Türen des Käfigs. Wege zum Subjekt in der Erwachsenenbildung*, Stuttgart: Klett-Cotta.

Mignolo, Walter D. (2009) 'Epistemic disobedience, independent thought and de-colonial freedom', *Theory, Culture & Society*, 26(7–8): 1–23.

Mill, John Stuart ([1861] 2001) *Representative Government*, Kitchener: Batoche Books.

Mistral, Gabriela ([1927] 1979) 'Los Derechos del Niño', in G. Mistral, *Magisterio y Niño*, Santiago de Chile: Andrés Bello, pp 62–65.

Mizen, Phil (2018) 'Bringing the street back in: Considering strategy, contingency and relative good fortune in street children's access to paid work in Accra', *The Sociological Review*, 66(5): 1058–1073.

Molyneux, Maxine (2007) 'Change and continuity in social protection in Latin America: Mothers at the service of the state?', in *Gender and Development Programme*, Geneva: United Nations Research Institute for Social Development (UNRISD/PPGD1/07/1).

Montgomery, Heather (2017) 'Anthropological perspectives on children's rights', in M.D. Ruck, M. Peterson-Badali and M. Freeman (eds) *Handbook of Children's Rights*, New York: Routledge, pp 97–113.

Moody, Zoe and Darbellay, Frédéric (2019) 'Studying childhood, children, and their rights: The challenge of interdisciplinarity', *Childhood*, 26(1): 8–21.

Moosa-Mitha, Mehmoona (2005) 'A difference-centred alternative to theorization of children's citizenship rights', *Citizenship Studies*, 9(4): 369–388.

Morales, Santiago (2020) 'Movimientos sociales y participación política de niñas y niños. Una aproximación a la experiencia político-pedagógica de La Miguelito Pepe', *Crítica y Resistencias. Revista de conflictos sociales latinoamericanos*, 10: 22–38.

Morales, Santiago Joaquín and Shabel, Paula Nurit (2020) 'El Gritazo. Análisis de una manifestación de niños y niñas por su derecho a trabajar y a participar', *MILLCAYAC – Revista Digital de Ciencias Sociales*, VII(12): 319–341.

Mutua, Makau (2002) *Human Rights: A Political and Cultural Critique*, Philadelphia, PA: University of Pennsylvania Press.

Nahuelpan Moreno, Héctor Javier (2019) 'Colonialismo republicano, violencia y subordinación racial mapuche en Chile durante el siglo XX', *HistorReLo – Revista de Historia Regional y Local*, 11(21): 212–247.

Nandy, Ashis (1983) *The Intimate Enemy: Loss and Recovery of Self under Colonialism*, New Delhi: Oxford University Press.

Nash, Jennifer C. (2019) *Black Feminism Reimagined: After Intersectionality*, Durham, NC: Duke University Press.

Neill, Alexander S. (1953) *The Free Child*, London: Herbert Jenkins.

Nentwig-Gesemann, Iris (2022) 'Kinder als Akteure in Forschungsprozessen – forschungsethische Standards und Herausforderungen', in M. Joos and L. Alberth (eds) *Forschungsethik in der Kindheitsforschung*, Weinheim: Beltz-Juventa, pp 70–87.

Neocleous, Marc (2013) 'Resisting resilience', *Radical Philosophy*, 178(March/April): 1–7.

Nichel Valenzuela, Fabián (2018) 'Experiencia de investigación militante como herramienta de transformación social con niños y niñas organizados de la comuna de Recoleta', *Trenza. Revista de Educación Popular, Pedagogía Crítica e Investigación Militante*, 1(2): 18–33.

Nieuwenhuys, Olga and Hanson, Karl (2020) 'Navigating between research, teaching and activism in children's rights and childhood studies', in R. Budde and U. Markowska-Manista (eds) *Childhood and Children's Research between Research and Activism*, Wiesbaden: Springer VS, pp 121–136.

Nogueira Beltrão, Beatriz (2020) 'El conocimiento cuerpo a cuerpo como forma de resistencia ante el racismo/sexismo epistémico', in I. Cornejo and M. Rufer (eds) *Horizontalidad. Hacia una crítica de la metodología*, Buenos Aires: CLACSO and Guadalajara: CALAS, pp 231–250.

Novaro, Gabriela and Hecht, Ana Carolina (2017) 'Educación, diversidad y desigualdad en Argentina. Experiencias escolares de poblaciones indígenas y migrantes', *Argumentos. Estudios Críticos de la Sociedad*, 84: 57–76.

Nuñez Patiño, Kathia, Rico Montoya, Angélica, Corona Caraveo, Yolanda and Alvarado S., Sara Victoria (2017) 'Presentación', in *Niñez y juventud: políticas públicas, educación y participación política. Argumentos – Estudios Críticos de la Sociedad*, 84: 9–14.

Nussbaum, Martha (2001) *Upheavals of Thought: The Intelligence of Emotions*, Cambridge: Cambridge University Press.

O'Kane, Claire, Barros, Ornella and Meslaoui, Nicolas (2018) *It's Time to Talk! Children's Views on Children's Work*, Duisburg: Kindernothilfe and Osnabrück: terre des hommes Deutschland.

Ofosu-Kusi, Yaw and Mizen, Phil (2012) 'No longer willing to be dependent: Young people moving beyond learning', in G. Spittler and M. Bourdillon (eds) *African Children at Work: Working and Learning in Growing Up for Life*, Zurich: LIT, pp 279–302.

Oliver, Christine M. and Dalrymple, Jane E. (eds) (2008) *Developing Advocacy for Children and Young People: Current Issues in Research, Policy and Practice*, London: Jessica Kingsley.

Opp, Günther and Fingerle, Michael (2007) 'Erziehung zwischen Risiko und Protektion', in G. Opp and M. Fingerle (eds) *Was Kinder stärkt. Erziehung zwischen Risiko und Resilienz*, Munich: Ernst Reinhardt, pp 7–18.

Osterhammel, Jürgen (2005) *Colonialism: A Theoretical Overview*, Princeton, NJ: Markus Wiener Publishers.

Österreichische Bundesregierung (2004) *Ein kindgerechtes Österreich. Nationaler Aktionsplan zur Umsetzung der Kinderrechte*, Vienna: Bundesregierung der Republik Österreich.

Oswell, David (2013) *The Agency of Children: From Family to Global Human Rights*, Cambridge: Cambridge University Press.

Ouviña, Hernán (2020) 'Movimientos populares, Estado y procesos comunitarios. Tensiones y desafíos desde América Latina', *MILLCAYAC-Revista digital de Ciencias Sociales*, VII(12): 441–464.

Oyěwùmí, Oyèrónkẹ́ (1997) *The Invention of Women: Making an African Sense of Western Gender Discourses*, Minneapolis, MN: University of Minnesota Press.

Oyěwùmí, Oyèrónkẹ́ (2016) *What Gender is Motherhood? Changing Yorùbá Ideals of Power, Procreation, and Identity in the Age of Modernity*, New York: Palgrave Macmillan.

Palominos, Simón (2016) 'Racismo, inmigración y políticas culturales. La subordinación racializada de las comunidades inmigrantes como principio de construcción de la identidad chilena', in M.E. Tijoux (ed) *Racismo en Chile. La piel como marca de la inmigración*, Santiago de Chile: Universidad de Chile, Editorial Universitaria, pp 187–212.

Parsons, Talcott ([1951] 1991) *The Social System* (new edn), New York: Routledge.

Patton, Stacey (2022) 'The children of children: Why the adultification thesis is a misguided trap for Black children and families', in C.J. Bergman (ed) *Trust Kids! Stories on Youth Autonomy and Confronting Adult Supremacy*, Chico, CA and Edinburgh: AT Press, pp 167–175.

Pease, Bob (2022) *Undoing Privilege: Unearned Advantage and Systemic Injustice in an Unequal World* (2nd edn), London: Zed Books.

Peleg, Noam (2018) 'Illusion of inclusion: Challenging universalistic conceptions in international children's rights law', *Australian Journal of Human Rights*, 24(3): 326–344.

Pérez, Diego (2016) 'Ubuntu y Sumak Kawsay. Paradigmas urgentes para una paz incluyente y sostenible en Colombia', in S. Gruner, M. Blandon and C. Mina-Rojas (eds) *Des/Dibjando el país/aje: Aportes para la paz con pueblos afrodescendientes e indígenas. Territorio, autonomía y buen vivir*, Medellín: Poder Negro, pp 51–64.

Perrin, Chris 'Kikila' (2020) 'The hall of mirrors and a landscape of multiple layers: Insurgent research, Indigenous resurgence, and challenging the university structure', *Verges – Germanic and Slavic Studies in Review*, 3(1).

Petermann, Franz (2000) 'Klinische Kinderpsychologie – Begriffsbestimmung und Grundlagen', in F. Petermann (ed) *Fallbuch der klinischen Kinderpsychologie und -psychotherapie*, Göttingen: Hogrefe, pp 13–26.

Piketty, Thomas (2020) *Capital and Ideology*, Cambridge, MA: The Belknap Press of Harvard University Press.

Piotti, María Lidia (2019) *Protagonismo Infantil y Trabajo Social*, Mendoza: Lengua Viva Editorial.

Poretti, Michele (2018) 'Unexpected allies: Expanding theoretical toolbox of the children's rights sociologist', in C. Baraldi and T. Cockburn (eds) *Theorising Childhood: Citizenship, Rights and Participation*, Cham: Springer Nature and Palgrave Macmillan, pp 111–134.

PRATEC (2005) *Dos Saberes*, Lima: Proyecto Andino de Tecnologías Campesinas.

PRATEC (2008) *Diálogo de Saberes y escuela rural andina*, Lima: Proyecto Andino de Tecnologías Campesinas.

PRATEC (2013) *Regeneración del Patrimonio Cultural Inmaterial en Comunidades Indígenas de los Andes Centrales. Ecuador – Perú – Bolivia*, Lima: Proyecto Andino de Tecnologías Campesinas.

PRATEC (2020) *Respeto y Buen Vivir*, Lima: Proyecto Andino de Tecnologías Campesinas.

Pritchard, Erin and Edwards, Delith (2023) *Sexual Misconduct in Academia: Informing an Ethics of Care in the University*, Abingdon: Routledge.

Pupavac, Vanessa (1998) 'The infantilisation of the South and the UN Convention on the Rights of the Child', *Human Rights Law Review*, 3(2): 1–6.

Pupavac, Vanessa (2001a) 'Misanthropy without borders: The international children's rights regime', *Disasters*, 25(2): 95–112.

Pupavac, Vanessa (2001b) 'Therapeutic governance: Psycho-social intervention and trauma risk management', *Disasters*, 25(4): 358–372.

Quennerstedt, Ann (2010) 'Children, but not really human? Critical reflections in the hampering effect of the "3 p's"', *International Journal of Children's Rights*, 18(4): 619–635.

Quennerstedt, Ann (2013) 'Children's rights research moving into the future: Challenges on the way forward', *International Journal of Children's Rights*, 21(2): 233–247.

Quijano, Anibal (2000) 'Coloniality of power, Eurocentrism, and Latin America', *Nepantla – Views from South*, 1(3): 533–580.

Quijano, Anibal (2008) 'Coloniality of power, Eurocentrism, and social classification', in M. Moraña, E. Dussel and C. Jáuregui (eds) *Coloniality at Large: Latin America and the Postcolonial Debate*, Durham, NC: Duke University Press, pp 181–224.

Quijano, Aníbal (2019) *Ensayos en Torno a la Colonalidad del Poder*, Buenos Aires: Edicones del Signo.

Rae, Gavin (2017) 'Between failure and redemption: Emmanuel Levinas on the political', in G. Rae and E. Ingala (eds) *Subjectivity and the Political: Contemporary Perspectives*, New York: Routledge, pp 55–73.

Rae, Gavin and Ingala, Emma (eds) (2017) *Subjectivity and the Political: Contemporary Perspectives*, New York: Routledge.

Rancière, Jacques (1998) *Disagreement: Politics and Philosophy*, Minneapolis: University of Minnesota Press.

Rappaport, Joanne and Ramos Pacho, Abelardo (2005) 'Una historia colaborativa: retos para el diálogo indígena-académico', *Historia Crítica*, 29: 39–62.

Rawls, John (1999) *A Theory of Justice* (revised edn), Cambridge, MA: Harvard University Press.

Reckwitz, Andreas (2008) *Subjekt*, Bielefeld: transcript.

Reivich, Karen J., Seligman, Martin and Mcbride, Sharon (2011) 'Master resilience training in the U.A. Army', *American Psychologist*, 66(1): 25–34.

Renaut, Alain (2002) *La libération des enfants*, Paris: Hachettes Littératures.

Rengifo Vásquez, Grimaldo (1991) 'Desaprender la modernidad para aprender lo andino. La tecnología y sus efectos en el desarrollo rural', *Revista UNITAS* (La Paz), 4: 32–36.

Restrepo, Gabriel (2016) 'Seguir los pasos de Orlando Fals Borda: religión, música, mundos de la vida y carnaval', *Investigación & Desarrollo*, 24(2): 199–239.

Reynaert, Didier, Bouverne-de-Bie, Maria and Vandevelde, Stijn (2009) 'A review of children's rights literature since the adoption of the United Nations Convention on the Rights of the Child', *Childhood*, 16(4): 518–534.

Reynaert, Didier, Desmet, Ellen, Lembrechts, Sara and Vandenhole, Wouter (2015) 'Introduction: A critical approach to children's rights', in W. Vandenhole, E. Desmet, D. Reynaert and S. Lembrechts (eds) *Routledge International Handbook of Children's Rights Studies*, London: Routledge, pp 1–23.

Ribeiro, Djamila (2020) 'Koloniale Maske der Stille', *die tageszeitung*, 23 June, p 12.

Richter, Elisabeth and Lehmann, Teresa (2016) 'Partizipation in der Kita zwischen deliberativer und Expertendemokratie', in P. Rieker, R. Mörgen and A. Schnitzer (eds) *Partizipation von Kindern und Jugendlichen in vergleichender Perspektive*, Weinheim: Beltz-Juventa, pp 39–63.

Rivera Cusicanqui, Silvia (1987) 'El potencial epistemológico y teórico de la historia oral: de la lógica instrumental a la descolonozación de la historia', *Revista Temas Sociales* (UMSA, La Paz), 11: 49–64.

Rivera Cusicanqui, Silvia (2010) *Ch'ixinakax utxiwa. Una reflexión sobre prácticas y discursos descolonizadores,* Buenos Aires: Tinta Limón.

Robertson, John A. (1996) *Children of Choice: Freedom and the New Reproductive Technologies*, Princeton, NJ: Princeton University Press.

Rodgers, Diane M. (2020) *Children in Social Movements: Rethinking Agency, Mobilization and Rights*, London: Routledge.

Rodin, Judith (2014) *The Resilience Dividend: Being Strong in a World Where the Things Go Wrong*, New York: Public Affairs.

Rodríguez, Rosana Paula and da Costa, Sofia (2019) 'Descolonizar las Herramientas Metodológicas. Una Experiencia de Investigación Feminista', *MILLCAYAC – Revista Digital de Ciencias Sociales*, 6(11): 13–30.

Rojas, Jorge (2010) *Historia de la infancia en el Chile republicano, 1810–2010*, Santiago: Junta Nacional de Jardines Infantiles, Junji.

Rollo, Toby (2018) 'Feral children: Settler colonialism, progress, and the figure of the child', *Settler Colonial Studies*, 8(1): 60–79.

Romm, Norma Ruth Ariene (2020) 'Reflections on a post-qualitative inquiry with children/young people: Exploring and furthering a performative research ethics', *Forum Qualitative Sozialforschung/Forum Qualitative Social Research*, 21(1): Art. 6.

Roose, Rudi and Bouverne-de Bie, Maria (2007) 'Do children have rights or do their rights have to be realised? The United Nations Convention on the Right of the Child as a frame of reference for pedagogical action', *Journal of Philosophy of Education*, 41(3): 431–443.

Rosen, David M. (2015) *Child Soldiers in the Western Imagination: From Patriots to Victims*, New Brunswick, NJ: Rutgers University Press.

Rosen, Rachel (2019) 'Poverty and family troubles: Mothers, children, and neoliberal "antipoverty" initiatives', *Journal of Family Issues*, 40(16): 2330–2353.

Rosenhaft, Eve (ed) (1982) *Organizing the "lumpenproletariat": Cliques and communists in Berlin during the Weimar Republic*, London: Routledge.

Rousseau, Cécile, Said, Taher M., Gagné, Marie-Josée and Bibeau, Gilles (1998) 'Resilience in unaccompanied minors from the north of Somalia', *Psychoanalytic Review*, 85(4): 615–637.

Rousseau, Jean-Jacques ([1755] 2016) *A Discourse Upon the Origin and the Foundation of the Inequality Among Men*, Charleston, SC: Create Space Independent Publishing Platform.

Rousseau, Jean-Jacques ([1762] 1979) *Emile, or on Education*, New York: Basic Books.

Rousseau, Jean-Jacques ([1762] 2017) *The Social Contract*, available at: www.earlymoderntexts.com/assets/pdfs/rousseau1762.pdf

Rufer, Mario (2020) 'No vamos a traducir. Instalar un secreto, negar la dádiva, redefinir el juego', in I. Cornejo and M. Rufer (eds) *Horizontalidad. Hacia una crítica de la metodología*, Buenos Aires: CLACSO and Guadalajara: CALAS, pp 277–302.

Rutter, Michael (1979) 'Protective factors in children's response to stress and disadvantage', in M.W. Kent and J.E. Rolf (eds) *Primary Prevention of Psychopathology*, Lebanon, NH: University Press of New England, pp 49–74.

Ruz Carrera, Natalia (2012) 'Del Palín a la boleadora. Niños y niñas mapuche en comunidades en conflicto', *NATs – Revista Internacional desde los Niños/as y Adolescentes Trabajadores*, XV–XVI(21–22): 67–76.

Said, Edward W. ([1978] 2013) *Orientalism*, New York: Vintage.

Salamanca Serrano, Antonio (2018) 'Filosofía Jurídica Latinoamericana en el siglo XXI. La (re)insurgencia histórica del derecho de los pobres y la naturaleza: el iusmaterialismo', in A. Rosillo Martínez and G. Luévano Bustamente (eds) *En torno a la crítica del derecho*, Aguascalientes: Centro de Estudios Jurídicos y Sociales Mispat and Universidad Autónoma de San Luis Potosí, pp 131–182.

Salazar, Gabriel (2012) *Ser niño 'huacho' en la historia de Chile (siglo XIX)*, Santiago de Chile: LOM Ediciones.

Sánchez Santoyo, Hilda Margarita (2003) 'La percepción sobre el niño en el México moderno (1810–1930)', in Y. Corona Caraveo and R.R. Villamil Uriarte (eds) *Tramas. Subjetividad y procesos sociales. Diversidad de infancias*, Mexico City: Universidad Autónoma Metropolitana, pp 33–59.

Sandel, Michael J. (2007) *The Case against Perfection: Ethics in the Age of Genetic Engineering*, Cambridge, MA: The Belknap Press in Harvard University Press.

Sarmento, Manuel Jacinto, Marchi, Rita de Cássia and Trevisan, Gabriela de Pina (2018) 'Beyond the modern "norm" of childhood: Children at the Marchins as a challenge for the sociology of childhood', in C. Baraldi and T. Cockburn (eds) *Theorising Childhood: Citizenship, Rights and Participation*, Cham: Springer Nature and Palgrave Macmillan, pp 135–157.

Save the Children (2002) *Children and Participation: Research, Monitoring and Evaluation with Children and Young People*, London: Save the Children Alliance.

Schibotto, Giangi (1988) 'La Niñez Invisible', in *Niños Trabajadores. Experiencias y reflexiones*, Lima: Instituto Publicaciones Educación y Comunicación José Cardijn, pp 95–110.

Schibotto, Giangi (1990) *Niños Trabajadores. Construyendo una identidad*, Lima: MANTHOC.

Schmidt, Christian (2021) 'Ermöglichung und Einhegung. Die Rolle der subjektiven Rechte bei der Gestaltung politischer Ordnungen', in E. Hilgendorf and B. Zabel (eds) *Die Idee subjektiver Rechte*, Berlin: De Gruyter, pp 135–152.

Segato, Rita Laura (2013) *La crítica de la colonialidad en ocho ensayos. Y una antropología por demanda*, Buenos Aires: Prometeo Libros.

Silva, Giselle (1999) *Resiliencia y violencia política en niños* (Colección Salud Comunitaria, Serie Resiliencia), Buenos Aires: Universidad Nacional de Lanús and Fundación B. van Leer.

Simison, Bob (2019) 'Investing in resilience: Disaster-prone countries are strengthening their ability to withstand climate events', *Finance & Development*, December: 22–25.

Sinervo, Aviva and Cheney, Kristen (2019) 'NGO economics of affect: Humanitarianism and childhood in contemporary and historical perspective', in K. Cheney and A. Sinervo (eds) *Disadvantaged Childhoods and Humanitarian Intervention: Processes of Affective Commodification and Objectification*, Basingstoke: Palgrave Macmillan, pp 1–35.

Singh, Surti (2017) 'The abject and the ugly: Kristeva, Adorno, and the formation of the subject', in G. Rae and E. Ingala (eds) *Subjectivity and the Political: Contemporary Perspectives*, New York: Routledge, pp 113–134.

Skillington, Tracey (2019) *Climate Change and Intergenerational Justice*, London: Routledge.

Sloth-Nielsen, Julia and Klep, Katrien (2020) 'Independent children', in J. Todres and S.M. King (eds) *The Oxford Handbook of Children's Rights Law*, Oxford: Oxford University Press, pp 615–637.

Spence, Tomas (1796) *The Rights of Infants*, London, available at: www.marxists.org/history/england/britdem/people/spence/infants/infants.htm

Spivak, Gayatri C. (1988) 'Can the subaltern speak?', in C. Nelson and L. Grossberg (eds) *Marxism and the Interpretation of Culture*, Urbana, IL: University of Illinois Press, pp 66–111.

Spyrou, Spyros (2011) 'The limits of children's voices: From authenticity to critical reflexive representation', *Childhood*, 18(2): 151–165.

Spyrou, Spyros (2018) *Disclosing Childhoods: Research and Knowledge Production for a Critical Childhood Studies*, Basingstoke: Palgrave Macmillan.

Stammers, Neil (2009) *Human Rights and Social Movements*, London: Pluto Press.

Stavenhagen, Rodolfo (1971) 'Decolonizing applied social sciences', *Human Organization*, 30(4): 333–357.

Stern, Bertrand (ed) (1995) *Kinderrechte zwischen Resignation und Vision*, Ulm: Klemm und Oelschläger.

Storck-Odabasi, Julian and Heinzel, Friederike (2022) '"Wofür braucht ihr das?" – Von der (Selbst-)Ermächtigung beforschter Kinder', in M. Joos and L. Alberth (eds) *Forschungsethik in der Kindheitsforschung*, Weinheim: Beltz-Juventa, pp 105–119.

Storey, John (2006) *Cultural Theory and Popular Culture*, Athens, GE: University of Georgia Press.

Strega, Susan and Brown, Leslie (eds) (2015) *Research as Resistance: Revisiting Critical, Indigenous and Anti-Oppressive Approaches*, Toronto: Canadian Scholars' Press and Women's Press.

Suárez Ojeda, Elbio Néstor (2001) 'Una concepción latinoamericana: la resiliencia comunitaria', in A. Melillo and E.N. Suárez Ojeda (eds) *Resiliencia. Descubriendo las propias fortalezas*, Buenos Aires: Paidós, pp 67–82.

Szulc, Andrea (2015) *La Niñez Mapuche. Sentidos de pertinencia en tensión*, Buenos Aires: Biblos.

Szulc, Andrea (2018) 'Entre la tutela y la represión. Nociones sobre la infancia y la identidad mapuche ante la participación política infantil en Neuquén, Argentina', in C. Fonseca, C. Medaets and F. Ribeiro (eds) *Pesquisas sobre Família e Infância no Mundo Contemporâneo*, Porto Alegre: Editora Sulina, pp 109–129.

Szulc, Andrea, Colangelo, María Adelaida, Shabel, Paula, Leavy, María Pía, Enriz, Noelia and Celeste Hernández, María (2016) 'Al rescate de la niñez indígena. Reflexiones antroplógicas a partir de una campaña de UNICEF Argentina', *Política y Sociedad*, 53(1): 123–142.

Taft, Jessica K. (2015) '"Adults talk too much": Intergenerational dialogue and power in the Peruvian movement of working children', *Childhood*, 22(4): 460–473.

Taft, Jessica K. (2017) 'Continually redefining protagonismo: The Peruvian movement of working children and political change, 1976–2015', *Latin American Perspectives*, 46(5): 90–110.

Taft, Jessica K. (2019) *The Kids are in Charge: Activism and Power in Peru's Working Children Movement*, New York: New York University Press.

Thangaraj, Miriam (2019) 'Commodification in multiple registers: Child workers, child consumers, and child labor NGOs in India', in K. Cheney and A. Sinervo (eds) *Disadvantaged Childhoods and Humanitarian Intervention*, Basingstoke: Palgrave Macmillan, pp 87–112.

Thiong'o, Ngũgĩ wa (1986) *Decolonising the mind: The politics of language in African literature*, London: James Currey.

Thomas, Nigel Patrick (2015) 'Children and young people's participation in research', in T. Gal and B. Faedi Duramy (eds) *International Perspectives and Empirical Findings on Child Participation: From Social Exclusion to Child-Inclusive Policies*, Oxford: Oxford University Press, pp 89–110.

Thomas, Nigel Patrick (2021) 'Child-led research, children's rights and childhood studies: A defence', *Childhood*, 28(2): 186–199.

Thomas, Nigel Patrick and O'Kane, Claire (1998) 'The ethics of participatory research with children', *Children & Society*, 12(5): 336–348.

Thomas, Peter (2009) *The Gramscian Moment: Philosophy, Hegemony and Marxism*, Chicago, IL: Haymarket.

Tlostanova, Madina V. (2019) 'The postcolonial condition, the decolonial option and the post-socialist intervention', in M. Albrecht (ed) *Postcolonialism Cross-Examined: Multidirectional Perspectives on Imperial and Colonial Pasts and the Newcolonial Present*, New York: Routledge, pp 165–176.

TRUST (2018) *Global Code of Conduct for Research in Resource-Poor Settings*, available at: www.globalcodeofconduct.org/

Tubino, Fidel (2005) 'La interculturalidad crítica como proyecto ético-político', presentado en el Encuentro Continental de Educadores Agustinos, enero 24–28, Lima, available at: https://red.pucp.edu.pe/ridei/wp-content/uploads/biblioteca/inter_funcional.pdf

Tuhiwai Smith, Linda (2005) 'On tricky ground: Researching the native in the age of uncertainty', in N. Denzin and Y. Lincoln (eds) *The SAGE Handbook of Qualitative Research* (3rd edn), Thousand Oaks, CA: SAGE, pp 85–107.

Tuhiwai Smith, Linda (2012) *Decolonizing Methodologies: Research and Indigenous Peoples* (2nd edn), London: Zed Books [third edn 2021].

Twum-Danso Imoh, Afua (2009) 'Situating participatory methodologies in context: The impact of culture on adult–child interactions in research and other projects', *Children's Geographies*, 7(4): 379–389.

Twum-Danso Imoh, Afua, Bourdillon, Michael and Meichsner, Sylvia (eds) (2019) *Global Childhoods beyond the North-South Divide*, Basingstoke: Palgrave Macmillan.

UN (1988) Protection of global climate for present and future generations of mankind. General Assembly Resolution 43/53, 6 December 1988.

UN (1992) Rio Declaration on Environment and Development. Adopted at the United Nations Conference on Environment and Development, Rio de Janeiro from 3 to 14 June 1992.

UN (2007) United Nations Declaration on the Rights of Indigenous Peoples, available at: www.un.org/development/desa/indigenouspeoples/declaration-on-the-rights-of-indigenous-peoples.html

UN (2015a) Sustainable Development Goals, available at: https://sdgs.un.org/goals

UN (2015b) Paris Agreement, available at: https://unfccc.int

UNCRC (2021) General Comment No. 25 on children's rights in relation to the digital environment, available at: /https://documents-dds-ny.un.org/doc/UNDOC/GEN/G21/053/43/PDF/G2105343.pdf?OpenElement

UNCRC (forthcoming) General Comment No. 26 on children's rights and the environment with a special focus on climate change (draft), available at: www.ohchr.org/en/documents/general-comments-and-recommendations/draft-general-comment-no-26-childrens-rights-and

UNDP (2019) *Human Development Report 2019. Beyond Income, Beyond Averages, Beyond Today: Inequalities in Human Development in the 21st Century*, New York: United Nations Development Programme.

UNESCO (1997) *Declaration on the Responsibilities of the Present Generations towards Future Generations*, available at: https://en.unesco.org/about-us/legal-affairs/declaration-responsibilities-present-generations-towards-fut ure-generations

Ungar, Michael (2005) 'Introduction: Resilience across cultures and contexts', in M. Ungar (ed) *Handbook for Working with Children and Youth: Pathways to Resilience across Cultures and Contexts*, Thousand Oaks, CA: SAGE, pp xv–xxxix.

Ungar, Michael (2013) 'Social ecologies and their contribution in resilience', in M. Ungar (ed) *The Social Ecology of Resilience: A Handbook of Theory and Practice*, New York: Springer, pp 13–31.

Ungar, Michael, Brown, Marion, Liebenberg, Linda, Othmans, Rasha, Kwong, Wai Man, Armstrong, Mary and Gilgun, Jane (2007) 'Unique pathways to resilience across cultures', *Adolescence*, 42(166): 287–310.

UNICEF (2009) *Campaña por los derechos de la niñez y adolescencia indígena*, available at: www.unicef.org/spanish/infobycountry/argentina_51266.html

UNICEF (2019) '16 children, including Greta Thunberg, file landmark complaint to the United Nations Committee on the Rights of the Child. Child petitioners protest lack of government action on climate crisis', available at: www.unicef.org/press-releases/16-children-including-greta-thunberg-file-landmark-complaint-united-nations

Uriarte, Juan de Dios (2013) 'La perspectiva comunitaria de la resilencia', *Psicología Política* (Universidad del País Vazco, España), 47: 7–18.

Valentine, Karen and Meinert, Lotte (2009) 'The adult North and the young South: Reflections on the civilizing mission of children's rights', *Anthropology Today*, 25(3): 23–28.

Valenzuela Arce, José Manuel (2020) *Heteronomías en las Ciencias Sociales. Procesos investigativos y violencia simbólica*, Buenos Aires: CLACSO.

Van Bueren, Geraldine (1995) *The International Law on the Rights of the Child*, Dordrecht: Martinus Nijhoff.

Van Daalen, Edward, Hanson, Karl and Nieuwenhuys, Olga (2016) 'Children's rights as living rights: The case of street children and a new law in Yogyakarta, Indonesia', *International Journal of Human Rights*, 24: 803–825.

Vandenhole, Wouter (2012) 'Localizing the human rights of children', in M. Liebel, K. Hanson, I. Saadi and W. Vandenhole, *Children's Rights from Below: Cross-cultural Perspectives*, Basingstoke: Palgrave Macmillan, pp 80–93.

Vandenhole, Wouter (2020) 'Decolonising children's rights: Of vernacularisation and interdisciplinarity', in R. Budde and U. Markowska-Manista (eds) *Childhood and Children's Rights between Research and Activism*, Wiesbaden: Springer VS, pp 187–206.

Vandenhole, Wouter and Erdem Türkelli, Gamze (2020) 'The best interests of the child', in J. Todres and S.M. King (eds) *The Oxford Handbook of Children's Rights Law*, Oxford: Oxford University Press, pp 205–224.

Vandenhole, Wouter, Roose, Rudi, Reynaert, Didier and De Bie, Maria (2008) 'Theorizing participation and citizenship of children: Towards an embedded approach of legal rights of children?', Working paper, *ESF Exploratory Workshop on Children's Participation in Decision-Making*, Berlin, 16–18 June.

Veerman, Philip E. (1992) *The Rights of the Child and the Changing Image of Childhood*, Dordrecht: Martinus Nijhoff.

Vergara del Solar, Ana, Llobet, Valeria and Nascimento, Maria Leticia (2021) 'South American childhoods since the 1990s: Between neoliberalisation and the expansion of rights – an introduction', in A. Vergara del Solar, L. Nascimento and V. Llobet (eds) *South American Childhoods: Neoliberalisation and Children's Rights since the 1990s*, Cham: Palgrave Macmillan/Springer Nature Switzerland, pp 1–43.

Vergès, Françoise (2021) *A Decolonial Feminism*, London: Pluto Press.

Verhellen, Eugeen (1994) *Convention on the Rights of the Child: Background, Motivation, Strategies, Main Themes*, Leuven: Garant.

Vinthagen, Stellan and Johansson, Anna (2013) '"Everyday resistance": Exploration of a concept and its theories', *Resistance Studies Magazine*, 1: 1–46.

Voß, G. Günter and Moldaschl, Manfred (eds) (2002) *Subjektivierung von Arbeit*, Munich: Rainer Hampp.

Voß, G. Günter and Pongratz, Hans-Joachim (1998) 'Der Arbeitskraftunternehmer. Eine neue Grundform der "Ware Arbeitskraft"?', *Kölner Zeitschrift für Soziologie und Sozialpsychologie*, 50(1): 31–58.

Voss, Martin (2008) 'The vulnerable can't speak: An integrative vulnerability approach to disaster and climate change research', *Behemoth – A Journal on Civilisation*, 3: 39–56.

Wagner, Wolfgang and Anholt, Rosanne (2016) 'Resilience as the EU global strategy's new leitmotif: Pragmatic, problematic or promising?', *Contemporary Security Policy*, 37(3): 414–430.

Wall, John (2017) *Children's Rights: Today's Global Challenge*, London: Rowman & Littlefield.

Wall, John (2019) 'From childhood studies to childism: Reconstructing the scholarly and social imaginations', *Children's Geographies*, 17(6): 1–14.

Wall, John (2021) *Give Children the Vote: On Democratizing Democracy*, New York: Bloomsbury Academic.

Wallerstein, Immanuel (2006) *European Universalism: The Rhetoric of Power*, New York: The New Press.

Walsh, Catherine (2005) 'Introducción. (Re)pensamiento crítico y (de) colonialidad', in C. Walsh, *Pensamiento crítico y matriz (de)colonial. Reflexiones latinoamericanas*, Quito: Editorial Abya-Yala, pp 13–35.

Walsh, Catherine (2007) 'Interculturalidad y colonialidad del poder. Un pensamiento y posicionamiento "otro" desde la diferencia colonial', in S. Castro-Gómez and R. Grosfoguel (eds) *El giro decolonial. Reflexiones para una diversidad epistémica más allá del capitalismo global*, Bogotá: Siglo del Hombre Editores, pp 47–62.

Walsh, Catherine (2009) 'Interculturalidad crítica y educación intercultural', presentation at the seminar 'Interculturalidad y Educación Intercultural', organized by Instituto Internacional de Integración del Convenio Andrés Bello, La Paz, 9–11 March.

Walsh, Catherine (2012) *Interculturalidad, crítica y (de)colonialidad: ensayos desde Abya Yala*, Quito: Instituto Científico de Culturas Indígenas.

Walsh, Catherine (ed) (2013) *Pedagogías decoloniales: Prácticas insurgentes de resistir, (re)existir y (re)vivir*, Quito: Ediciones Abya Yala.

Walsh, Catherine (2018) 'Decoloniality in/as praxis', in W.D. Mignolo and C. Walsh (eds) *On Decoloniality: Concepts, Analytics, Praxis*, Durham, NC: Duke University Press, pp 13–102.

Walsh, Sarah (2019) 'The Chilean exception: Racial homogeneity, mestizaje and eugenic nationalism', *Journal of Iberian and Latin American Studies*, 25(1): 105–125.

Wells, Karen (2018) *Childhood Studies: Making Young Subjects*, Cambridge: Polity.

Werner, Emmy E. (2007) 'Entwicklung zwischen Risiko und Resilienz', in G. Opp and M. Fingerle (eds) *Was Kinder stärkt. Erziehung zwischen Risiko und Resilienz*, Munich: Ernst Reinhardt, pp 20–31.

Werner, Emmy E. and Smith, Ruth S. (1982) *Vulnerable but Invincible: A Longitudinal Study of Resilient Children and Youth*, New York: McGraw-Hill.

Werner, Emmy E. and Smith, Ruth S. (1992) *Overcoming the Odds*, Ithaca, NY: Cornell University Press.

Wiggin, Kate Douglas ([1892] 1971) *Children's Rights: A Book of Nursery Logic*, Ann Arbor: Gryphon Books.

Williams, Chris (2010) *Ecology and Socialism: Solutions to Capitalist Ecological Crisis*, Chicago: Haymarket Books.

Wilson, Shawn (2008) *Research as Ceremony: Indigenous Research Methods*, Manitoba: Fernwood.

Wink, Rüdiger (ed) (2016) *Multidisziplinäre Perspektiven der Resilienzforschung*, Wiesbaden: Springer VS.

Wissen, Markus and Brand, Ulrich (2022) 'Emanzipatorische Perspektiven im "Anthropozän". Über die Grenzen des grünen Kapitalismus und die Notwendigkeit einer radikalen Alternative', *PROKLA 207*, 52(2): 263–281.

Woodhead, Martin, Montgomery, Heather and Burr, Rachel (2007) 'Adversities and resilience', in H. Montgomery, R. Burr and M. Woodhead (eds) *Changing Childhoods: Local and Global*, Bingley: Willey, in cooperation with Open University, pp 1–34.

Woodhouse, Barbara Bennett (2008) *Hidden in Plain Sight: The Tragedy of Children's Rights from Ben Franklin to Lionel Tate*, Princeton, NJ: Princeton University Press.

World Bank (2013) *Building Resilience: Integrating Climate and Disaster Risk into Development*, available at: https://openknowledge.worldbank.org/bitstream/handle/10986/16639/826480WP0v10Bu0130Box37986200OUO090.pdf?sequence=1&isAllowed=y

World Bank (2017) *Unbreakable: Building the Resilience of the Poor in the Face of Natural Disasters*, Washington, DC: The World Bank Group, available at: http://documents.worldbank.org/curated/en/512241480487839624/pdf/110618-PUB-Box396333B-PUBLIC-PUBDATE-11-24-16-UNIT-ITSKI.pdf

World Economic Forum (2011–2012) *Systemic Financial Resilience*, Network of Global Agenda Councils Report 2011–2012, available at: http://reports.weforum.org/global-agenda-council-2012/#view/global-agenda-council-2012/councils/systemic-financial-resilience/

World Economic Forum (2012) *Global Risks 2012. Seventh Edition. An Initiative of the Risk Response Network*, available at: www3.weforum.org/docs/WEF_GlobalRisks_Report_2012.pdf

World Inequality Lab (2018) *World Inequality Report 2018*, coordinated by F. Alvaredo, L. Chancel, T. Piketty, E. Saez and G. Zucman, available at: https://wir2018.wid.world/files/doload/wir2018-full-report-english.pdf

World Resources Institute (2008) *World Resources 2008. Roots of Resilience. Growing the Wealth of the Poor*, Washington, DC: World Resources Institute.

Wright, Michael, Culbong, Margaret, Jones, Tanya, O'Connell, Margaret and Ford, Danny (2013) 'Making a difference: Engaging both hearts and minds in research practice', *ALARj – Action Learning, Action Research*, 19(1): 36–61.

WTO (2021) *World Trade Report 2021: Economic Resilience and Trade*, Geneva: World Trade Organization.

Young, Iris Marion (2001) *Justice and the Politics of Difference*, Princeton, NJ: Princeton University Press.

Young, Iris Marion (2002) *Inclusion and Democracy*, Oxford: Oxford University Press.

Zander, Margherita (2008) *Armes Kind – starkes Kind. Die Chance der Resilien*, Wiesbaden: VS Verlag.

Zermatten, Jean (2007) 'The Convention on the Rights of the Child from the perspective of the child', in C. Bellamy and J. Zermatten (eds) *Realizing the Rights of the Child*, Zurich: Rüffer & rub, pp 36–52.

Zibechi, Raúl (2007) *Autonomías y Emancipaciones: América Latina en Movimiento*, Lima: Universidad Nacional Mayor de San Marcos, Fondo Editorial de la Facultad de Ciencias Sociales.

Zibechi, Raúl (2017) *Movimientos sociales en América Latina. El 'mundo otro' en movimiento*, Mexico City: Bajo Tierra Ediciones.

Index

References to endnotes show the page number,
note number and chapter number (207n5[ch7]).

251

Printed in the USA
CPSIA information can be obtained
at www.ICGtesting.com
JSHW011550110923
48257JS00005B/21